'S

ROADS

TERROR

ON THE
HIGHWAY

PAUL EBERLE

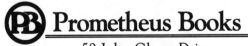

Prometheus Books

59 John Glenn Drive
Amherst, New York 14228-2197

Published 2006 by Prometheus Books

Inquiries should be addressed to
Prometheus Books
59 John Glenn Drive
Amherst, New York 14228-2197
VOICE: 716-691-0133, ext. 207
FAX: 716-564-2711
WWW.PROMETHEUSBOOKS.COM

10 09 08 07 06   5 4 3 2 1

Library of Congress Cataloging-in-Publication Data

Eberle, Paul, 1928–
    Terror on the highway : rage on America's roads / Paul Eberle.
        p. cm.
    Includes bibliographical references
    ISBN 13: 978-1-59102-379-1 (pbk. : alk. paper)
    ISBN 10: 1-59102-379-3 (pbk. : alk. paper)
    1. Road rage—United States. 2. Automobile drivers—Psychology. 3. Traffic safety. 4. Aggressiveness. I. Title.

TL152.35.E25 2006
363.12'51—dc22

2005032630

Printed in the United States of America on acid-free paper

CONTENTS

Acknowledgments 7

1. Car Wars: "I Shot Him Because
   He Was Driving Too Slow" 9

2. Aggression: "I Shot Him Because
   He Passed Me" 47

3. Women Warriors and Leading Citizens:
   "I Shot Him Because He
   Looked at Me with Disrespect" 61

4. Choices: "I Can't Believe I Shot Her" 95

5. How Are We Going to Fix It?
   Dealing with the Madman 111

6. Public Perceptions:
   What the Cars Are Saying 115

CONTENTS

7. New Legislation and Programs:
   Some Immodest Proposals   123

8. Warning Signs: Spotting Trouble
   before It's Too Late   135

9. Outside Agitators: Ambient Precursors of Aggression   151

10. Density: Too Many Cars—Not Enough Roads   175

11. The Car as Sacred Icon:
    "Do Not Kick the Holy Virgin"   193

12. Road Rage Psychology: The Roads Scholars   211

13. Dos and Don'ts: Avoiding the Land Mines   229

14. Reinventing the City: Leave Your Guns at Home   257

Glossary   273

Resources   277

Bibliography   281

ACKNOWLEDGMENTS

This book is for Shirley Eberle, my lifelong partner, accompanist, traveling companion, and beloved wife, who brought a steady stream of information, research, and concept formation to the table. We work well together.

I would like to thank Chris Harris, media expert and legendary publicist, who generously opened his archives and shared his knowledge and insight with me.

Many thanks to Eleanor Goldstein of SIRS Knowledge Source for her generous assistance in sending me valuable articles and research materials, which I badly needed as I began this project.

I would also like to thank the AAA Foundation for Traffic Safety and the National Highway Transportation Safety Administration for their help.

Let him not pass but kill him . . .
—William Shakespeare (*Othello*, Act V)

**To each and every problem there's a solution
that's neat and quick, and wrong.**
—H. L. Mencken

1

CAR WARS

"I Shot Him Because He Was Driving Too Slow"

On August 31, 1998, Mike Tyson was a passenger in a car driven by his wife in Gaithersburg, Maryland. They had gone shopping. Another car slammed into their rear bumper with a loud bang, jerking them backward, then forward. Tyson is one of that small number of adepts who are paid hundreds of millions of dollars for their services. He had once been the heavyweight boxing champion of the world, but a string of misadventures had left him with his assets depleted. He had been tried and convicted in Indiana on allegations of rape and had spent some time in prison. His Nevada boxing license had been revoked. Now, he was out of prison but still on probation for the Indiana conviction and, if he were convicted of another criminal offense, he could be ordered to serve up to four more years on that sentence.

The Nevada Athletic Commission had recently given him a new lease on life—the right to practice his profession—but he knew that his future hung by a slender thread. The commission had warned Tyson that another jail sentence could result in permanent revocation of his boxing license—a revocation that other states would follow. If ever there was a time to be gentlemanly and restrained, this was it. He turned and looked back. Two men got out of the other car. Mike Tyson got out of his car, kicked one of them in the groin, and punched the other, according to witnesses. Tyson said he was angered when the occupants of the other car did not inquire as to whether his wife was hurt or make any expression of apology. When he appeared before Montgomery District Court Judge Stephen P. Johnson for arraignment, he pleaded no contest. The judge dispatched him to jail for one year and said that Tyson "lashed out at two innocent people" with "the hands and feet of a professional fighter." He further stated that the two men were spared serious injury only by the intervention of Tyson's bodyguard.[1]

It is easy and somewhat comforting to dismiss this behavior as the act of a young man who has been surrounded by violence all of his life, or attribute it to his lack of acculturation or to head trauma after too many bouts in the ring. But millions of other people have behaved in almost exactly the same way—with only minor variations while driving or riding in a car. Not all of them have provided the other driver with such inspirational therapy, but many have committed far more egregious acts—including murder.

O. J. Simpson, as if he had not had enough of the court system, was involved in a road rage confrontation on December 5, 2000. The driver of the other car, Jeffrey Pattison, age fifty-five, told police that Simpson ran a stop sign, that Pattison sounded his horn, and that Simpson stopped in the middle of the road, walked to Pattison's car, snatched his glasses, and scratched his face. Flanked by his lawyers, Simpson surrendered himself at the Miami-Dade County Jail on February 9. He was charged with assault and "burglary of an occupied vehicle." He was booked, fingerprinted, and released on $9,000 bond. People asked for his autograph and some shook his hand, including a peace officer.[2] Perhaps we all want to be the invincible, strong man who does as he pleases and fears no one. At the trial in October 2001, Simpson faced up to sixteen years in prison. Pattison testified that Simpson acted like a madman; nearly hit his car, forcing him to slam on his brakes; and that when he honked his horn, Simpson stopped in front of him, walked angrily to his car, reached in, and snatched off his glasses. Simpson testified that Pattison pursued him and provoked the confrontation after Simpson ran a stop sign and then turned in front of him. The jurors acquitted Simpson in less than two hours. One of the jurors said there wasn't enough evidence to support the charge of "burglary of an occupied vehicle,"[3] a felony. But sometimes it can be inexpedient—and costly—to get out of your car.

Actor Jack Nicholson is not an alumnus of the ghetto or of the penal system. He is exceptionally bright and gifted. He cannot be unaware that persons of substantial wealth are targeted for lawsuits, and that the county jail system needs more guests, which brings more money. He was driving in North Hollywood on February 8, 1994, when a rude or incautious driver in a Mercedes-Benz changed lanes too quickly and cut in front of him, forcing him to brake. Something snapped. When both cars were stopped for a red light, Nicholson got out and whipped the Mercedes-Benz with a golf club, smashing the windshield and the roof, then got back into his car and drove away. The occupants of the other car jotted down the license plate number. Police said the number matched that of Nicholson's car.[4]

The owner of what was left of the battered Mercedes, Robert Blank, filed a lawsuit in Los Angeles Superior Court, seeking an unspecified amount in general and punitive damages. The civil complaint alleged that Blank had suffered assault and battery, emotional distress, false imprisonment, physical injuries, and pain and suffering.[5] Police and the city attorney's office filed a misdemeanor vandalism charge against the actor, a charge that carries a possible six months in jail. However, on March 3 the lawsuit was settled, effectively dismissing the misdemeanor charges and barring authorities from prosecuting Nicholson. Shortly thereafter, Nicholson served as celebrity host of the annual Police-Celebrity Golf Tournament.[6]

It feels good to discharge anger, to whip the insolent offender, to humiliate him, to see him cringe, tremble, grovel, cry out in agony, and beg for mercy. Some may gain satisfaction from seeing his car crumpled and ruined, his bones broken, his blood spilled. Metaphorically at least, many would like to stand over him, smiling, and ask, "Do you want to mess with me again?"

Everything else vanishes except the elated rush of winning. People will risk, and often suffer, devastating losses for one brief moment of personal triumph. You can live for years as a civilized, benign, loving parent and spouse—and then one day, when you're preparing to take revenge upon your enemy, be suddenly cognizant, with foreboding clarity, that there is another self inside your shell who is crazy and frightfully dangerous to yourself as well as to others. This is not another entity. It is you, the *real* you, removed from the artificial constraints of the office, the family, or a polite social gathering, a rudiment that was present in the embryo when you first were formed, but requires certain stimuli to raise it up to full power.

Once it is fully aroused it is extremely difficult, sometimes impossible, to restrain.

Gene Hackman, another legendary film actor, engaged in a fistfight with a motorist after a minor fender bender. According to a story in *USA Today*, Hackman was driving his Volvo sedan on Sunset Boulevard when his car made contact with another Volvo that cut in front of him to make a right turn from a left-hand lane.

Hackman and the other driver parked in front of the Wolfgang Puck Cafe. When Hackman tried to exchange insurance information, the other driver and a man who had been riding with him began shoving Hackman and shouting homophobic slurs at him. Fists began flying. Hackman, according to his publicist, hit one of the men, who went down. By the time police arrived, the fight had ended. All three men were bruised but none wanted to file a complaint.[7] Many publications have published stories listing celebrities who have engaged in similar behavior. Hackman really wasn't given a choice, but many people who are at the top of their careers have foolishly rushed into this kind of reckless behavior without first thinking about how much they had to lose—and how little to gain. Some of them were people of prodigious intellect. Why did they not think of the consequences before rushing into such dangerous, self-destructive situations?

When a motorist was shot to death by another driver in 1996, the shooter was asked why he did it. His answer: "He was driving too slow."[8] In Lansing, Michigan, a sixty-seven-year-old man was arrested and charged with stabbing another man in the chest because, he said, the other man was driving too slowly. His victim was driving on a road for which the speed limit was thirty-five miles per hour.[9] A California man fired a handgun while driving, fatally injuring the driver of another car. When he was caught and asked why he killed the other driver, he told police he did it because the other driver had passed him.[10] After another fatal driving duel the shooter told police, "He wouldn't let me pass."[11] A teenager who shot the occupant of another car was caught and taken into custody by police. They asked him, "Why?" He said he did it because the man looked at him with disrespect.[12]

In June 2000 a sixty-nine-year-old Colorado man, angry over a parking space dispute, shot and killed another man who had parked too close to his space.[13]

There are several kinds of acts that are likely to trigger a road rage duel. If you perform them habitually and frequently, you are virtually guaranteed to get into hair-raising combat sooner or later. These are the common currency of road rage.

TAILGATING

Tailgating (following too close) is one of the most common forms of aggressive driving, according to a study commissioned by the American Automobile Association (AAA) Foundation for Traffic Safety.[14]

Flashing high-beam headlights is a close second; it typically accompanies tailgating, along with excessive use of the horn and shouting foul epithets. Tailgating usually occurs when one car is moving more slowly than the surrounding vehicles. Even when there is a red light only a short distance ahead and an impenetrable logjam of stopped cars, when someone slows down it often enrages the driver behind him, thwarting her need to speed.

When you see a car following you too closely, nearly touching your rear bumper, glance up and take a look at the driver's face. Some drivers tailgate casually and habitually because they are mimicking the driving habits of other people and because they believe that is the way a seasoned driver drives in traffic. It also tends to immunize them from the rage of other tailgaters. They are never driving too slowly. When you look back at this kind of driver the face you see usually will not be particularly combative.

But when you look into your rearview mirror and see a face bulging with anger, tilted imperiously upward, eyes boring into you with hate, head and shoulders jerking forward—beware. It is unwise to underestimate the potential for mindless violence, injury, and even death that may surround you. You are seeing a person whose rage has burgeoned to such a pitch that she is no longer in control of her fate. She has lost the power of reason. If you slow down to make a turn or to park, forcing her to brake and reduce her speed, she will experience this as a further insult and her rage will greatly increase. She may lose all control, put her foot to the floor, and crash her car into yours—even if you do not taunt her or make a gesture of defiance. I have seen it happen many times. It has happened to me, even in bumper-to-bumper traffic where there was no way for me to move forward to accommodate the bully's demands. If you can move away from her before she crashes into your car, she is likely to pursue you with the intent to do violence to you and your vehicle. Be especially attentive. Anything can happen. If she continues to follow you each time you make a turn or change lanes, you may be in a state of deadly combat. The longer she follows you, the greater the danger. How you deal with it may determine whether you get away unscathed or suffer great bodily damage and the destruction of your property.

Not all tailgaters are mentally deranged thugs or obtuse-witted office robots. I know a noted psychologist who is a chronic tailgater.

"I can't stand it! I get so goddamn mad when I want to get home and those other idiots won't move!" she told me indignantly as we crawled through a stop-and-go traffic jam.

"Why don't you just lean back in your seat, relax, take some deep breaths, turn on the radio, or just think, meditate, contemplate. There's no way you can fly over those cars. Just think about something else for a while. Go with the flow. Think about all the good things in your life. Make a list of things you have to do or plan a vacation you've always wanted to take. Just go with the flow, accept the inevitable, and wait out the traffic tie-up, with malice toward none and charity for all," I told her.

"Gee, I never thought about that," the psychologist said.

Tailgaters are extremely dangerous and it is absolutely imperative to distance yourself from them as quickly as possible, or you may not be going home again. More about that in chapter 3.

Trying to placate a tailgater is usually a waste of time. If you attempt to reason with him the tailgater will probably believe you are patronizing and "top-dogging" him, since you are behaving with more dignity, showing yourself to be stronger and more in control, behaving more like an adult. The tailgater may perceive your effort to negotiate as a sign of weakness and fear. If you get out of your car, the tailgater is likely to assault you. One of the cardinal rules of survival in car war is: Don't get out of your car![15]

You cannot communicate with a tailgater if he is pursuing you at high speed. That's when you really need to think coolly, quickly, and know exactly what to do. You must get as far away from him as possible.

Tailgating is a manifestation of one of the most primitive animal instincts. Like a fox chasing a rabbit, the tailgater is not susceptible to reason, censure, or disgrace. As with the fox, abandoning the chase is not an option. There is only one sensible way to deal with this situation: Look around you, plan your moves carefully, and get away from him, beyond his reach, where he cannot harm you.

TAILGATING IN REVERSE

Tailgating in reverse is another common act of car combat. When an enraged tailgater who wants to speed finds himself behind a slow car, she rides the slow car's rear bumper, dangerously close, changing speed in sync with the slow car, remaining inches from its rear bumper like a doppelganger, flashing her high beams, stridently shouting her frustration and outrage from her open window, and leaning on the horn, trying to terrify the slow driver. Many slow drivers enjoy torturing the tailgater by touching the brake pedal, which flashes the bright brake lights, causing the tailgater to panic, stomp on his brakes, and possibly lose control of his car and crash. Or the slow driver may softly ride his break pedal, decelerate, and slowly bring the tormented hotshot to a complete stop, perhaps moving forward a few yards and doing it again, bringing her car and the tailgater's car once again to a stop. The slow driver may raise the phallic middle finger and watch while the tailgater twitches, jerks, screams, leans on her horn, and raises her fist, seized with anger more powerful than she can contain.

This is called a *brake job*. I have seen it happen many times, and I have heard the deafening crash of metal against metal and the shattering of glass that often accompanies freeway dueling. It is an extremely provocative act. If you try it you must be ready—combat ready. You have brought up all the defeats the tailgater has suffered. You have brought back the night when he was walking with his girlfriend, the love of his life, and he got into a fistfight during which he was brutally and decisively beaten, and watched as his girl left with the other young man, laughing with him as they got into his car and drove away. You have brought back all the insults and humiliations he has absorbed and buried in that dark chamber where he deposits the memories that are too ugly and too painful to think about. They remain there. They rot and ferment. You have added one more—maybe the decisive one that pushes this individual to do something that you both will regret.

You have tormented a person who already is barely able to contain his aggression and you have raised his rage to a level at which the tank ruptures and all of that noxious miasma ignites. It has been my observation during many years of driving that it is almost certain that he will follow you, no matter how fast and recklessly he has to drive, determined to punish you. He will follow you until he overtakes you or until he is so belated in the race that he no longer can see you. If he is unable to overtake you he may stalk you for weeks, months, or years, consumed by his obsession. It has happened to me and to several people with whom I am acquainted.

An inordinately sadistic driver may lead the tailgater into a narrow street where he cannot pass and then do a brake job again and again, riding her brake pedal, watching the other driver jerk to a stop, and seeing his implosive torment. I have seen it happen many times. This is a dangerous act and it must be performed with extreme attentiveness: The other driver may suddenly burst into a paroxysm of rage and destroy himself and you. You must be ready for anything, including a gun, a knife, a baseball bat—anything. His frontal cortex is shut down and there is only one thought in his mind: *I'm going to kill that punk or die trying.*

But when a person is as angry as this driver is, he tends to malfunction because he moves too fast and reacts too fast. He is not thinking; he is reacting instinctively, like a frog or a cat or a reptile. He is at a disadvantage. If you continue to torture him, he will wreck his car and probably do himself considerable harm. And he may very well hurt you, too.

CHANGING LANES

Another common offense is to change lanes and move in front of the car just behind you in the next lane. Even if you are not cutting him off, even if you give him plenty of room, even if you have no malicious intent, it often hits a raw nerve in the other driver. It is similar to what you experience when you are standing in line at a theater, waiting to get in, and another person squeezes in front of you and remains in front of you, making the unspoken statement that you are too weak, too timid, or too confused to resist. It may, and often does, ignite in the other driver a burst of rage so overpowering that he will go to any lengths, at dangerously high speed, putting his life in great danger, to avenge this insult if he is unable to pass you and retaliate. The adrenaline rises up and takes control, obliterating the power of reason. I have spent a large part of my life behind the wheel of a moving car, and I have always been perplexed at the number of drivers who will suddenly become enraged at a driver who, objectively speaking, has given no offense.

No matter what happens—even if the other car manages to overtake you, trap you, or corner you—do not get out of your car.[15] You do not know what weaponry he has in his car, in his jacket, in his pocket, or under his belt. It is not necessary to get out of your car. Just be calm and smile. Never show fear; the appearance of fear attracts violence. Use your imagination, do your dance. If you see a gun, floor it and get out of there, even if it is necessary to damage your car in order to get away from him. Keep your head down.

CUTTING ANOTHER CAR OFF

At first glance this may sound like a repetition of the last section, but it is a very different situation. Changing lanes while giving the driver behind you plenty of room can, and often does, produce anger. But changing lanes and cutting off the other driver so that he finds it necessary to slam his brakes to avoid a collision generates far more anger and may result in violence. Occasionally this is done by an inattentive or inexperienced driver, but more often it is done as an act of retaliation for a prior offense or as a gratuitous and deliberate insult. In any case, it will be perceived as an affront and a challenge. If you cut another driver off with a look of expansive, pleasurable sadism, the face of a person gloating over his victory, and then unfurl the triumphant third finger, you can expect trouble. The other driver will know that it is a challenge, an act of war, and is likely to feel that it must be punished with massive retaliation at any cost.

BLOCKING TRAFFIC

Blocking traffic, even if it is not intentional (for instance, if your car has stalled), thus interfering with the traffic flow, can bring down considerable wrath upon you from those sharing the road with you. Blocking the left lane (the passing lane) is one of the most frequent causes of road rage violence. A Seattle woman was driving in dense morning traffic when her engine failed, leaving her and her car stuck in the passing lane. A male driver, stuck behind her, leaned on his horn, blasting his rage at her in even, orderly cadence, like a farmer whipping his horse. The woman tried to start her engine but succeeded only in flooding the carburetor. The man continued to rattle her with his horn. She quietly walked back to the man's car and spoke to him: "If you'll come up and help me start my car, I'll stay back here and work the horn for you."[16]

He did. Most tailgaters are not that civilized. I have seen drivers get out of their cars and rage at a helpless driver stalled in traffic: "Get that goddamn junk off the road! We want to get to work." I once saw a large truck pushing a stalled car off of the road while the terrified driver in the car tried to get out.

TAUNTING GESTURES

When you brandish the phallic third finger at a driver who has already been seized with scalding anger, you are symbolically violating him and penetrating him. You are instructing him that it is you who have the phallus and it is he who will be penetrated—that you are hard and he is soft—that you are strong and he is weak. There is a high probability that this will lead to an act of extreme displeasure, particularly if he perceives you as being smaller and/or weaker than himself. That lowers the threshold.

Other taunting gestures include waving one's fist in a threatening manner and turning one's head from side to side in an expression of extreme disapproval and contempt. Sometimes just staring at the other driver with a look of loathing and scorn will be sufficient to provoke a fight. Leaning on the horn and/or revving up the engine to rattle the other driver is another common gesture of hostility. Cutting the other car off and then hitting the brakes is another. Some drivers will open their windows and shout their indignation: "Hey, you dumb . . . !"

Another taunting gesture is to put the headlights on high beam, causing retinal pain to the driver in front. Some irate drivers will make movements with their hands that communicate the message that the driver in front is mentally deficient.

RACING

Racing is the rudiment, the first principle, of road rage. In some cultures the greatest disgrace is lying, theft, fraud, heresy, bringing dishonor upon one's family, being unchaste, engaging in forbidden delights, reading unauthorized books, or listening to unauthorized music. But in America, the greatest disgrace for many is being passed on the highway by another car. Even if the highway is not overcrowded, even if there are only two cars on the highway, they are likely to race. Nobody wants to lose. Nobody wants to be second best—unless she aspires to more rewarding achievements that she is unwilling to put at risk for such a trivial victory. Does everybody race? No, not everybody, but virtually everyone experiences the urge to race at one time or another. It's in all of us in varying degrees, the young and the elderly, males and females, the highly educated and illiterates. Racing is in our blood, is encoded in our DNA and in that of other animals.[17] Life is a race. Female birds mate with the male that flies fastest and wins fights. Human females mate with the man who wins the race for self-advancement, the fight for affluence. And they mate with the man who wins car races. Professional race car drivers are showered with attention by women who long for the opportunity to touch the glamorous driver and and take possession of him. That's not true of *all* women. But it is true that each woman is looking for *some* particular characteristic and mate with the man who meets it. For many, the car is a powerful attraction.

Before the invention and proliferation of the car, drivers of horse-drawn wagons got into road rage duels in New York and other crowded cities. The drivers frequently threw vegetables at other drivers. The W. C. Fields motion picture *If I Had a Million*, made in 1932, is about road rage. An elderly couple, after years of enduring rudeness, assault, and fright at the hands of road rage bullies, inherit a million dollars. They purchase a fleet of cars, hire several skilled drivers, go out on the road and smile with satisfaction as the bullies are forced off the road and their cars demolished. People race with one another in the supermarket, the hotel lobby, the taco stand, the post office, the bank, the parking lot, the airport, and the sidewalk, in order to cross in front of the other person and score some small victory. What is the logic behind this behavior? Each of us reacts differently. No two drivers are quite the same. Some experience anger of a greater intensity than others. Some merely mutter and scowl. Others kill. Some of us are aware of the savage killer that lives inside of us; most of us deny that he exists and delegate the blame to others.

But for most drivers, aggressive driving is a natural part of our macho warrior culture. A "real" American does not shrink from combat. He says, "Nobody does that to me and gets away with it." He looks at the other car and says, "I'm gonna take that guy out of his car and beat the hell out of him."

I have spent a large portion of my life behind the wheel, and I have tried to estimate the number of people out of one hundred who will race if passed by another car. If you run the gauntlet of peak traffic overload on a busy artery like Ventura Boulevard in Los Angeles or the Ventura Freeway, or any main highway in the county's inter- and intrastate highway system and if you observe what is going on around you, you will notice that nearly everywhere you look a car is trying to pass the car in the next lane, overtake the car in front of her, or outrun and block the car that is trying to pass her or simply trying to get on or off the freeway. Not everybody races on the road, but you can almost always see pairs of cars racing with each other. This may seem hyperbolic, but it's not. If you drive in Las Vegas, Dallas, Chicago, Seattle, Los Angeles, or Florida you will be able to witness it for yourself. I have witnessed this phenomenon, at all times of the day and night, for many years, and I have observed that most of the drivers have a look of desperation and urgency on their faces. The noise is deafening—the roar of thousands of engines; the shrill, harsh blast of car horns; the squealing of tires; the shouts; the sirens. Occasionally you see a driver biting his lip in rage and frustration, eyes bulging. It has repeatedy been my observation that when a driver is passed by another car, he reacts as though he has lost his penis. You can see it in his eyes and on his face. A woman is no different. She feels naked, stripped of the garments of self-respect, and she can be redeemed only by overtaking and passing the other car. There is a look of desperation, of inexorable resolution, in the driver's face as he quickly changes lanes and pursues his opponent in order to restore his manhood, or, in the case of a woman, her self-respect. If he passes the other driver, his manhood is automatically refunded. He has been redeemed. Women may not experience the fear of emasculation, but there are many women who are every bit as violent and vindictive as any man. A woman may be at a disadvantage because of her smaller musculature and lighter weight, but a woman in control of a two-ton vehicle is as powerful as a man. More powerful, perhaps.

Not everybody races, but the U.S. Department of Transportation has estimated that two-thirds of the fatalities resulting from car crashes are at least partially caused by aggressive driving.[18]

When I first began driving in dense urban traffic, when I was very young, it occurred to me one morning that when you do something spiteful to anger another driver—when you race with her, defeat her, gloat and humiliate her—she carries that hot, stinging anger with her and inflicts it upon another driver, who passes it on to still another driver. This repeating relay system moves outward in expanding waves. By the end of the day, you may have set in motion a series of actions that result in the death of another person. Everything you do goes out in expanding oscillations. The automobile gave us freedom from the relative confinement of travel on horseback or on foot. In some people's minds, it also gave us freedom from responsibility.

OTHER COMMON ACTS OF ROAD RAGE

Some other common acts of road rage and acts that provoke road rage are:

- Closing the gap between your car and the car in front of you to prevent another driver from entering traffic or changing lanes.
- Running another car off the road.
- Ramming another car.
- Throwing objects, paint, or other damaging materials at another car.
- Getting out and kicking another car.
- Hitting the rear bumper of another car when it is moving slowly.
- Blasting your horn excessively at another car.
- Getting out of your car, pulling another driver out of his car if he isn't already out, and trading blows, rolling in the dust, punching and kicking.
- Shooting, stabbing, or clubbing another driver.

The list is only as finite as your imagination.

There are more than 215 million cars and light trucks in the United States,[19] and nearly as many drivers. Most of them are angry.[20] Those who are not can often be provoked when other drivers breach and violate their borders, and will retaliate in some way. When traffic is light, the drivers race. When traffic is dense, they cut each other off, tailgate, give each other brake jobs, raise the third finger, and bump each other. When traffic is at a standstill, some get out of their cars and confront each other. These confrontations sometimes lead to fights and killings. In the morning, drivers tend to be more restrained because of the imperative of getting to work and clocking in on time. In the afternoon, when the day's work is over, they tend to become more reckless. The duels are lengthier and more violent.

It would be simpler if the road rage combatants came from one class of people, one ethnic group, or one gender, or were simply mentally deficient, irresponsible thugs and bums who have less to lose. There are also those who are so dwarfed by regimentation—powerless folks who live their lives in cringing, groveling servitude—that they cannot act or speak without a command or a dispensation. But when they get behind the wheel and go out on the freeway, they enter another world: the solitary interior of the car. The mask falls away and we see the vampire.

But there is no one profile for the aggressive driver.[21] You might see a fashionably dressed middle-aged woman in an expensive new car dueling with another driver. You are just as likely to get a middle-aged pillar of the community who masks his craving for power, domination, and control over others behind his conservative, pin-striped, three-piece suit and tie and an impeccable haircut. When he's not driving, he conceals his sadism behind pious rhetoric about law and order, blind obedience to authority, blind belief in dogma, and abhorrence of sex, drugs, art, music, dancing, and the adventurous spirit. He speaks of service to the community and to the Lord, but when he sits behind the wheel, all of that is left behind and what remains is a reptilian killing machine. My wife and I knew a physician who was like that, as well as a clergyman and a prestigious psychologist. Women have more traffic accidents than men, but men are three times more likely to be killed in battle on the freeway.[22] Studies show that once size and physical strength are taken out of the equation, women are more likely to inflict violence upon a man than the reverse. A Michigan study found that 53 percent of aggressive drivers are women. The same study concluded that 80 percent of drivers are angry almost all the time while driving.[23]

The interaction between drivers replicates the aggression we see when we are away from the car, in public spaces and in private spaces, too, but it is more primal, unadorned by etiquette and the public pretense of civility. On the freeway you're just a steel structure, a set of wheels.

A few years ago I designed an experiment. I was driving on a six-lane main road. It was early afternoon. Traffic was sparse. I searched for the most respectable, conservative-looking driver I could find. I found her. I recognized her face. She is a very conservative member of one of California's legislative bodies, an extremely ambitious careerist who never misses an opportunity to exhibit herself on television and in newspaper headlines, proclaiming the need for obedience to the laws, some of which are of her own making. She was impeccably dressed in her fashionably conservative business suit, driving a shiny new car. Her hair was flawlessly coifed in one of those short, boyish haircuts that are fashionable with female executives and politicians, not one shaft out of place. Her attaché case and her telephone were on the car seat. We were driving at the same speed, side by side.

TERROR ON THE HIGHWAY

I pushed down on the gas pedal slightly and moved a few feet ahead of her. She accelerated and passed me, leaving me a few feet behind. I pushed down on the gas again and sailed leisurely past her, remaining just a few feet ahead. She retaliated, passing me and driving just a few feet ahead. We repeated this dance several times. Finally, I observed that the traffic control light, about three hundred feet ahead, had turned yellow and was about to turn red. I pressed down on the gas pedal and passed her, loudly revving up my motor. She gunned her motor and passed me. Very gradually, very inconspicuously, I slowed down so that I would be able to stop. She did not slow down. She sped up and ran the red light, determined to win the final round and leave me sitting ignominiously behind the red light as she triumphantly sailed away. A large bus was crossing the intersection in front of her. I froze. She missed it by only a few inches. If the bus had been moving just a bit slower she would have been goulash. I have repeated this experiment many times, trying not to put another driver in danger and trying to estimate what percentage of the drivers out there will take the challenge and race. The results, although they are imprecise, are about 80 percent. Some of them make only a feeble effort to win the race and quickly abandon it. Some will chase you all the way to Omaha. Some of those who do not compete are men and women who are able to control the savage killer inside and know that life is more important than attempting a petty, spiteful victory. There are also those inexperienced drivers who are afraid to do battle on the road. These are the future freeway fusiliers. But no two drivers are identical. There are those who are friendly and kind. But if you spend enough time driving, you will occasionally encounter one who is extraordinarily aggressive, blazing with homicidal anger, one who will not abandon the contest until he has destroyed you or been destroyed, or left sufficiently far behind that he cannot find you. But if that happens he may be waiting in ambush for you the next day. I've seen it happen more than once.

Some metropolitan areas, such as Manhattan and San Francisco, are surrounded by water and can only grow upward since they lack the land area to spread out horizontally. In these places, it is possible to get around without a car, using the buses and rail systems in place. But in cities like Los Angeles, where the urban sprawl extends for nearly one hundred miles in all directions, it is difficult—if not impossible—to earn a living without driving a car. Los Angeles has an embryonic rail system, but a one-way ticket costs as much as $8.50 on some routes. That's $17 a day. Or you can buy a ticket that is valid for one month: only $276—approximately the amount of a monthly payment for an inexpensive car. And the buses are few and far between.

It is really a hardship to be without a car in a city like Los Angeles. Those drivers who are unable to control their anger and their desire to race, and practice other road rage behaviors sometimes lose their driver's licenses after being ticketed too many times by police. Not surprisingly, many drivers find it necessary to acquire a fraudulent driver's license, using an assumed name and an entire new identity to accompany and corroborate it. The Department of Motor Vehicles (DMV) has periodically taken steps to make it more difficult to acquire and use false driver's licenses, but whatever people are willing to pay for, someone will provide. On July 6, 2000, several employees of the California Department of Motor Vehicles were arrested for allegedly selling licenses to drivers who would be denied a driver's license if their true identity and history were known to the DMV. There are more complicated, more sophisticated ways to acquire a new identity. Several interesting books on the subject have been published.[24] Many people who are not criminals drive with fake licenses because they have been the victims of racial profiling or some other selective and discriminatory enforcement. Getting a new license and a new set of cards and papers will not change the color of your skin or preclude the police from harrassing you, but it will wipe the slate clean and give you a fresh start. People who accumulate too many traffic tickets pay higher fines and are ordered to perform many hours of "community service." They also suffer the suspension of their licenses or pay higher insurance premiums. A new set of identification gives them a fresh start—if they don't get caught. To a person who has spent his life in the cloistral, air-conditioned ambience of the corporate office, insulated from the real world, this may seem shocking and even dangerous, but it is no more so than the misconduct of government and its oily patrons, who steal millions while poor people go to prison for stealing an old television set.

There are many variations on these basic patterns. These are just the outer layers of the onion, not the real source of road rage. It is necessary to peel away these outer layers to get to the central truth at the heart of the matter. But first, we will dispose of some of the superficial advice and analysis we are given by the authorities and the experts, those whom I call the "roads scholars."

There is a sense of anonymity, an absence of accountability on the freeway.[25] On the freeway you are just a steel box on wheels, and at night your face is not seen. But sometimes this is illusory. Recently, an angry young man flipped the bird at the driver of another car—only to discover that the driver was his employer's wife. He fell from grace and found it expedient to seek other employment.

It's not just anonymity. The average driver—particularly of the white-collar, middle-class variety—spends her life hedged in and compressed by a superabundance of tight little prohibitions. The bosses don't want anything embarrassing, or anything they perceive as bizarre that rises up unpredictably. She must be a regular gal, a model of propriety at all times, or suffer the loss of her livelihood. She cannot say what she really thinks and feels; she cannot show her anger; she cannot be a free-wheeling, fun-loving libertine, even if her libertinism is perfectly wholesome and harmless. She cannot be real. As she becomes older she grows stiffer, robotic, and becomes one of *them*. But when she gets behind the wheel of a car, all that unravels as Dr. Jekyll vanishes, displaced by Mr. Hyde.

There is also the fact that most of the people on the road feel powerless and, indeed, they *are* powerless by reason of poverty, ignorance, and a general sense that there is nothing they can do when they are the victims of injustice. But when they get behind the wheel, they have a 300-horsepower engine, the open road ahead, and a sense of being no longer powerless—free at last.

Firearms, knives, clubs, and fists are frequently used to settle aggressive driving disputes, but the weapon most frequently used is an even more dangerous weapon: the car itself. According to an AAA study, in 35 percent of road rage disputes, the aggressor uses his or her car as a weapon to ram another driver.[26] If you fight with a stranger, face-to-face, armed only with your fists, you take the risk of getting a humiliating, brutal beating before the eyes of your mate, your family, and your children—and you may find yourself lying ignominiously on the ground, bleeding and hurting, while your adversary mocks you, insults you, boasts, and loudly dares you to get up and continue. And you will probably carry the scars, the broken nose, the segmented eyebrows, and toothless gums for the rest of your life, reliving your humiliation every time you look in the mirror. There are men who like to fight and who don't care if their faces are smashed, scarred, and mutilated. They wear it as a badge of authority and as a warning to others: "If you mess with me, you will look like this." But most people are not accomplished street fighters and most do not want to risk going through life facing the world with a broken, deformed face, the emblem of the loser.

Most drivers prefer to do combat inside the protective structure of the car. It is less humiliating to be defeated in a battle between two machines than in a battle between two individuals stripped to their essentials. In car combat you might be able to ram, crush, and destroy the other car and its driver. But the stakes are higher. You could do some hard time. In the ensuing chapters you will read the stories of people who lost years of their lives in prison for an event that could easily have been avoided. Nothing is worth going to prison.

For some people, driving a car is just a means of getting from point A to point B. But for many others it is a challenge, a test, a rite of passage: It is a chance to prove one's mettle in combat, a way to establish one's supremacy and humiliate the other driver. The aggressive driving phenomenon is nothing new, but in recent years the alliteration "road rage" has become part of our common vernacular and has captured the attention of the media. Several "experts" and public figures have claimed authorship of the phrase. Nobody knows who first used it, but it was Chris Harris, the virtuoso media expert and publicist, who first introduced the term in the news media and made it part of our language, and several other languages. Consequently, in 1998 there were more than four thousand media stories on some aspect of road rage.

There are other phrases commonly used to describe this phenomenon: freeway fury, asphalt assault, motor mayhem, car wars, and mad car disease, to name a few. Some experts use the terms "road rage" and "aggressive driving" interchangeably. The AAA Foundation for Traffic Safety defines "road rage" as uncontrolled violence in which a driver "intentionally kills or injures another motorist or attempts to kill another motorist," while it defines "aggressive driving" as behavior that "does not rise to the level of criminal conduct."[27]

Road rage has become a generic term, and it is poorly understood.

In 1998 the California Highway Patrol (CHP) recorded 209 incidents of assault with a deadly weapon in which the weapon used was the vehicle, 524 persons carrying concealed firearms, 390 carrying loaded firearms, and 260 throwing an object at a vehicle. According to the CHP, every two hours and twenty-three minutes one person is killed in a vehicular mishap; every fifty-one seconds someone is injured; one out of every fifty-nine drivers will be involved in a fatal collision; and 26 percent of all collisions are the result of excessive speed.[28]

For nearly a century we have speculated about this enigma. An ordinarily civilized, pleasant person gets behind the steering wheel and is transformed into a raging sadistic killer. Several years ago when I was visiting a friend at the American Federation of Musicians in Los Angeles, I saw a list of names on the bulletin board. It was a list of the names of members of the local Musicians Union who had been killed in automobile accidents that year. I was astounded. I asked a man who was standing nearby, "How many people are killed in car accidents in the United States?"

"Several every day," he said.

But are they really accidents?

In 1997, 5,307 pedestrians were killed by automobiles.

Six hundred forty-four were children. Some of these deaths

were caused by inattention on the part of the pedestrians—especially the deaths of children—but most were caused by drivers who were driving too fast or recklessly, without regard for the safety of pedestrians. Many drivers openly confess their hatred of pedestrians because pedestrians cause them to slow down or stop.

A study conducted recently by the Surface Transportation Policy Project[29] disclosed that more than eleven hundred child pedestrians were injured or killed in Southern California in 1996, according to an editorial in the *Los Angeles Times*. Students at Hollywood High School were quoted as saying that it is a life-threatening experience just to walk across Sunset Boulevard after school.

Usually, road rage occurs between two combatants, one-on-one, but not always. On a Los Angeles freeway in 1997, nearly one hundred cars were damaged in a sudden chain of rear-end collisions. What does this have to do with road rage? It was filmed from helicopters, and television viewers could plainly see that most of the drivers were following too closely, driving too fast, racing, and trying to thwart the hated stranger who was attempting to change lanes to get on or off the freeway. Some of the cars were totaled. Ambulances were carrying away the wounded. Tow trucks towed away the wreckage.

A similar chain of rear-enders occurred a few months earlier on the I-15, the conduit that connects Los Angeles to Las Vegas. It takes about five hours to drive from Los Angeles to Las Vegas—less than that if you drive over seventy miles per hour. It is boring. What you see is mostly desert: sand and rocks. Most drivers go too fast, even when the weather is fair, but when there is poor visibility they do not usually slow down. The imperative of beating the other car is too powerful. This chain reaction involved more than one hundred cars, most of them following too closely at excessive speed, most of them angry, most of them racing with each other. It happens with dismal regularity.

For most drivers it is a game—like checkers, chess, football, backgammon, or parcheesi—but I know of no game that engenders such incendiary passions. I have known professional boxers, top-ranked contenders, who, after giving each other a bloody, brutal bashing, went out afterward and enjoyed an evening of food and drink together. Not so with aggressive driving. The hot, killer rage does not evaporate when the race is over. It is not uncommon for a driver to stalk another for weeks—or months—after a humiliating defeat, determined to assault the other driver once more, to prove his superior strength and settle it, once and for all.

A man in Seattle, a salesman, drove constantly, day and night. One day, another driver did something that angered him so violently that he followed the man at a distance and discovered where he worked. The next evening he followed the man to the place where he stopped for beer with his friends after work. Then he followed him to his home. He waited for the right moment, when he would not be seen. He was able to corner the man in his garage and beat him. Then he took out his knife. The final result was that two lives were ruined: one man died, and the other spent nine years in prison. Why? Because one man taunted the other by braking in front of him and slowing him down. And perhaps because the knife-wielding man was a lightweight who was tired of being targeted by bullies, mocked, and treated with contempt.

Road rage has several levels. Some drivers can disconnect their anger and move on to more productive thoughts. Some cannot transcend the instinctive animal urge to retaliate by overtaking the aggressor and soiling him with the raised, erect finger, thus purging themselves of their defeat. For some, that is not enough.

Some drivers cannot restrain the overpowering, burning, compelling need to overtake and pass the other driver, to brandish the third finger, to cut in front of him too close, and then stomp the brakes, forcing him to skid and/or lose control of his vehicle. For some drivers, that is not enough.

Some drivers will pursue the other car with the fanatic awareness that there can be no turning back until the other car is a crumpled wreck, the driver's bones broken, his blood spilled, his terrified voice crying out in supplication. For some, even that is not enough.

No two drivers are quite the same. But there are some in whom the prehistoric savage killer is out of control and has totally taken possession of its host. That driver is out there, waiting to intercept you.

There was a dispute on the 101 freeway in Los Angeles several years ago. A small, ungainly, excessively thin young man driving a small car insulted a very large man driving a pickup truck. The large man in the truck pursued him for over an hour with somber eyes that had blanked everything else out. Finally, he had the other car trapped on a dead-end street. The small man in the small car tried to drive around and flee, but each time he tried the large man in the pickup moved in front of him, blocking his way, moving him further into a corner from which he could not escape. The small man tried to circle around and go behind the pickup, but the pickup backed up and demolished his front-end suspension and his steering rods. He could go no farther. It was very much like a fox running down a rabbit until he has him cornered. The small man in the small car panicked. He locked his doors. The large man smashed the windows, pulled him out, and inflicted a brutal beating upon him. When his victim was down, groggy and defenseless, the large man took out a knife and butchered him like a side of beef. The small man miraculously survived, but he hasn't much to live for. The large man in the pickup lost the best years of his life in one of California's correctional facilities. When he was released, he quickly learned that most of the doors of opportunity were closed to him.

Who won?

On Memorial Day weekend in 1997, 513 people were killed in automobile crashes during the sixty-hour period from 6 P.M. Friday to 6 A.M. Sunday. On the weekend of the Fourth of July during the same year, 508 persons died on the roads and highways of the United States.[30]

Studies by the AAA and the Department of Transportation show that the most dangerous drivers are young males under the age of thirty-five. That is hardly surprising, since those drivers have an overload of youthful energy combined with a deficiency of experience and skill in handling a car. But we also see the embittered older person—male or female—who is angrier and has greater driving skills. We see him everywhere, almost like repeatedly seeing the same person. His face exudes self-betrayal: He doesn't care about anybody and nobody cares about him. He does not love and he is not loved. His life has been a failure, a monotonously unending series of losses: hard, exhausting work and little compensation; a life of being ignored and excluded. He is willing to risk death for one small win. He is everywhere.

There are at least 12 million licensed drivers in Los Angeles County, which, according to the *Los Angeles Times*, has the worst traffic congestion in the nation. But other metropolitan areas are rapidly catching up. Other areas of greatest freeway overload are Florida, particularly Miami; Phoenix; Chicago;

Washington, DC; Las Vegas; Dallas–Fort Worth; Seattle; Denver; New York City; and New Jersey. Smaller cities such as Albuquerque, New Mexico; Atlanta, Georgia; Austin, Texas; and Charlotte, North Carolina, are also beginning to feel the crunch of traffic congestion and filthy air.[31]

In Ohio on August 28, 2001, a thirty-six-year-old former Cleveland SWAT police officer, Geoffrey Stevens, fired his gun into the car of another motorist while shouting at him, missing him by inches. The victim asked the judge to be lenient with the former cop. The judge gave Stevens two years probation, ordered him to undergo psychological counseling and anger management, and ordered him to give a written apology to the victim. He also ordered him not to handle a gun. If he violates the terms of his parole he will serve three years in prison.[32]

On June 21, 2002, in San Antonio, a twenty-three-year-old off-duty correctional officer, Tobie Garcia, was shot in the head after a car cut off a pickup truck. At the time of the most recent news report, Garcia was still alive but in critical condition.[33]

In Chicago on October 2, 1999, five white deputy sheriffs were arrested for allegedly pursuing and firing on a black couple. The deputies were off duty. They told authorities that the other driver had cut them off. Two were charged with attempted murder. The others were charged with official misconduct and obstruction of justice.[34]

With such an overload of vehicles surrounding your car, you can get an almost infinite variety of drivers in your proximity. You can get a driver who is hearing voices because he was released, too early, from a mental hospital and has neglected to take his antipsychotic drugs. The voices may be telling him to kill you. Or you may be driving alongside a person who has taken several prescription drugs and is unable to control his arms and legs. It would be more pleasant if you could choose your freeway neighbors, but they all look alike, just your garden-variety cars and trucks and drivers.

Two years ago, when we were parked in a shopping mall, we saw an elderly lady driving a Cadillac toward our van. Fortunately, we were not in the van. We stood and watched as she drew closer. She did not slow down. With a look of grim determination, she accelerated and caved in the side of our van. It was totaled. We watched as she got out of her Cadillac.

"I'm so sorry!" she said.

"Why did you do that?" I asked.

"I don't know!" she replied. "I tried to take my foot off the gas and put my foot on the brake but my foot just went down on the gas."

Then, after we had talked for some time and she felt more comfortable with me, she opened her handbag and took out six prescriptions, which she showed me, one by one.

"Are you taking all six of those drugs? At the same time?" I asked.

"Yes," she said. "My doctor told me to."

"Did your doctor warn you that all of those drugs have side effects, and when you combine two, or three, or six, anything can happen?"

"No. He never said anything about that."

Dr. Arnold Nerenberg, a clinical psychologist who specializes in road rage, has stated that twenty-nine thousand Americans died because of aggressive driving in 1996.[35] An Australian study concluded that about half of all traffic accidents in Austalia may have been caused by road rage. A study conducted by Lex Research in the U.K. indicates that of Britain's nearly 3 million company car drivers, about 83 percent have been victims of road rage. These are people who drive almost constantly because that is how they earn their living. Collectively, they are probably one of the best sources of observations of road rage. Some law enforcement officials believe that nearly all of the automobile crashes in the United States are caused by road rage. There is no scientific research to support this belief, but the U.S. Department of Transportation has estimated that two-thirds of traffic fatalities are at least partially caused by aggressive driving.

The story that follows came to me in pieces from various eyewitnesses, including an ambulance driver and a cop.

"Elliot" was doing well. He was an acquaintance of one of my friends. He had a glamorous, interesting job that paid well. He was married to a beautiful young woman he had met during his second year at college and they had two small sons. They had bought a house, a boat, and a glistening new car with a powerful engine. He was clever, resourceful, and somewhat overcompetitive. The other men at work were continually carrying defamatory tales about him to his boss, hoping to get him fired, because they knew the inevitable comparisons between his performance and theirs would be made. But that, too, was a challenge and the bosses valued him because he brought in more money than the others. Although he was only twenty-seven years old, he was earning more money than many men twice his age. He and his beautiful wife, "Barbara," lay awake at night, looking forward with exhilaration to a glorious future, filled with vacation trips to faraway places; distinguished, stimulating friends; and the joy of watching their children grow into adulthood. They had an expensive, high-quality stereo; a large-screen television; an outdoor barbecue; and all the gadgetry of suburban living. They liked to party and dine with friends and clients. They stringently avoided extramarital affairs, although there were many invitations, because their bonding was too strong and too precious to be put at risk.

He was in a hurry. There was something he needed to tell his wife in order to avoid an embarrassing situation. He was driving on the freeway in his new Thunderbird, surrounded by moderately heavy traffic. He was annoyed. He did not like to see anybody get ahead of him, even though they were already there before he entered the freeway. He wanted to win. He wanted to be number one.

He signaled for a lane change but a car pulled up alongside him, blocking his way. The driver was a grim-faced, white-haired man. His hard, merciless eyes said it all: Me in front, you in back. I'm the boss. No son of a bitch is gonna get in front of me.

Elliot floored it and tried to leave the other driver behind, but he was stuck in a slow-moving lane. The older man also accelerated, passed him, changed lanes, cut in front of him, and left him far behind. Elliot pushed it to the floor, weaving through traffic until he found an open lane and passed the older man at about 85 MPH. The older man tried to pull in front of him, but Elliot was able to swing around him, seized with the ecstatic adrenaline rush of victory. As he passed the older man he flipped him the finger with an elated grin and gave him a brake job. The enraged older man changed lanes and pursued Elliot. His eyes were fixed on Elliot like dual laser beams. Elliott looked back at him in the rearview mirror. His face said: I'm gonna take him out of that car. But Elliot was far ahead and still gaining. He maintained his speed, going about 90 or 100 MPH so that the other car would not overtake him and rob him of his victory before he could find an off-ramp. At that speed the sounds of the tires and the motor rise to a higher frequency, producing a high-pitched tone like the soundtrack music on an eerie horror movie when the big chase is beginning. It's an elated adrenaline buzz, the precarious high of winning. It elevates your arousal. Elliot had already gone far beyond the exit closest to his home. Although he was traveling at a frightfully dangerous speed, he felt no fear, only the transcendental exhilaration of winning.

Once you gun your motor, accept the challenge, and go after the other car you have crossed the line and entered another world where nothing else exists. A high-speed race releases mind-altering chemicals in the brain, and everything vanishes but the thrill of winning or the crushing, stinging agony of being beaten. Aggressive driving is contagious and addictive. Like the vampire, once bitten, you become one of them.

A deceleration from 20 MPH to zero in one second can rupture your aorta and end your life. Elliot knew that, but it was not a matter of great concern to him at that time. He knew he was riding dangerously close to that bottomless crevasse, but he had no sense of the enormity of death or its finality, the imminent danger of loss of all the wonderful things in his life. It is always like that during these contests. It wasn't until the race was over that he thought of his wife and how sad she would be if their beautiful new car was smashed and ruined, if *he* was smashed and ruined—or killed. He wondered why he found it irresistible to do such a reckless thing. Elliot saw an off-ramp. He let up on the gas and put his foot on the brake pedal, being careful to decelerate slowly enough to avoid skidding and losing control of the car.

It had been a good day for Elliot. He had defeated two other cantankerous drivers, leaving them far behind with their scalding anger and humiliation. This would be the crowning victory at the end of a near-perfect day. He was still going at a velocity of about 80 MPH. He did not see the stalled truck until it was too late.

He awoke in something that looked like a tunnel, but it was moving and bouncing, spinning and tumbling. He was lying on his back and there were two men kneeling over him. He heard a loud siren coming from overhead. Then he remembered. He knew he was badly injured.

"Listen!" he said urgently. "I've got to get a message to my wife! Tell her . . ."

They shushed him as he spoke and told him to lie still. He pleaded with them again: "Please! Tell my wife . . ." But they told him to be quiet. When they arrived at the emergency entrance to the hospital one of the men spoke to him, then examined him and looked at the other paramedic.

"What's the matter?" the other man asked.

"He's dead."

They put him on a gurney and rushed him into the emergency room, ignoring the nurses who, one by one, told them:

"You'll have to wait."

"The doctor is busy."

"You'll have to wait."

"You'll have to wait your turn."

"We've got to get him in there right away! He stopped breathing! There's no pulse or respiration!" the ambulance driver shouted.

"Aaaah, don't get excited," an older nurse said in her harsh, oversmoked voice as she sat at the counter playing solitaire.

Once they entered the emergency room—over the protest of the nurses—the doctors did what they could, trying to revive him, but to no avail. It was too late.

Why did he gamble so much? And for what? When the answer to that question is generally understood we will have come a long way toward eliminating slaughter on the highways, and a good deal more than that.

NOTES

1. Katherine Shaver, "Tyson Gets One Year for Assault on Motorists," *Los Angeles Times*, February 7, 1997, p. A-12.

2. Mike Clary, "Simpson Faces Road Rage Charges," *Los Angeles Times*, February 10, 2001, p. A-3.

3. Dana Canedy, "Jury Acquits O. J. Simpson in a Trial on Road Rage," *New York Times*, October 25, 2001, p. A-19.

4. Julie Tamaki, "Jack Nicholson Accused of Breaking Man's Windshield," *Los Angeles Times*, February 23, 1994, p. B-1.

5. Julie Tamaki, "Motorist Settles Civil Lawsuit against Jack Nicholson," *Los Angeles Times*, March 11, 1994, p. B-5.

6. Thom Mrozek, "Arraignment Delayed for Jack Nicholson," *Los Angeles Times*, April 15, 1994, p. B-3.

7. *USA Today*, October 31, 2001, and *Time* magazine published the story on November 12, 2001. I called *USA Today* and got left on hold forever. There are about seventy-five pieces on the Web about Hackman and his road rage adventure: Celebritywonder.com/html /Gene Hackman.html; G.H. Biog http://www.angelfire.com /celeb2/genehackman/bio/html; and naturally, the *National Enquirer*. *USA Today* is a better source but I was unable to find the articles from *USA Today* and *Time* on the Web, maybe because they are five years old.

8. Dominic Connell and Matthew Joint, *Aggressive Driving: Three Studies* (Washington, DC: American Automobile Association Foundation for Traffic Safety, 1997), p. 6.

9. Ibid.

10. Ibid.

11. Ibid.

12. Ibid., p. 7.

13. Ibid., p. 11.

14. Ibid., p. 12.

15. This advice has been given repeatedly by police, government spokespersons, and academics. It can be found in virtually every book, article, and publication on road rage.

16. Radio Station KJR and other Seattle radio stations carried this story after the female driver called it in.

17. Konrad Lorenz, *On Aggression* (New York: MJK Books, 1963), pp. 181, 201.

18. Connell and Joint, *Aggressive Driving*, p. 3.

19. Stephanie Paul, Media Communications Director, AAA Foundation for Traffic Safety, 1440 New York Avenue, Washington, DC (oral interview).

20. Art Levene, "How Angry Drivers Are Putting You in Danger," *Redbook*, March 1997, p. 90. Also *Time*, January 22, 1998, p. 64. See also "Agressive Driving Is America's Car Sickness Du Jour," January 12, 1998, http://www.time.com/time/magazine /1998/com/980112/society.road_rage.html.

21. Joint and Connell, *Aggressive Driving: Three Studies*, prepared by AAA Foundation for Traffic Safety, Washington, DC, p. 3.

22. Ibid., p. 3. See also David Everett, "Women Catching Up with Men in One Area: Driving Deaths," Knight Ridder News Service, June 29, 1994. Also Dianne Hales, "The New Road Warriors," *Ladies Home Journal*, April 1998, p. 96. Also Jessica Snyder Sachs, "Road Warriors," *Parenting Magazine*, November 1998, p. 2, http://www .parenting.com/parenting/article/article_general/0,8266,5,99,00. html.

23. Gerry Byrne, *New Scientist*, London, England, December 9, 2000, pp. 38–41.

24. *New I.D. in America* (Port Townsend, WA: Loompanics Unlimited, 1999). The Loompanics Catalog has a section with several pages of titles on "alternative" I.D.

25. Russell Geen and Edward Donnerstein, eds., *Human Aggression: Theories, Research, and Implications for Social Policy* (Washington, DC: Academic Press, 1998), p. 23.

26. AAA Three Studies, p. 10; also p. 6.

27. Stephanie Faul, Media Information Director, AAA Foundation for Traffic Safety, oral interview. This definition of road rage and "agressive driving" has been published in various AAA literature. AAA Foundation for Traffic Safety's URL is http://www.aaa foundation .org.

28. California Highway Patrol, oral interview.

29. The Surface Transportation Policy Project is a national coalition of more than two hundred organizations working to promote transportation policies that motivate neighborhoods to provide better travel choices. It also provides assistance to local agencies.

30. California Highway Patrol, Public Information Office, oral interview.

31. Hugo Martin, "No Idle Boast: L.A. Traffic Worst," *Los Angeles Times*, June 21, 2002, p. B-1.

32. Former SWAT Officer Apologizes for Road Rage Incident," WEWS-TV, www.newsnet5.com/news/1530069/detail.html (June 25, 2002).

33. "SAPD SWAT Situation and Arrest," San Antonio Police Department news release, www.sanantonio.gov/sapd/pdf/Adv _062002.pdf (June 21, 2002).

34. http://www.APBnews.com/newscent.../1999/10/02_01. html (October 2, 1999).

35. Arnold Nerenberg is somewhat "over the top." He makes many reckless and unfounded statements.

2

AGGRESSION

"I Shot Him Because He Passed Me"

S cientists have been trying for decades to identify the causes of humans' aggressive behavior toward their own species: internecine wars, tribal wars, race riots, gang wars, religious wars, world wars, witch-hunts, and now, road rage. They fail to understand that these are innate behavior patterns encoded in our genes—and those of our most ancient predecessors. We have little hope of redirecting our aggression without understanding how it functions, how we acquired it, and the conditions that formed it.

According to the Nobel Prize–winning scientist Konrad Lorenz, aggression is an instinct that, like other instincts, evolved for the purpose of preserving the species. He draws a distinction between attacking a member of another species to get food, which is aggressive but is done without anger, and aggression in the proper sense, which is directed against a member of the same species but is not without anger. Most vertebrates fight their own species, including *Homo sapiens*.[1]

What are the sources of Lorenz's theories? His *On Aggression* includes a lengthy bibliography, but no notes or references. His is original work, based on a lifetime spent observing many species of fish, birds, and mammals, including primates, for which he was awarded the Nobel Prize in Physiology or Medicine in 1973 for "discoveries concerning organization and elicitation of individual and social behavior."

Widely renowned as the father of animal behaviorism, Lorenz states that intraspecific aggression serves the purpose of spreading the members of a species evenly over an inhabitable area, because overcrowding causes depletion of food, exposure to contagious diseases, the inability to hide, and excessive fighting. Intraspecific aggression, he writes, is directed toward members of a neighboring tribe, herd, or flock, not toward members of the same family, herd, or tribe—in other words, toward the stranger. On the freeway, the "stranger" is the other car. During the Early Stone Age, Lorenz asserts, there were wars between hostile neighboring tribes. This was the influence that caused humans to acquire the vicious warrior virtues that many people still admire. This is why there are always dozens of wars in progress on the planet at any given point in time. Many reasons are given by the ruling groups: religion, the need for food, the depravity of the other tribe, but the fact is, it is in our nature to fight our own species. There are strong instinctive and cultural influences that act as deterrents to killing members of one's own tribe or family, but they don't always hold back the paleolithic killer. We have a natural appetite for combat. When a war ends, we enslave the losers and execute their leaders, clean up the rubble, bury the dead, and house the disabled. Then we begin killing each other again.

I watched an old interview of former president Richard Nixon by Brian Lamb on C-SPAN. Nixon stated that there have been 140 wars since World War II in which a total of 8 million people have been killed. That was 1992. On CNN in 2000, presidential candidate Bill Bradley stated that there were thirty-two ethnic wars going on "right now."

Lorenz views intraspecific aggression as the greatest threat to the survival of humans, because the invention of artificial weapons has changed our environment so rapidly that our inhibitions against killing, both instinctive and cultural, are not equal to the task of controlling it. We are a species filled with the brutish, aggressive passions of a Stone Age man. But instead of holding an ax, we hold the hydrogen bomb in our hands.[2] Another of these artificial weapons is the car.

Lorenz writes that because of our invention of artificial weapons, our aggressive instinct has been derailed and is malfunctioning; our only hope for survival is in understanding that it is a powerful, species-preserving instinct, more powerful than rational thought.[3] Why was it necessary for us and so many other animal species to acquire such fierce intraspecific fighting instincts? And why do so many people want to prohibit the study of evolution, which might be our salvation? Why do we not teach drivers that our intraspecific aggression is more powerful than reason—unless the driver gains insight into the nature of his aggression and the consequences of not keeping it in check? The driver *must* understand the measure of its power and also understand that to be drawn into a road rage duel is to blindly obey, and be controlled by, a master who will sacrifice you as casually as one would crush a cockroach.

Explaining the ways in which aggression goes wrong, Lorenz states that we must dispose of "certain inner obstacles which prevent people from seeing themselves as a part of the universe and recognizing that their own behavior too obeys the laws of nature."[4]

Another product of intraspecific selection, Lorenz notes, is the frightfully stressful, overcompetitive lifestyle of contemporary people, a condition that is unnecessary. We could as easily live and work in friendly cooperation, mutual assistance, and do without renal atrophy, high blood pressure, and its lethal consequences.[5] This, too, is a race, a form of combat not unlike road rage. Like the tattooed street thug and the paleolithic anthropoid, the corporate worker has no room in his life for cultural or humanistic interests. Typically, he has no values. He has a car. It is his escape from boredom. He thirsts for battle.

Lorenz observes that aggression is not the essence of everything evil; that without aggression there is no bonding, no love, no friendship, no motivation to achieve, no creativity. The most highly developed love bonding is found in humans and geese.

Aggression is as old as the class of reptiles, but bonding between individuals did not appear until the Tertiary period, somewhere between 12 and 60 million years ago, and exists only in animals with fierce intraspecific aggression. "Thus," he states, "intraspecific aggression can certainly exist without its counterpart, love, but conversely there is no love without aggression."[6]

Aggression is the worst and the best of who we are, depending on what we do with it. Aggression is what enabled Thomas Edison to persevere when his assistants advised him to give up. When George Washington and his ragged, barefooted followers made war upon the mightiest army in the world against hopeless odds, that was the manifestation of a high degree of aggression—unlike the pampered Tories, who could not understand why he would do such a vulgar thing.

What makes aggression even more dangerous is that it is

spontaneous. It does not require external stimuli but is activated by endogenously produced stimuli in the limbic system.[7] This explains why there are so many acts of homicidal violence by drivers against strangers who have done nothing to offend them. Who among us has not had the experience of suddenly being verbally and/or physically assaulted by a person to whom we have caused no real harm or annoyance? Lorenz states that the belief that animal and human behavior is predominantly reactive is erroneous. He writes, "The fact that the human nervous system does not need to wait for stimuli . . . before it can respond, but that it can itself produce stimuli which give a natural, physiological explanation for the 'spontaneous' behavior in animals and humans has found recognition only in the last decades."[8]

A series of experiments found that the deprivation of any outlet for an instinctive behavior pattern progressively lowers its threshold to zero. In other words, when our instinctive aggression is bottled up and has no outlet, it is compressed and becomes more volatile. The modern office worker is usually deprived of any outlet for her aggression. But when she gets into her car it is, at last, released! The obsequious bureaucrat is transformed into a valiant warrior-avenger. In order to preserve the species, new ritualized behaviors evolve to inhibit aggression and divert it into innocuous behavior. In birds and other animals there are rituals, certain physical movements and gestures, that serve to prevent the killing and injuring of members of the same species.[9] In humans there are rites that are not hereditarily fixed but are traditions learned by each new generation: for example, the smoking of the peace pipe by mutually hostile Native American chiefs to resolve a dispute, or the etiquette of various human ethnic groups that also serves to avert violence. They redirect aggression. Without them, we would be extinct.

With the invention of long-range artificial weapons, a person can kill by remote control and not see what he has done. The balance between aggression and inhibition has been skewed. When a driver loses the ability to inhibit his aggression and rushes into battle, roaring toward his target on the highway, he does not see a man, a woman, and an infant. He sees a car. According to Lorenz, "Conceptual thought and speech changed all man's evolution by achieving something which is equivalent to the inheritance of acquired characters. . . . Thus, within one or two generations a process of ecological adaptation can be achieved which in normal phylogeny and without the interference of conceptual thought, would have taken a time of an altogether different, much greater order of magnitude." Our social inhibitions, he writes, could not keep pace with these rapid changes.[10] In other words, the larger, more powerful human brain has changed our behavior, our environment, and technology so rapidly that it is out of control and could extinguish all life on the planet. The human being, he warns, is "a jeopardized creature."

I once watched an interview of Werner von Braun, the aging German rocket whiz kid, conducted by a television network newswoman. Braun was boasting of his latest project: an orbiting space station.

"But what could an orbiting space station do that would justify such an enormous cost?" the newswoman asked.

"It would have many great benefits to mankind," he said, his eyes glowing with enthusiasm. "Entire cities could be destroyed in a few seconds!"

"And what other great benefits to mankind would it have?" she asked in a tone of icy sarcasm.

"Entire nations could be wiped out in a single raid!" he exulted.

I know this brief excerpt may appear surreal or out of context, but I saw it with my own eyes and heard it with my own ears and I can assure you that he was perfectly serious.

Lorenz, who spent his life observing fish, birds, and mammals of almost every species, identifies four types of social organization: (1) The anonymous flock, which lacks the awareness of its members as individuals. (2) The family and social life of certain birds, such as the heron. Although they nest in colonies, their only structural basis is territorial. (3) Rats, which do not recognize each other as individuals but by tribal smell and which treat members of their own tribe with benignity while they viciously attack any member of another tribe. (4) The type of social organization in which the bond of love and friendship prevents members from harming each other. This bond he observed in humans and geese. He defines war and other forms of slaughter as the aggressive instinct malfunctioning and warns that with the technology we now possess, it could extinguish all life on the planet.

The most primitive grouping of animals is the anonymous flock. The members of the anonymous flock do not recognize each other as individual entities, only as components of the flock. "Under certain horrible conditions," Lorenz writes, "even man can regress to anonymous herd formation."[11] This regression occurs in times of mass panic. There is also, too often, a regression to horrible primitive behavior when an individual gets into his car.

Another undesirable result of intraspecific selection, Lorenz asserts, is the grotesque, overblown gluttony of certain individuals afflicted with the instinctive compulsion to amass an enormous body of monetary assets and property. This, too, is a race that engages those who possess a dangerously high degree of self-assertion, another manifestation of the same aggressive instinct that produces road rage. "Commercial competition today might threaten to fix hereditarily in us hypertrophies of these traits. . . . It is fortunate that the accumulation of riches and power does not necessarily lead to larger families—rather the opposite—or else the future of mankind would look even darker than it does."[12]

Lorenz expresses the hope that rational, moral responsibility will prevail and be sufficient to manage the growing menace of lethal technology. He also predicts that *Homo sapiens* will mutate into a higher, more intelligent species. There is certainly no reason to believe that *Homo sapiens* is the final product of evolution, which is apparently going on all of the time.

In the meantime, we can only hope that all obstacles to learning, knowledge, and insight will be removed. Censorship is as great a danger to our survival as aggression.

Philip Zimbardo, one of the most respected contemporary psychologists, asserts that America has a collective fascination for violence.[13] We are not the only people who have an affinity for violence. Zimbardo writes that in 1983, "the nations of the world spent nearly $1 trillion on military weapons."[14] Many nations spend more on weapons than on food and agriculture. "In 1986, declared the 'Year of Peace' by the United Nations, five million people died in thirty-six wars."[15] There is a shared belief among psychologists that human beings are "instinctively aggressive animals." Sigmund Freud's theory of aggression (the death instinct), Zimbardo writes, "has little scientific utility to predict or control behavior."[16]

According to Zimbardo, there is compelling evidence that aggression is encoded in our genes. In a 1986 study that compared 286 monozygotic (identical) twins to 179 bizygotic (fraternal) twins, the bizygotic twin pairs' scores were uncorrelated, while in the identical twins the correlation of aggressiveness scores was significantly higher.[17] Those who conducted the study also concluded that very little of the twins' aggressiveness was caused by shared environment. "Brain disease of the limbic system and temporal lobes has been found in persons exhibiting . . . senseless brutality . . . or repeated serious automobile acidents."[18]

Other scientists argue that aggressiveness is a contagious disease that is most prevalent in the eleven southern states.[19] Zimbardo writes that violent behavior is more frequent when temperature and air pollution are high.

In 1939 a group of psychologists at Yale University presented an alternative view that aggression was learned, not instinctive, but it became clear that aggression was not always preceded by frustration. One of the interesting facts presented by Zimbardo is that the death penalty does not deter people from murdering others. In fact, murders actually *diminish* slightly when the death penalty is abolished.[20] Expressing or acting out aggression is not a catharsis, but may have an opposite effect.[21] In other words, "letting off steam" is not a panacea for aggression, but may stimulate the desire for aggression. According to Zimbardo, "Expressing anger against one's enemies, verbally or in overt action, directly or vicariously is not likely to reduce our tendencies toward aggression. Learning how to negotiate conflicts verbally, however, can reduce the need for physical aggression against them."[22] The same is likely true of road rage.

As for the influence of media violence, Zimbardo asserts, "There is little convincing evidence that viewing violence on television . . . causes an increase in subsequent aggressiveness."[23]

In *The Territorial Imperative*, Robert Ardrey presents substantial evidence that we are territorial animals who will defend our space against all members of our own species, a concept generally accepted in the biological sciences. Like Lorenz, he presents observations on territorial behavior in other animals and demonstrates that humans obey the laws of many other species. Of particular interest to those who wish to understand the nature and source of road rage is the ferocious rage and animal energy that is released in a smaller and weaker territorial defender when a larger and more powerful intruder invades his property. Our military chiefs of staff did not factor that into their plans when they invaded Vietnam. Neither did the Arab League when they launched the 1967 war against Israel.

In some species the female is sexually unresponsive to an unpropertied male and the male who has not taken possession of territory is incapable of copulating with the female. Similarly, one cannot deny that human females want sexual affection, but they want it at a good address—with a male who has a good car.

In his chapter titled "The Amity-Enmity Complex," Ardrey has put the duality of animal and human behavior into a simple equation:

$$A = E + h$$

which means that amity (A) is directly proportional and equal to the enmity (E) and hazard (h) that assail any human and most higher animals. Enmity (E) is defined as emanating from within the species; hazard (h) represents any external threat that comes from outside the species: war, floods, fire, drought, snakes, predators, and other life-threatening conditions.[24] For primitive humans, there was also the supernatural. In other words, amity between members of the same species will be equal to the sum of enmity and hazard that assail them. But there is very little amity without enmity and hazard. It is well known that war brings the people of a state or tribe together; they fight less among themselves and join in amity and camaraderie to combine their collective aggression against the common enemy. "With every addition to the value of E, there has been produced an additional value of A."[25] When there is a war, the people are thoroughly indoctrinated to become enthusiastic about invading the enemy long before the assault is launched. Before World War II my father was one of the principal authors of a massive media campaign to create the belief that the enemy were fiendish monsters, repulsive and unspeakably cruel, killers of children and mothers—which was true, but not everybody in the United States concurred with that belief. Many people were infatuated with Hitlerism, but they quickly became 100 percent American, and equally anti-German, in the face of such propaganda. Even Americans of German origin, which then comprised the second largest ethnic group in the United States, quickly became enthusiastic about the war. Understanding the duality of human and animal behavior could be a potent tool in the hands of those who want to put an end to road rage, or at least greatly diminish it. Subtle messages could be implanted in motion pictures and television dramas portraying the road rager as a repulsive creature whom nobody would want to have anything to do with. Most people are very frightened of ostracism. A few would continue to drive aggressively, but most would find it too embarrassing. One is not really anonymous in the car.

Ardrey quotes an article by Ibenaus Eibl-Eibesfeldt, who writes, "A growing body of evidence from observations in the field and experiments in the laboratory points to the conclusion that this vital mode of behavior is not learned by the individual but is innate in the species. . . ."[26] Paraphrasing Lorenz, he writes that:

The Lorenz approach to human aggression is, first, that we must recognize that it is healthy, that it is necessary, that it is innate, that it is ineradicable; the second, that the solution to the human problem is to be sought in the direction of nature, in other words by the enlargement of all those less-than-lethal competitions, ritualizations, and displays, whether between individuals or groups, which absorb our hostile energies and turn them to ends, either harmless or constructive.[27]

Enmity, Ardrey states, is the stuff that amity is made of, but "the human being is an incalculable stew of evolutionary endowment, individual genetic variation, and personal experience never common to identical twins, so man lies beyond all mathematics."[28] Ardrey stated that in 1965, only about 3 percent of all land under cultivation in the Soviet Union was in private hands. Yet it produced almost half of all the vegetables consumed and three-quarters of all eggs. "The territorial nature of man is genetic and ineradicable. . . . This territorial species of which you and I are members has been the source of all freedom, the curse on the despot, the last desperate roadblock in the path of the aggressor's might."[29] Apparently the members of the politburo were not aware of the human territorial instinct, nor were Karl Marx and Friedrich Engels.

The psychologists who have become the experts on road rage refer to aggressive drivers as "emotionally impaired" and "mentally disordered." Generally speaking, they are not. They are simply doing what they were engineered to do. Must we either resign ourselves to this condition, or attempt genetic engineering or psychosurgery? No. Although we have powerful instincts, as do other animals, we also have large frontal lobes in our brains that give us the power to manage and control aggression, once we understand the consequences of not controlling it. Unfortunately, many people do not want to understand evolution and instinctive behavior, and many teachers do not want to teach their students about these phenomena. Our television and educational institutions have not been eager to address this subject.

What we do to each other on the road in no way differs from what we do to each other in other settings. It is the same instinctive, paleolithic animal aggression—powered by a 300-horsepower engine, a 3,000-pound battle wagon, and concealed from view much of the time, giving us the illusion of anonymity.

This is where we need to look. Once we understand aggression and know that it is an integral part of the human organism and how it functions, we will know everything we need to know about road rage.

NOTES

1. Konrad Lorenz, *On Aggression* (New York: MFJ Books, 1966), p. 30.
2. Ibid., p. 241.
3. Ibid.
4. Ibid., pp. 222–24.
5. Ibid., p. 217.
6. Ibid.
7. Ibid., pp. 49–53.
8. Ibid., p. 51.
9. Ibid., p. 67.
10. Ibid., p. 238.
11. Ibid., p. 139.
12. Ibid., pp. 42, 246.
13. Philip G. Zimbardo, *Psychology and Life* (Glenview, Ill.: Scott Foresman, 1985), p. 643.
14. Ibid.
15. Ibid.
16. Ibid., p. 644.

17. Ibid., p. 645.

18. Ibid., p. 646.

19. Ibid., p. 647.

20. Ibid., p. 648.

21. Ibid.

22. Ibid., pp. 645, 649–50.

23. Ibid., p. 651. See also J. L. Friedman, "Effect of Television Violence on Aggressiveness," *Psychological Bulletin* 96 (1984): 227–46.

24. Robert Ardrey, *The Territorial Imperative* (New York: Atheneum, 1966), pp. 269–70.

25. Ibid., p. 274.

26. Ibid., p. 297. Also see Irenaus Eibl-Eibesfeldt, "Fighting Behavior in Animals," *Scientific American*, December 1961.

27. Ardrey, *The Territorial Imperative*, p. 302.

28. Ibid., p. 272.

29. Ibid., pp. 111–17.

3

WOMEN WARRIORS AND LEADING CITIZENS

"I Shot Him Because He Looked at Me with Disrespect"

WOMEN WARRIORS

Many people uncritically accept the prevalent but unexamined notion that road rage is a "guy thing." Wrong! Police often refer to these battles as "dueling testosterone," but that is a misnomer. It's adrenalin. Until recently, statistics showed that about 55 percent of road rage incidents involved male drivers and only 45 percent were caused by women. More recent traffic studies indicate that women are driving more aggressively and causing more fatal accidents. Soon, they will have achieved full parity in freeway slaughter. A woman driving a car is faster and more formidable than any man—unless he, too, is driving a car. Over the past two decades car crashes involving female drivers have increased by 18 percent.[1] According to the AAA Foundation for Traffic Safety, men do most of the road rage shootings, while women do most of the rammings. A recent Michigan survey found that 56 percent of drivers who admitted to high levels of anger were women. The study concluded that men and women were equally likely to act out their anger while driving.[2] A road rage study conducted by Paul Overberg in 1999 concluded that "aggressive drivers were women as often as men."[3] The study also showed that women were more likely than men to tailgate, block lanes, and punish other drivers.

Thirty-four-year-old Gena Foster was on her way to pick up her child from school in an affluent suburb of Birmingham, Alabama. She entered the slow lane in front of a car driven by Shirley Henson, a forty-year-old secretary. Henson flashed her brights. Foster slammed her brakes. The challenge was accepted and returned. The two angry drivers got into a four-mile duel, racing and crossing lanes. When one car left the freeway, the other followed. Later, when both cars were stopped, Foster approached Henson's automobile, shouting. Henson drew a .38 caliber revolver and shot Foster in the face, killing her.[4] Henson is a former Cub Scout leader with a son in college. Her neighbors describe her as a friendly person who loves dogs and children. Foster was the mother of three children and had only recently moved into her new home on three acres of land. Neither had any criminal record. But the county's rapid growth had turned their commutes into an ordeal of stop and go traffic. Law enforcement officials stated that about half or more of the drivers in this area have firearms in their cars.[5]

This incident is a demonstration of the power of mindless animal rage that is frequently triggered when one car changes lanes and moves in front of another. It is also an example of what can and does happen when one driver gets out of her car to confront an angry, out-of-control road rager. It also reflects the alarming increase in road rage behavior on the part of female drivers. Since the 1980s fatal combat involving female drivers has risen 18 percent and women are now involved in more nonfatal accidents than men.[6]

Sharane Kearney, age twenty-four, was driving a borrowed Lincoln Continental toward an intersection on a Salt Lake City street. She slowed down for a red light. She was unfamiliar with the large Continental, two tons of rolling weight, and she had just taken an amphetamine. She unwittingly put the transmission in reverse, and when the light turned green she pushed down on the gas pedal, backing up and hitting the car behind her with a loud bang, accompanied by the shatter and tinkle of broken glass. The driver of the other car, fifty-year-old Joann Collett, followed Kearney into a parking lot to exchange insurance information. But Kearney had no insurance and she had no driver's license. Both drivers got out of their cars. A dispute ensued that burgeoned into a shouting match. Kearney got into the Lincoln, backed out of the parking space, and started to drive away, but Collett stood in front of the Continental and demanded that she stop, backing away as the car moved forward. Kearney pushed down on the gas pedal and Collett disappeared under the front end. Kearney gunned her motor, dragging Collett's broken body for a distance of fifteen hundred feet, crushing and grinding her, leaving a trail of flesh, blood, hair, bone fragments, teeth, shreds of clothing, cosmetics, paper, and other scraps of Joann Collett's life. Then she turned the corner and the body rolled free from under the car. Joann Collett was dead.

Kearney drove the borrowed car back to a friend's house and asked her friend to hide it. They washed away the blood, the fragments of Collett and her clothes. Then they went out and spent a pleasant afternoon shopping at the mall.

But Kearney had left too many witnesses and she did not

abscond. She thought it was over until the police came, arrested her, and took her to the county jail, where she remained for several months.

At her sentencing hearing the defense argued that "Miss Kearney suffers from a debilitating set of illnesses that would hamper her ability to deal with a situation of stress." The defense further stated that Kearney had been a victim of child abuse, that she suffered from "anxiety disorders," migraine headaches, and chest pains.

Her lawyer, Judith Jensen, did her best to argue that Kearney was not responsible for Joann Collett's death because of a long list of disabilities that impaired her judgment and made her unaware of what she was doing:

> She suffers from a diagnosed major depression and abuse that Dr. Gregory considers to exhibit signs of post-traumatic stress syndrome, your honor . . . and there are other underlying mental illnesses that are documented. Miss Kearney has disabilities in perception . . . when she looks from the left to the right she requires a moment that most of us do not require. She can't understand it. . . . She also has Reynaud's disease that prevents her . . . from manipulating things. She is a loving, caring mother.

Kearney had an excellent lawyer who did as much as a lawyer could do for her client. She plea-bargained down to manslaughter rather than face the penalties for first-degree murder. She tried to persuade the judge to give her client "an alternative placement, not prison."

When she had finished the judge spoke: "Anything from the defendant?"

Kearney replied, "I would like to say I'm terribly sorry to the family."

"The court will hear from anybody who wants to be heard today," the judge announced. A young girl stood.

"My name is Andrea Cleff," she said. "I would just like to say most people that see someone in front of the car would immediately stop the car. And my mom probably thought she would have stopped. Miss Kearney didn't and my mom died. We have heard a lot about the defendant and what kind of a person she is. I would like to tell you about my mother. She was caring, thoughtful, would never do nobody wrong. If you need help she was always there. I loved my mom and I miss her."

The prosecutor reiterated the testimony of witnesses who stated that Sharane Kearney "punched it" and accelerated when Joann Collett stood in front of her car. The judge strongly asserted that, contrary to the defense's representations that Kearney was unaware of what was happening, she knew exactly what she was doing, that she had a prior hit-and-run offense as well as driving under the influence.

Before sentencing Kearney, the judge said:

The defendant did not lack the ability to reason and to be rational. She took the car home, told her friend to hide it, they wiped the blood off the car. Then what did they do? They went shopping.

Now, the husband mourns, the children mourn, the grandchildren mourn, friends and neighbors mourn . . . because of this horrendous act of violence.

It is this court's observation that violence is becoming an everyday occurrence in this city. And in the lives of many people it is the preferred way to resolve problems. Unfortunately, vehicles are now becoming the means in which angry people intimidate, maim, and kill others. Cars and trucks of every description are now used by out-of-control people to vent their hostilities and their anger to solve problems. It is a problem of no small proportions. . . . This crime has to stand alone in its indescribable detail. The court simply does not have the words to describe the situation.

The court finds that there is no legal reason why sentence should not be imposed. The defendant is committed to the Utah State Penitentiary for the term prescribed by law. The defendant is fined ten thousand dollars. The defendant is ordered to pay restitution to the dollar, determined by Adult Probation and Parole at an appropriate time when she is released. And it is the expressed opinion of the court the defendant should serve fifteen years in the Utah State Prison.[7]

Court was in recess. Kearney was taken away; she will be away for a very long time. The lawyers and spectators departed, leaving the courtroom vacant. The defense attorney may have been correct when she said Sharane Kearney fled because she was afraid. But most reasonable people would not kill another driver. That was the act of a person who did not care about anyone, including herself. There are so many people who do not care about anybody, not even themselves. I have lived and worked among them.

So have you. A neighbor of the defendant was interviewed by reporters and asked what she thought of the incident. Her answer: "Sharane wouldn't do that."

In 1997, in a widely publicized road rage incident, Renée Andrews, a twenty-nine-year-old Ohio woman who was six months pregnant, was driving to work when she discovered she was about to miss her off-ramp and hastily changed lanes. She cut in front of a car driven by Tracie Alfieri, age twenty-three, who became so enraged that she pursued the car driven by Andrews at high speed and "got even" by cutting in front of her then stomping her brakes, causing Andrews's car to crash into a diesel tractor-trailer. Alfieri drove away without stopping, high on her victory, and arrived at her place of employment, grinning and boasting to her coworkers, "Nobody cuts in front of me and gets away with it!" and "I don't take any shit when I'm driving." She didn't know she had caused Andrews to lose her baby and nearly lose her life until the police came and arrested her. For her victory, she was rewarded with 548 glorious days and nights in a state prison. Nearly every bone in Andrews's body was broken. The bones in her limbs were reconstructed and held together with steel rods. She lost her baby and can never have another child. We saw her sitting sadly with her husband, surrounded by the crib, toys, and baby clothes they had bought and received as gifts before the accident. Alfieri spoke to the television cameras with the demeanor of a person who has been the victim of a calamitous injustice. She said it was unfair that she should be prosecuted and sent to prison, that she was not culpable.[8]

In Dale City, Virginia, in July 1999, Natalie Davis, age twenty-five; her two small children, ages two and four; and four other family members were driving in her car when they encountered a car blocking the entrance to the cul de sac on which their home was situated. The other car was surrounded by several teenage girls. When Davis asked the teens to move their car and let her pass they refused. When Davis managed to maneuver her car around the teenagers' car, circumventing their roadblock, the teens became angry. They pursued her, according to police. A short distance down the road, one of the teenagers, a sixteen-year-old girl, grabbed Davis by the hair and pounded her head against the pavement. Another girl, eighteen years old, began stomping on Davis's head and kicking her in the face, right in front of her children, police said. A police officer arrested the assailants and Davis was taken to a hospital, where she was listed in critical condition. The two teenagers were held without bond and charged with aggravated malicious wounding.[9] Two days later, Natalie Davis died from her injuries. Prosecutors said they would seek to try both of the teenage girls as adults.

These girls did not think. They simply obeyed the more powerful commands of their animal instincts and threw away their lives. This case is an excellent example of aggression and the spontaneity of aggression. The teens could easily have allowed Natalie Davis to pass and enjoyed an evening with their contemporaries instead of years in jail.

In West Palm Beach, Florida, on January 14, 1999, Lisa Vedovelli stopped at an intersection just as the yellow light was turning red. The driver in the car behind her, Charlene Canales, screamed and leaned on her horn. Then, according to police, Canales got out of her car, walked to Vedovelli's car, punched her, and pushed her in front of a moving car, which ran over her foot. Canales bent her license plate so that nobody would be able to read it, but she was arrested, charged with aggravated battery, and released on $5,000 bail.[10]

PILLARS OF THE COMMUNITY

Even those who are theoretically our exemplars are not immune to road rage. In North Carolina, a driving instructor was sitting in his car with a student driver at the wheel when another driver cut too close in front of the car. The instructor became so angry that he ordered his student to speed up and pursue the car. When both cars were stopped at a red light the instructor got out, ran to the other car, and punched the driver in the face.[11]

In Potomac, Maryland, Robin Ficker, a prominent lawyer who had been a member of the state legislature, was driving his car when he accidentally rear-ended a car driven by a woman who was six months pregnant. The woman reported that when she got out of her car the man struck her in the face, breaking her prescription glasses and leaving her with a black eye. He was arrested, tried, and convicted of battery and malicious destruction of property.[12]

In Massachusetts Donald Graham, a soft-spoken white-haired man, was driving at night. He was a deacon of his church, a pillar of the community, a role model to all those who serve the Lord. When he saw a driver tailgate another car and flash his high beams on, he was angered. He decided to punish the driver by tailgating him, high beams on, for eight miles. Finally, the other car swerved onto the shoulder. Two men got out and said, "Hey! What's your problem?" The deacon opened the trunk of his car and took out a crossbow, aimed, and shot an arrow. One of the men turned to the other and said, "Hey! I've been shot!"

The weapon was not one of those toy bow-and-arrow sets of the kind given to children on their birthdays. It was as sophisticated and precisely tooled as a firearm. It had a telescopic sight. The arrows were tipped with razor-sharp blades that extended outward when the arrow hit its target, cutting the surrounding tissue. The wounded man was taken to a hospital, but by the time he arrived he had lost too much blood and the hospital staff were unable to save him. The deacon was tried, convicted, and sentenced to spend the rest of his life in prison. His wife divorced him.

In a lengthy interview with a television newsman the deacon, in the pious tone of a holy man, recounted the events that occurred the night of the killing. Finally, the television newsman commented, "I haven't heard you say you're sorry."

The deacon replied, "I'm not gonna apologize for doin' the right thing."[13]

According to the *Boston Globe*, the deacon had been previously convicted four times for drunken driving in Massachusetts and cited for causing a traffic accident and failing to stop for a red light.[14]

It should come as no great surprise that so many prestigious community leaders engage in such shockingly brutal, irresponsible behavior. There is that Dr. Jekyll–Mr. Hyde cohabitation in all of us. The very fact that so many "pillars of the community" commit serious, violent crimes triggered by road rage attests to the shallow mentality of those who should know better. Our leadership has been less than inspiring, and the consequences are visible everywhere.

PRINCE OF PEACE

In 1999 in Minneapolis, a doctor was charged with assault after chasing a seventy-year-old woman in his BMW and hitting her in the face. Witnesses said the elderly woman turned too close in front of the doctor's BMW. They reported seeing him speed up and pull in front of her and then stop, blocking her. He got out of his car, swore at her, and punched her, according to spectators. When police arrived she was crying and her face was swollen. The doctor works as a pain specialist at Queen of Peace Hospital.[15]

An Ohio man was charged with assault after allegedly punching a driver who cut into a funeral procession.[16]

In Florida a teenager squirted a car with a water pistol. The driver returned, raised a firearm, and shot him to death.[17] In Washington State a teenager who threw an egg at a car was shot to death by its driver.[18] There have been enough incidents of assault with a firearm by one driver against another to fill several large volumes. Women, children, infants, and the elderly have been the victims. These skirmishes are happening all the time. It never stops.

MEET THE BULLY

Aggression usually takes the path of least resistance. The aggressor usually chooses someone who appears to be smaller and weaker than himself, not a person who is large and powerful, whose face is bulging with raging, punitive anger. That is why the word "bully" has found a permanent place in our vocabulary. The bully has an imperative to be boss, to be unobstructed by others, to arbitrarily bark his orders, and to be obeyed. Bullies are everywhere. To some degree it's in all of us, as Konrad Lorenz has demonstrated.

In April 1996 a twenty-five-year-old mother picked up her baby daughter and began driving toward her home in Westchester County, New York, when a large, heavy truck began tailgating her.

The truck driver was in a hurry and he became impatient with the mother in her little car. He relentlessly ran her down and struck her rear bumper with considerable force. She tried to get out of the way but the truck rammed her car again and sent it crashing into a tree. The young mother suffered fractured ribs, as well as kidney, back, and neck injuries. Her five-month-old daughter died of head trauma. After inspecting his bumper, the truck driver drove off, leaving mother and child trapped in their car.[19] This is one of the most dangerous situations in which you, as a driver, can find yourself: being tailgated by a large, heavy vehicle while driving a smaller passenger car—particularly on a narrow road where there are no witnesses, no guardrails to protect you from being pushed off the road, and no place to escape or call for help. Many inexperienced drivers believe that driving is no more dangerous than riding the bus. Not so. It is frightfully dangerous. Like playing the piano or violin, driving is a skill that takes years to master, and even those who have decades of experience make mistakes, just as seasoned professional athletes sometimes drop the ball. When you are driving a small or standard-size car and you are being tailgated by a much larger, heavier machine whose driver wants to wreck your car and do bodily harm to you, you must be prepared. You must not let your fear cause you to lose control. You must be vigilant, and when another vehicle begins to follow too closely, you must be aware of it at the earliest stage so you can assess the situation and take evasive action. You must know the limitations of your vehicle, what it is capable of doing and what it is not. You must also know the limitations and vulnerabilities of the other vehicle. A driver who has acquired skill in handling a car can outmaneuver a larger vehicle, causing it to miss you and possibly crash. It is imperative to remember the first indispensable principles of driving in traffic: (1) Fear is your greatest enemy. You must disconnect your fear. (2) One second of inattention can cause you to suffer great bodily injury or death. I have asked law enforcement officers what a driver should do in this circumstance. The answers I received were somewhat vague. Most of them told me that there are too many variables to take into consideration but all agreed on one point: Don't panic. Keep your cool. Try to escape. Try to call for help.

THE LONE AVENGER

Arthur Caenen was driving his car in Wichita, Kansas, when he saw Jordan Palmer, age sixteen, carrying a can of gasoline on the grassy median of a divided road. Caenen hit the young man from the rear and ran him over at a speed of about 40 MPH. Palmer was flung into the air, rolled off the hood of the car, and was run over. He was dragged underneath the car for more than one hundred feet, suffering massive head injuries, from which he died. Caenen was standing close to the body when a spectator asked him, "Did you see what happened?" He calmly replied, "Yes. I ran him over." He also said he intentionally ran Palmer over. He pleaded not guilty by reason of insanity but the jury didn't buy it; they convicted him of murder in the first degree.[20] Was he a deliberate, calculating monster—or a product of defective DNA? Or was Caenen driven to madness by repeated insults and frustrations—or all of the above? Why would he kill someone who had done nothing to harm or insult him, a boy he didn't even know? This is another example of the spontaneity of aggression. And perhaps when his attorneys pleaded him not guilty by reason of insanity they were correct.

A DUEL

There was a spectacular road rage duel in 1996 on the George Washington Memorial Parkway just outside Washington, DC, when two men, both twenty-six years old, raced at a velocity of about 80 MPH for a distance of eight miles. One was slightly behind the other. With a roaring engine and squealing tires as his battle hymn he pursued the other car, eating up the parkway between them, drawing closer. It ended suddenly when both drivers lost control and their cars tumbled over the divider into oncoming traffic, killing two other drivers. Only two of the four drivers survived. One was convicted of involuntary manslaughter and sentenced to ten and a half years in prison.[21]

He almost certainly knew the risks and the consequences of his behavior, but his need to defeat and crush the intransigent young man driving the other car and his instinctive animal rage blotted out the abhorrence of death, overpowering the thinking frontal lobes of his brain. He was unable to abort his deadly sortie. These high-speed duels are extremely common.

Some drivers will not take the challenge because they have too much to lose: a loving family, a beautiful house, money, and substantial assets that could be lost in a lawsuit, resulting in bankruptcy and indigence. But for some, this is not enough to restrain the madman inside. There are some who have wonderful relationships with their mates and loved ones, happy lives, wonderful careers, and brilliant futures, and are unwilling to put that at risk. For a great many, these are sufficient to restrain the mad beast inside.

But for others they are not enough.

There are people who have all of the above, yet they go racing into annihilation like a mad panzer commander, or a kamikaze pilot. These are your fellow travelers.

I knew a man named Jeff who was a builder and an electrical contractor. He was a self-made man, the son of a semi-illiterate couple in the rural South. He had little education, but he had become a wealthy man. He lived in a beautiful house situated in one of Seattle's posh, subtropical, upscale communities. He belonged to the clubs that businessmen join, and attended church regularly in search of new clients. He was a well-dressed man, well liked by the businesspeople who lunched with him. He was a tough boss. He did not like to be disobeyed or beaten. Though he was a model citizen, Jeff had one very serious flaw. He could not endure the humiliation of being passed by another car when he was driving. He did not merely get angry; he pursued the other car, even if it became necessary to chase him for miles into another county at dangerously high speeds. Occasionally I saw him on the freeway while driving only a short distance behind him. He was driving a Corvette, a car built for speed and rapid acceleration with a lightweight fiberglass body and a huge, powerful engine. He moved like a football player carrying the ball, outrunning one driver after another, cutting in front of one car, then going after another. He was all over the freeway, changing lanes, defeating one car after another in rapid succession. I delicately and diplomatically asked him about it one day after lunch when we were sitting in his office. He had had a few drinks and was more candid than he would otherwise have been. I asked him, "What do you do when some guy passes you and cuts in front of you?"

"Well, I don't generally let him pass me," he said. "A Corvette can take most of those cars in just a couple of seconds. Now and then one of 'em gives me a run, but I always take him sooner or later. One guy got away from me while I was stuck in a slow lane and he got off the freeway so he could quit while he was ahead, but I followed him and saw where he went. He was hiding behind a restaurant. He figured if I didn't find him he would be the winner by default.

"But when he came out I hit it and passed him and cut him off twice and gave him a brake job and flipped him the finger. Then I took off and left him behind in the dust and went home. When it was over I was a happy man." He grinned.

I asked him, "What do you experience in your mind when someone passes you and cuts in front of you?"

"It fills you with hate. I can't even describe it in words. Something snaps. Everything else vanishes. I know I have to take him and make him know that I'm the boss. I have to make him go home knowing that I'm the winner and he's the loser. It sounds kinda gross but once that contest starts there's no way I can quit until it's over. If he gets away I'll catch him the next day on his way home from work." He also told me that he was having a new, custom-built racing engine that nobody would be able to beat installed in his Corvette.

The problem with Jeff's competitive driving is that he was too conspicuous and caught the attention of the police. He received too many tickets, and one day he stood before a judge and his driver's license was suspended for a year. But that didn't stop him. He went to Idaho, where he got a driver's license in that state. He also acquired another driver's license in Montana when he was there on business, and he even procured a bogus California license using a different name. But he could not control his wildly overcompetitive driving. For him, the freeway was a battlefield and to suffer defeat was something he could not endure. It is like losing his mate to another man or being defeated in a fight, humiliated and disgraced. Introspection was not an option. He did not read anything but the real estate and sports sections of the newspaper. He had neither the inner strength nor the insight to understand that being passed by another driver does not have to be the ultimate defeat, that there are more important issues in our lives, that you can ignore it without suffering the loss of your dignity. Jeff was eventually arrested. The judge was generous enough not to send him to jail, but his driving days were over. He sat at his desk and told me, with wounded eyes, "It's not fair."

The bully becomes angry when another driver passes him.

A California driver, a karate instructor, passed another car.

The elderly man driving the other car was so enraged that he pulled the martial arts instructor out of his car, beat him up, and drove away. How was an elderly man able to beat up a martial arts instructor? I don't know, but stranger things have happened. A sixty-five-year-old Northridge, California, man was drawn into a road rage duel with a teenage boy. They exchanged angry words and unfurled their bellicose third fingers. The elderly man got out of his car, beat up the teenager, and drove home, charged with the euphoria of victory. His happiness was short-lived. After dinner he suffered a heart attack and died.

MENTORS AND ROLE MODELS

Law enforcement officers are generally regarded as mentors and role models. In Millington, Tennessee, police officers saw a car driven by seventeen-year-old Rodie Gossett run a stop sign. With red lights blazing they pursued him. He did not stop. According to his companion, it was night and Gossett wanted to get to a well-lighted place with witnesses present before surrendering to police, because he feared that he would be beaten or executed. In some places, driving while black can be a capital offense. There was a brief chase. Gossett drove his car into a brightly lit gasoline station adjacent to an all-night convenience store, got out of his car, raised his hands, and surrendered. Several police cars surrounded him. Officer Peter Nichelson walked up behind him, drew his gun, and shot Gossett in the head, killing him instantly. The gun, according to witnesses, was only a few inches from Gossett's head. A jury found him not guilty of murder but convicted him on the lesser included charge of criminally negligent homicide.[22] Judge L. T. Lafferty handed Nichelson the minimum sentence under Tennessee law: one year of probation, after which his record will be wiped clean if he complies with the requirements of his probation. Rodie Gossett's mother has sued Nichelson, the city of Millington, its police department, the mayor, and the chief of police for $15 million.[23]

TERROR ON THE HIGHWAY

In 1993 the ACLU Foundation of Southern California began a study of high-speed police pursuits in the area, based on data from law enforcement agencies. The study disclosed the unsettling news that police have a tendency to mete out "street justice" at the conclusion of a pursuit. Rodney King's brutal beating was not simply an isolated incident.

In a sample of 1,707 police pursuits conducted during 1992, the number of suspects killed numbered 12 while the injured totaled 374. Of the injured suspects, 221 were injured during the chase and 153 were injured after the pursuit ended. That's 40.9 percent. Twelve southern California agencies conducted pursuits that resulted in 47 deaths, 1,240 injuries to "suspects," and 314 injuries to "others," people whose only misdeed was being in the path of the pursuit. Sometimes these unwitting victims of circumstance are arrested, charged with a crime, and imprisoned. Police generally are exempted from any liability for loss of life and limb resulting from their driving at unsafe speeds if they are in pursuit of a car. In California in July 2002, a black teenager was brutally beaten while being taken into custody. Another young man videotaped the beating and was subsequently arrested. The youth who was beaten was charged with assaulting a police officer.

Amnesty International has published a disturbing report of cases in which unarmed civilians were beaten, tortured, and some even killed by police under extremely questionable circumstances in the United States. The victims are mostly people of color, the mentally ill, paupers, teenagers, homeless persons, and gay, lesbian, and transgendered individuals. According to the publication, "while there have been criminal prosecutions in several high profile cases, such action is generally rare."[24]

In a unanimous decision the US Supreme Court ruled on May 26, 1998, that police cannot be held liable in lawsuits arising from death and injury caused by high-speed police pursuits, even if the victims are innocent bystanders and even if the police act in reckless disregard for human life.[25] About three hundred persons are killed each year in the United States in accidents involving police chases, approximately the same number that are killed in police shootings.[26]

Law enforcement data shows that in 4,842 pursuits during the years 1993, 1994, and 1995, the chases were overwhelmingly initiated by trivial traffic code infractions. Very few were related to serious, violent crimes.

A typical incident occurred recently in Los Angeles when a young African American man discovered he was being followed by a police car. His only offense was driving with a crack in his tail light lens. But he was afraid. He did not want to become another Rodney King and carry the wounds, scars, and other irreversible damage that occurs as the result of a brutal beating for the rest of his life. Inhabitants of the ghetto know that black people are routinely abused and frequently killed by police. They know that what happened to Rodney King has been going on long before the Rodney King incident occurred. But the white middle class who watch the carefully sanitized, filtered news on television generally do not.

The young man fled from the police but was captured. He was charged with six felonies: fleeing from a police officer, refusing to obey an order, and several other redundant charges. The judge sentenced him to a term of eight years in state prison. His only crime was fear. Panic. Did he deserve to have eight years taken from him?

Shirley Ann Padalecki, an eighteen-year-old college student, was driving home from a wedding reception shortly before midnight in April 2001. She, too, was engaged to be married. As she drove her car homeward she converged with a high-speed pursuit in which both the police and the truck being pursued were moving at a velocity of about 100 MPH. The truck crashed into her car, fracturing her skull. She was taken to a hospital where she lay in a coma for two weeks. Since then she has had numerous brain and reconstructive surgeries. According to her family, she suffers from memory loss, "doesn't think straight," and is unable to return to work or continue her education.

"It's been a vicious nightmare," her father said. "Nobody could repair the damage and the trauma we went through." He said that his family had spent hundreds of thousands of dollars to cover her medical expenses. The family is suing the city of Simi Valley, California, for negligence, recklessness, and speeding on city streets and intersections where there were other vehicles and people.

"They authorize officers to chase anyone for anything at any speed," the family's lawyer said. Despite state law and the recent Supreme Court decision, both of which immunize police from being held accountable for the consequences of high-speed pursuits, the trial court judge refused to dismiss the case. The city appealed, but both the State Court of Appeals and the US Supreme Court declined to review the judge's decision, so the case is still very much alive.[27]

Killing suspects, bystanders, and passersby at speeds of 95 or 100 MPH is hardly necessary. The police have helicopters in the air most of the time; some small cities that don't can still cut off all avenues of escape and surround the fleeing outlaw. Most fleeing suspects can be found without mass demolition and carnage. But cops are not much different from the rest of us. They like their cars. They like to race. They like to win. And they like to gloat: "I bet you don't feel so smart now, do ya?"

Racing with a cop is not an optimal way to spend your leisure hours, particularly if you belong to a group that is outside the protection of the law. Cases of police firing at suspects at the conclusion of pursuits continue to be reported with dismal frequency. A disproportionate number of the victims are minorities and people who are "different."[28]

Nevertheless, there are several high-speed police pursuits every day in Los Angeles County. In some cities, such as Baltimore, high-speed police chases have been prohibited. Early in 2003, Los Angeles' new police chief, William J. Bratton, persuaded the city's police commission to prohibit high-speed pursuits initiated by trivial infractions such as driving with a cracked tail light or running a stop sign. Bratton said the new rules will enable officers to weigh the necessity of a high-speed chase based on probable cause and reasonable suspicion that a crime has been committed. Until now they had had virtual carte blanche to pursue with or without probable cause. Officials have stated that the new rules will substantially reduce the number of collisions and injuries caused by high-speed pursuits.[29]

In September 1999 there was a more bizarre chase on the five o'clock news. The vehicle leading the police on a lengthy race was a garbage truck. This spectacle occupied about a half hour of the newscast. There were three high-speed police pursuits on the television that evening. Such things are televised because people love a race. It gets ratings. It sells advertising.

A chase is a form of combat. In the initial stage of the pursuit, one of the combatants may lead the other into a trap where the pursuer is at a disadvantage. This often occurs in road rage duels. In any case, the state of mind of the pursuer is almost always the same: "When I catch that bastard, I'm gonna kill him."

The police are in a position similar to lawyers. The reprehensible conduct of some lawyers has spawned a massive body of extremely cruel lawyer jokes, some of which might be perceived as too revolting for general circulation. But if it were not for lawyers, our Constitution and our Bill of Rights would be a dead letter by reason of long disuse. We would have no human rights and no one to protect us from the pirates.

Similarly, the conduct of some police officers has generated a sense of distrust in the public mind. Many intelligent, respectable people tell their teenage children, "Don't trust the police. Don't talk to the police. Don't make eye contact with the police." Yet if it were not for the presence of the police, we would be living under seige in a condition of savagery. Our lives would be short and violent. There are excellent police officers, but there seems to be an absence of competent leadership. It is also a well-known fact that police departments in American cities have not found it easy to recruit personnel who would make the best kind of police officers. The police are a quasi-military organization. When soldiers are allowed to act autonomously without due process of law, without responsible leadership and discipline, the seeds of a police state will grow and thrive. Like a doctor's, the cop's work is dangerous, sensitive, and stessful.

We need to dismantle the wall of silence that conceals medical, police, and government malpractice. When the government and the media tell us that bad cops are "only a tiny fraction of 1 percent," they are not serving our best interests. I have several friends who are law enforcement officers and retired cops. The brightest and best of law enforcement will tell you privately, if they know you and trust you, that there are bad cops and that these cops are indeed a serious problem. It would be better if we could bring it all out in the open. We have nothing to fear from public scrutiny. Most people like the police and want to support them. Every day they put themselves in danger to protect us.

What doctors, cops, and government officials do is often shrouded in secrecy. They do not answer our questions. They do not share their experiences with us. If they did, it would improve the quality of their services and the quality of our lives.

On April 24, 2001, the US Supreme Court ruled that police have unlimited power to stop and search a vehicle and make a full custodial arrest of its driver, taking her to the city jail, even if the alleged infraction is one that would result in only a small fine and no jail time if there were a conviction. The offense may be real, illusory, or pretextual. In other words, there may be no "probable cause" at all, but police have now been given extremely broad power to stop and search cars on the roads and arrest the occupants. The court upheld the arrest and jailing of a woman who was driving with her seat belt unfastened and her children's seat belts unbuckled. She was handcuffed and taken into custody, booked, fingerprinted, and placed in a jail cell. After paying her fifty-dollar fine, she decided to sue. The American Civil Liberties Union (ACLU) took up her case in the hope of salvaging what's left of the Fourth Amendment prohibition of unreasonable search and seizure. But the court disagreed.[30] (On the same day, the court held that states and schools cannot be sued for racially biased policies.) One cannot but suspect that the justices are somewhat out of touch with the social realities of America. Her appeal was denied.

Kareem Abdul-Jabbar, the NBA's all-time leading scorer who led the Los Angeles Lakers to five NBA championships, was charged with attacking another driver. He was behind a fifty-eight-year-old man, waiting to turn into a shopping mall. He began honking his horn. Then, according to the police, Abdul-Jabbar got out of his car, grabbed the man driving the car in front of him, pushed his face against a plate glass window, then shoved him to the ground and held him there. He was ordered by a West Los Angeles court to undergo thirty-six hours of anger management counseling and pay $5,000 to a Police Department program for at-risk youth.[31] The fact that so many top-level professional athletes are involved in road rage incidents and other forms of violence certainly corroborates Lorenz's conclusions on aggression. These are men endowed with a high degree of aggression. A timid, passive man does not get to be a professional athlete.

MAD CAR DISEASE

Sometimes even courtesy doesn't pay. William Wilson, a forty-five-year-old commuter driving on Interstate 494 in St. Paul, Minnesota, changed lanes to allow a truck to enter the west-bound lane of the highway. In so doing, he cut in front of a lumber truck driven by twenty-six-year-old Brent Rau. Rau was angered and aimed his truck at Wilson's car, according to witnesses. Rau motioned for Wilson to pull over to the side of the road. Wilson complied. Rau punched Wilson repeatedly in the face, breaking his nose. Wilson was hospitalized and required both internal and external stitches. Another driver stopped the fight and called 911. State troopers arrested Rau, and he was charged with assault. According to a local television station that covered the incident, Rau had a string of traffic violations, including flight from police.[32]

In Richfield, Minnesota, Richard Halldorson was driving a dump truck on Highway 77 when a pickup swerved in front of him and stopped, forcing him to stop. The driver of the pickup opened his door, dashed to the dump truck, opened Halldorson's door, dragged him to the pavement and beat him with his fists, then dashed back to the pickup and hastily departed.

Halldorson was not seriously injured. In an interview with WCCO-TV he said, "We all got to be on the road. We all got to share it, you know. . . . You don't have to hit people to get your point across."[33]

In St. Petersburg, Florida, a fifteen-year-old bicyclist was arrested for allegedly shooting a motorist three times in a road rage dispute. He was charged with attempted murder. Police said he was laughing when he was arrested and booked. He was also a suspect in another incident in which a bicyclist shot a man who was driving a pickup truck. The bicyclist complained that the truck driver came too close to his bicycle while making a turn. The truck driver got out of his pickup. There was an argument as to who had the right of way. When the driver of the pickup walked back to his truck, the bicyclist drew a gun from his waistband and shot him three times. The driver of the pickup positively identified him from a photo lineup. Police said he will be tried as an adult.[34]

In Dallas, a forty-one-year-old financial analyst said it was road rage that caused him to shoot and kill two truck drivers and wound a man he suspected of being a truck driver in August 1998. In a letter to a friend written after his arrest, he wrote: "I found it quite pleasurable to kill those two men. . . . If you are an angry person and someone provokes you to violence . . . it feels wonderful to cause their death and watch their pain." The prosecutor read the letter to the jurors, and the analyst also confessed to shooting a third man. The jurors deliberated for less than ninety minutes before sentencing him to death by lethal injection.[35]

The saddest stories of road rage are the ones that involve animals. Tim Hill was driving his truck with his dog, Toba, tied in the back by a leash. He stopped the truck when he saw five ducks crossing the street. He waited so they could reach the other side of the street and go on their way. The car behind him began indignantly honking its horn. Witnesses said they saw Gary Priddle, who was stopped behind Hill's truck, get out of his car and strike the dog with a nine-iron golf club while Hill waited for the ducks to cross. Hill said he heard his dog yelp and saw Priddle walk back to his vehicle holding a golf club. The dog's skull was fractured in four places and he lost his left eye. Priddle was sentenced to fifteen months in jail. There was court testimony that Priddle has a condition that can result in loss of control and violent outbursts. Don't we all?[36]

On a February morning at about 7:30, Sara McBurnett was driving on Airport Road in San Jose. Her little dog, Leo, a bichon frise, was riding with her in the car. She loved her pet and enjoyed taking it with her in the car. A black SUV with Virginia license plates swerved in front of McBurnett's car, causing a minor fender bender with little damage to either vehicle. The driver of the black SUV got out of his vehicle, approached McBurnett's car, and knocked on the window. McBurnett opened it. Leo jumped on her lap to greet the stranger as McBurnett apologized, but explained that he had suddenly cut her off and had not given her sufficient time or space to avoid the collision. The enraged driver reached into her car, grabbed the dog by its neck, and threw it into oncoming traffic. The dog was hit and crushed by a car. The dog's pitiful screams were heard within a radius of nearly a mile. The other driver ran back to his car and sped away, swerving into traffic that was moving in the opposite direction, and was gone. McBurnett got out of her car, ran out into traffic in an effort to save her beloved pet, but Leo died on the way to the veterinary emergency hospital. Several witnesses said they could identify the other driver, but he had vanished.

When this story was published in the newspapers and broadcast on the electronic media, many people sent in contributions to a reward fund to be paid to any person able to find the driver and provide information leading to his arrest. The reward fund grew and grew, but nobody was able to find the dog killer. Almost certainly he changed his appearance and abandoned the SUV. The San Jose Police gave the man a long head start. The written report of the 911 call was shelved for two weeks. The police took no action on the case until the story was broadcast in the media. Donations continued to pour in to the reward fund at the Santa Clara Valley Humane Society. For more than a year nobody was arrested, but dog lovers and sympathizers raised $120,000 to help find the killer. McBurnett said that the money already received was enough to motivate people to identify him and asked that would-be donors send the money to the Humane Society and to their local animal shelters.

After a year of searching and coming up empty, the police charged a man they believed to be the dog killer. He was indicted by a grand jury and charged with "killing or maiming or abusing an animal," a felony punishable by up to three years in state prison. Although McBurnett's identification of the man was inconclusive, he was already in custody, charged with an unrelated offense. His name is Andrew Burnett. Apparently he was foolish enough to tell someone who found the reward offering of $120,000 too attractive to resist. He was tried and convicted. On Friday, July 13, 2001, Superior Court Judge Kevin J. Murphy sentenced him to the maximum: three years in state prison. During a ninety-minute sentencing hearing Burnett, his mother, and others pleaded with the judge for a more lenient sentence, but the judge was not moved. McBurnett said that although some people might think the sentence was harsh, "they do not know the depth of my pain." She also told the court that watching Leo die was like seeing the death of her own child.[37]

TERROR ON THE HIGHWAY

Three teenage girls were driving home from Virginia Beach in the westbound lane of Interstate 64 on a Sunday in August 1999. They had a series of confrontations with another driver, who followed them, pulled up alongside the girls' car, and began firing at them with a handgun. One of the shots hit the driver in the head and killed her instantly. A passenger in the car, an eighteen-year-old girl, was shot in the leg. The car went out of control and struck an embankment.

Five off-duty sheriff's deputies were riding in a car in Chicago when, according to charges, they believed another car had cut too close in front of theirs. They chased the car. One of the officers drew his firearm and fired at the vehicle, shattering a window. The shooter and the driver were charged with attempted murder and aggravated discharge of a firearm. The other three were charged with two felonies: official misconduct and obstruction of justice. One of the five was suspended, three were stripped of their police powers, and the fifth resigned.[38]

If you were the judge or a member of the jury, how would you rule on this one? Around midnight, Brett Tonkin and his wife, Margaret, heard the sound of a dog barking. Brett looked out of his bedroom window and saw several teenage girls "rolling" his house, yard, trees, and shrubbery with toilet paper. It was the third time this had happened. The Tonkins were proud of their yard. It was bad enough the first time, but three times in three months was more than they could endure. They ran out of the house, shouting at the girls. The teenage girls fled in two cars. One was a white passenger car with twelve girls in it; The other carried six more. The Tonkins jumped into their pickup truck and began chasing the teens in the hope of getting their license plate numbers. One of the cars sped away recklessly at high speed with its lights turned off, according to Tonkin. After a 1.6-mile chase the driver lost control of her car and hit a tree at high speed. She and one other girl were injured, but three of the passengers were killed. Tonkin saw a police patrol car and told the officer what had happened.

Tonkin was tried for vehicular homicide and reckless driving. Prosecutors said that he was responsible for the girls' deaths. If convicted on all of the charges, he faced a possible eight years in prison and an $8,000 fine. The driver of the crashed car testified that Tonkin should bear most of the blame. The mother of one of the dead girls looked at Tonkin and said, "You killed my daughter." The police officer also testified. He did not blame Tonkin for the accident but placed responsibility on the teenage driver who, he said, was driving on a dark road at high speed with her headlights turned off. Her memory had been slightly impaired by the accident.

Brett Tonkin broke down and wept on the witness stand, saying that all he wanted was that the teenagers be held responsible for vandalizing his home. He was acquitted on all nine counts of vehicular homicide and one count of failing to obey a stop sign, but he was convicted of driving too fast for conditions, following too closely, and speeding. He received a twelve-month suspended sentence and a $400 fine, plus a $400 surcharge. Apparently the toilet-paper-wielding teenagers felt anger toward the Tonkins' daughter, who was an exceptionally attractive and popular cheerleader but was younger than the girls. Brett and Margaret Tonkin testified that the first time their house was "rolled" it was embarrassing, but that the second time, the girls also threw cat litter on their home. Margaret Tonkin testified that shortly before the third "rolling" of their home, their daughter had received an ugly note from one of the pranksters, and that there had been rumors at the high school that their home would be "rolled."[39] I think that any reasonable person of sound mind would not believe that Brett

TERROR ON THE HIGHWAY

Tonkin deserved to be sent to prison, as the prosecutors had wished. He was, after all, not the aggressor. But wouldn't it have been more efficient and less dangerous to photograph the girls and their cars? He could have disabled the cars by deflating their tires. Then, even if they had fled on foot, police would have been able to identify the leaders.

*   *   *

This is just a small sample of recent road rage incidents. We will sort them out later on. We could go on endlessly. Each month brings another crop of horror stories. There are thousands, maybe tens of thousands, of these skirmishes. Most of them, including some fatal ones, don't even get mentioned in the media.

Aggressive drivers are not drooling, snarling vampires with green skin and long white fangs. They are very ordinary people. When you drive on an expressway or a surface road, these are your fellow travelers. They are all around you, alongside you, in front of and behind you. Are you sure you want to duel with them?

These are contests that do not have to happen and would not happen if each of those involved knew what to expect and what to do. Does anybody win? If nobody wins, there's something wrong with the game.

Reams of literature have been published by various sources, both public and private, on road rage. Psychologists, cops, and radio talk-show hosts have proclaimed themselves to be experts. Politicians, posturing for votes, have enacted voluminous laws.

Programs have been funded. Nearly all have a monotonous, one-size-fits-all approach that has had little or no effect. Despite all of this literature, "analysis," and rhetoric, road rage violence continues to increase at an alarming rate: according to the media and the AAA, about 7 percent each year. We need to look deeper. We need to look at the real source of road rage and how it can be managed. Endless preoccupation with superficial symptoms hasn't worked and isn't likely to work. It isn't something we can afford to ignore. At the rate road rage is increasing, our roads and highways will soon be a demolition derby.

During more than forty thousand hours behind the wheel I have observed and isolated several types of drivers:

(1) The driver who aggressively engages the other car in battle for no discernible reason. He goes out on the road looking for battle, thirsting for battle. It is spontaneous, compulsive, and virtually irresistible. Even the threat of severe consequences does not mitigate his aggression.

(2) The driver who is normally friendly, generous, and kind, but loves to fight and loves the hyperarousal of battle. For him, witnessing a fight is a glorious event, but to participate is the ultimate, apocalyptic experience.

(3) The compulsive racer who cannot endure being passed. She will follow another driver for any distance, no matter how long it takes. If she loses she will hunt the other car down with the resolve to even the score and turn defeat into victory, no matter how long and difficult the undertaking. For her, the freeway is a test that will prove her to be either a powerful, rakish winner or a contemptible weakling.

(4) The speeder. Speed, like combat, is a macho thing. There are many men who have an urgent need to prove their maleness over and over again by speeding and doing battle. If you pass one or belittle him he will take the challenge as quickly and zealously as he would

respond to the flirtatious smile of a beautiful woman. There are men who do not speed or fight but admire those who do. An extremely common phenomenon is the atavistic man who indignantly proclaims that it is the slow driver who causes accidents. That is about as logical as saying that it is the man who refuses to fight who is the cause of violence. Slow drivers can cause collisions, but far more crashes are caused by speeding and reckless driving.

(5) The driver who would be a more civilized driver if she were treated more kindly. But unless you begin life with certain advantages, you are probably destined to spend your years in groveling, obsequious servitude and exhausting, stressful overwork. Not all of us can enroll at Harvard and ascend into the aristocracy.

There are other distinct types. No two drivers are exactly the same. But they all have one thing in common: the primitive, overpowering animal instinct to attack, kill, maim, and torture.

NOTES

1. Karyn Sultan, "Woman's Role in Road Rage Up, Statistics Show," *Woman Motorist*, April 18, 2001.

2. EPIC-MRA, a Lansing, Michigan, firm that conducts telephone surveys.

3. *Columbia Journalism Review* (1999).

4. *Washington Post*, November 16, 1999.

5. http://www. washingtonpost.com.

6. Dominic Connell and Matthew Joint, *Aggressive Driving: Three Studies* (Washington, DC: AAA Foundation for Traffic Safety, 1997), p. 10.

7. *Twin Falls (Idaho) Times News*, August 20, 1997. See also the *Salt Lake Tribune*.

8. *Newsweek*, June 2, 1998. Also *Current Health*, November 2, 1998.

9. Associated Press, Dale City, Virginia, July 2, 1992, http://www.apbnews.com.

10. Associated Press, West Palm Beach, Florida, January 16, 1999.

11. Reuters, April 10, 2001.

12. Connell and Joint, *Aggressive Driving*, p. 3.

13. *48 Hours*, September 18, 1997.

14. John Ellement, *Boston Globe*, February 24, 1994.

15. Jim Adams, *Minneapolis Star Tribune*, September 2, 1999.

16. "Road Ragers—Road Rage vs. Defensive Drivers," Active Dayton.com, July 19, 2002. http://www.roadragers.com.

17. Mizell, Joint, and Connell, *Three Studies*.

18. Ibid., p. 12.

19. This occurred in Westchester County, NY, in April 1996.

20. The opinion of the Kansas Supreme Court gives a lengthy narrative of the case: No. 83,288.

21. *Washington Post*, April 9, 1996.

22. http://www.plp.org/cd97.html.

23. http://www.courttv.com/trials/nichelson.

24. Amnesty International USA, *Race, Rights, and Police Brutality*. The full report is available online at www.amnestyusa.org /RIGHTS FOR ALL/police.

25. *County of Sacramento et al* v. *Lewis*, 96–1337 (decided May 26, 1998).

26. "Not Just Isolated Incidents: The Epidemic of Police Pursuits in Southern California," a report by the ACLU Foundation of Southern California.

27. Anna Gorman, "Suit Challenges Police Pursuit Policy," *Los Angeles Times*, April 19, 2001.

28. Several are included in Amnesty International USA's *California Update on Police Brutality*.

29. Andrew Blankstein, *Los Angeles Times*, January 8, 2003, p. B-1.

30. *Atwater v. Lago Vista*, 532 US 318 (2001).

31. *Los Angeles Times*. See also *USA Today*, January 30, 1998.

32. "Charges Filed in 'Road Rage' Case," WCCO-TV, www.channel4000.com/news/stories/news-971010-213641.html (October 10, 1997).

33. "Another Case of 'Road Rage' . . . ," WCCO-TV, www .channel4000.com/news/stories/news-980213-070851.html (February 13, 1998).

34. http://www.apbnews.com.

35. Dallas, Associated Press, September 1, 1999.

36. http://www.apbnews.com. Also Reuters, July 1, 1999.

37. *San Jose Mercury News*. See also *Los Angeles Times*, July 14, 2001, sec. B, p. 1. (Also www.interstice.com/leo.)

38. Chicago, Associated Press, October 2, 1999.

39. Court TV (New York) broadcast July 1, 2002.

4

CHOICES

"I Can't Believe I Shot Her"

Shirley Henson, who was mentioned in the last chapter, was, according to all media reports, an ideal suburban mom, a Cub Scout den leader. If you asked her before the fateful incident in November 1999, "What would you do if another driver cut you off on the interstate, gave you a brake job, flipped you the finger, and made you really mad? Would you engage her in a four-mile battle, then shoot her and be arrested and charged with murder?" She would almost certainly have said, "No. I'm not that stupid." Yet she did exactly that. She could not have been unaware of the statutory penalties for such behavior. When it was over and Gena Foster's lifeless body lay next to her car she said, "Oh my God! I can't believe I shot her."

If you asked Tracie Alfieri, the young woman in Ohio, "If another driver cut in front of you and made you mad as hell, would you race her, cut in front of her, give her a brake job, and put her into a collision that would kill her unborn baby and cause her nearly fatal injuries, and get you a prison term?" she would probably say, "No!" But she did exactly that.

THE BEHEMOTH

Michael Eck started early for his daily commute from his home in Baltimore to work so that he would have no need to hurry. He was a family man who enjoyed spending time with his wife and his baby daughter, Christina. He was moving along smoothly when he saw a huge, blue eighteen-wheeler rig in front of him, pulling a heavy load. There was a steep hill ahead and the truck driver, although he would not be able to maintain highway speed going up the hill, refused to move over to the slow (right) lane so that other vehicles could pass. Eck signaled for a lane change and passed the big rig from the right side, then reentered the left lane. When he saw traffic ahead he slowed down—and then he felt a tap on his rear bumper. Then he saw the big rig behind him, so close it was almost touching his car. Eck changed lanes, moving toward the right shoulder in order to exchange insurance information. He waited for the truck to pull off on the shoulder, but instead, the truck slammed into his Chevrolet, crashing into him with such power that his engine was disabled by an electrical failure and it took all of his strength to turn the steering wheel. The power brakes also stopped working. Roaring like a mad beast, the truck slammed into the Chevrolet again and again.

Eck punched 911 on his hands-free cell phone and shouted urgently, telling the operator that he was being rammed repeatedly by the tractor-trailer. His engine was dead and he had little control over the car. The truck was literally pushing him across the pavement. He gave the 911 operator his position as the truck driver continued to smash into his car. He didn't know how much more the car could take without breaking up. He managed to get the car into the right lane and heaved a sigh of relief, but the truck changed lanes behind him and slammed him again. A state trooper sped to the scene, but traffic was backed up for miles. The truck driver was pushing his giant truck up against the Chevrolet's rear end, swerving from side to side, nearly causing the Chevy to roll over. Up ahead was another big rig, also moving slowly. Eck suddenly realized that the truck driver intended to crush him between the two big rigs. Since it was almost certain that if he did not bail out of the car he was going to die, he grasped the door handle. The police car finally arrived and brought the two vehicles to a stop. The truck driver, James Trimble, was a sixty-five-year-old man with white hair. He was trembling with rage as he told the state trooper that the entire incident was Eck's fault: "He pissed me off so I hit his car to get him out of my way." Later, in a written statement, he said he wanted to teach Eck a lesson. He had pushed the car for twelve miles. Eck still suffers from pain in his shoulder, neck, and back, and is being treated by a physician. The truck driver was charged with a long list of offenses, including aggravated assault. He pleaded guilty to one count of aggravated assault and six lesser charges and agreed to permanently surrender his commercial driver's license. He was sentenced to a prison term with a maximum of nearly two years.[1]

If you had asked Trimble a day or two earlier if he ever would do such a thing he probably would have told you, "I'm driving $80,000 worth of equipment, not to mention the freight. I'm making a good living. Why would I blow all of that and end up with nothing except a prison cell?" But that is what he chose to do. Why did he try to destroy this harmless commuter, destroying what was left of his own life? What was he thinking? He wasn't.

This is one of the classic models of the road rage duel: the bully, inside the protective walls of a massive fortress on wheels, trying to crush the smaller vehicle. He doesn't think. He acts on an instinctive impulse that exists in all vertebrates. He has to make up a story to justify his behavior, not just to try to diminish the penalties, but because he doesn't know why he did it.

THE GROWING BODY COUNT

As the overcrowding and density of traffic on our public roads continues to grow, we hear and read more horror stories of road rage combat. But we still do it. Until one has been an eyewitness—up close—to the gore and agony that lie in the wake of a high-speed car crash, or until it happens to a loved one, we tend to think that it happens only to other people. But sooner or later we will be the other person.

The US Department of Transportation (DOT) estimates that eight thousand people are killed and at least a million are injured each year as a result of "road rage" or "aggressive driving," as opposed to garden-variety "accidents." The National Highway Traffic Safety Administration (NHTSA) has stated that two-thirds of the forty-two thousand people killed in car crashes in 1996 were victims of aggressive driving.[2] The same agency announced that in 1997 forty-one thousand were killed in vehicular crashes and that two-thirds of these were caused by road rage.[3] According to the National Motorists Association, only forty of these crashes were caused by road rage.[4] Various experts and agencies, both public and private, have offered their estimates of the body count, ranging from hundreds to thousands to tens of thousands. These numbers contain a lot of zeroes and they are highly speculative.

Incidents in which one driver assaults another with the intent to kill or injure have risen by 51 percent since 1990, according to the AAA Foundation for Traffic Safety. And they continue to rise substantially each year at a rate of about 7 to 8 percent.[5] Automobile accidents are the leading cause of death among children over the age of one year, according to a commission appointed by Rodney Slater, former Secretary of Transportation during the Clinton administration.[6] Why do otherwise intelligent persons commit such senseless, self-destructive acts?

According to the DOT, 3,580,000 occupants of cars are involved in crashes each year.[7] Other experts estimate that as many as 6 million people are injured each year as a result of road rage duels, and more drivers are injured than passengers.[8] Light trucks are three times more likely to roll over than passenger cars.[9]

The AAA Foundation for Traffic Safety reports 41,967 fatalities and 3,399,000 injuries on the roads and highways of the United States during 1997. But it doesn't end there. Many of those involved suffer crippling, paralytic injuries and lie helplessly in hospital beds for the rest of their lives. Some are blinded. Some are horribly burned. Every day, hospitals see the damaged skulls, limbs, kidneys, livers, hearts, brains. Many of them don't make it.

It doesn't end there. Grief affects our biochemistry and weakens the immune system. Widows and widowers have a higher-than-average probability of dying within two years of losing a spouse, and it is most likely to happen to those who had the best and most lasting marriages.

These are just "round numbers." Nobody knows how many

people lose their lives in road rage altercations. Nobody knows how many are disabled. David K. Willis, president of the AAA Foundation for Traffic Safety, states that "for every aggressive driving incident serious enough to result in a police report or a newspaper article there are hundreds, or thousands more, which never get reported to the authorities."[10]

HIDDEN DAMAGE

The human body can withstand impact roughly equal to the speed of a man running: about five MPH. It was not designed to withstand solid impact at 50, or 80 MPH. If you have ever been riding in a car when it crashed at 5 MPH, imagine that impact multiplied by ten—or sixteen. Most people believe that an impact at 60 MPH is twice as powerful as one at 30 MPH. Not true. It is four times as powerful. If you cannot restrain your urge to speed, to pursue and destroy another car, or to beat up its driver, you could be one of those fifty thousand people who suddenly cease to exist. Or you could be paralyzed by a spinal injury and spend the rest of your days lying in a hospital bed while your friends and loved ones gradually drift away. It's your choice.

Another of the "rewards" of road racing is jail time in the local lockup or a state prison term. Even if the crash wasn't your fault, you should be aware that eyewitnesses and cops often accuse the wrong person. It could happen to you. Judges and jurors are extremely unpredictable. It may give you some momentary satisfaction to wreck the other car, but is it worth it?

In the past few years we have had a tidal wave of disclosures of false arrests, false convictions, and false imprisonments resulting from dishonesty, sadism, ambition, malice, incompetence, and laziness on the part of police, prosecutors, lawyers, and judges. In the past, editors obediently deleted these stories from the media without having to be told, but a new generation of less corrupt, less obedient journalists has supplanted them. Most incidents of police and prosecutorial malpractice still are reported timidly and briefly, if at all, leaving out the most salient elements of the story because reporters don't want to be removed from the list of people to be called when there is a big story to be disclosed at a press conference. Even when it is clear that a defendant is not guilty, judges tend to have a blind allegiance to the police and the prosecutor's office—certainly not all judges, but this has been the rule rather than the exception. This is especially true in California where we have had sixteen years of ultraconservatives who appointed only prosecutors to the bench, never defense attorneys. I am personally acquainted with several Republican lawyers who have tried for years to get appointed to the judicial bench, believing that being active in the Republican Party would give them an advantage over other candidates, only to be told that the governor appoints nobody aligned with the defense. Judges are the nearest thing we have to monarchs. A judge can have you thrown in jail for the slightest gesture of disrespect to his or her person, or simply for speaking when he orders you to be silent. That kind of power, held by anyone but a very exceptional person, brings out the very worst, the darkest in the repertoire of human behavior. Many judges are not very exceptional people; many are failed lawyers who somehow got themselves appointed to the bench. You cannot always trust the authorities to do the right thing if you and your family have no ties to powerful people, which is one of the most compelling reasons not to engage in behaviors that attract their attention. Yet many people choose to do so.

JUSTICE

Charles Beatty, age sixty-six, was driving toward his home in Los Angeles when he was blocked by a car that was stopped in front of him. The occupants were engaged in conversation with a pedestrian. Beatty waited patiently through two or three signal light changes, then became impatient, pulled around the car, and drove away. He did not know that the occupants of the car were police officers working in plain clothes, driving an unmarked car.

The officers hastily pursued him, stopped him, and issued him a ticket. Beatty complained, but accepted the ticket and complied with the officers' orders. As he got into his car, Beatty said, "I'll see you in court." According to Beatty, one of the officers tried to pull him out of his car, using abusive language, and the other officer drew his gun and shot Beatty four times in the back. Miraculously, he survived. In court, Beatty said he had done nothing to offend the officers except to question the propriety of their behavior. "I believe we're in a day when these things will not be swept under the rug," he told the reporters. The officer who fired the shots was given a five-year prison sentence. Beatty still carries a bullet near his spine.[11] Certainly the officers' actions were inexcusable, but it would have been more prudent for Beatty to say nothing.

There has also been a plethora of reports of torture, murder, and rape in state prisons and jails at the hands of both guards and inmates. On August 5, 2001, Los Angeles County agreed to pay a $27-million settlement of five class-action lawsuits alleging illegal detention of inmates in the county jail. Some of the litigants were held beyond their release dates. Some complained of being subjected to strip searches including digital penetration of body cavities. Others were found to have been held on warrants for other persons—the police had arrested the wrong person. The Sheriff's Department announced that it is now releasing inmates at the courthouse when they are ordered released by a judge. Previously they were taken back to the jail where they were held for days before being freed. About four hundred thousand former inmates were plaintiffs in the class-action lawsuit.[12]

The prison population in the United States has tripled and continues to grow. The sentences are longer, even for trivial, nonviolent offenses. Prison construction and maintenance are an extremely profitable industry. In California the prison industry is one of the largest contributors to political campaigns.[13]

Do you want to entrust your life to their custody? Their caring staff of highly trained personnel are waiting with smiling faces. To falsely convict and send a person to prison for ten years—or twenty—is a partial murder. A life should be a progression to a better quality of existence, a process of learning, acquiring skills, wisdom, and humanity. Prison is not the best setting in which to accomplish this. A prison term breaks that continuum. Even if you are fortunate enough to come out alive, you will never be quite the same person. It can happen to you if you choose to recklessly place yourself in the wrong place at the wrong time. If you are driving at a dangerously high speed, the police tend to suspect that you may be a wanted fugitive. This is not unreasonable but there is often a lack of careful investigation. Early in 2002, a Los Angeles man was released after spending two years in a state prison because police had warrants for the arrest of a man with the same name.[14]

GAMBLING YOUR BRAIN

If you are involved in a crash and someone is killed or disabled as a result of the crash, you could be charged with a felony and face a jury. Who will the jurors believe?

Hardly a day goes by without a media report of a person who was released after spending ten, twelve, eighteen, or even twenty years behind bars for a crime he did not commit. Most were guilty only of being in the wrong place at the wrong time, in the company of the wrong people.

One of the worst and most common injuries that occur in car crashes is brain damage. According to the NHTSA, during the average year between 1992 and 1994, 118,154 people suffered brain injuries in car crashes, 8,563 persons suffered skull injuries, and 15,994 received "other" head injuries. Another 718,263 crash-involved car occupants received injuries to the face, neck, shoulder, and back.[15] When you add in the injuries to other body parts, the total comes to 3,623,142.

According to the same publication, 43,555 occupants of crash-involved light trucks suffered brain damage, 5,207 suffered skull damage, and 4,366 received "other" head injuries during the same period in time. The total of injuries to occupants of crash-involved light trucks comes to 1,055,679.[16]

Vehicular crashes are by far the leading cause of brain damage. Head injuries designated as "skull" and "other," and probably all of the injuries that occur in automobile accidents, are possible causes of brain damage because brain damage often is inapparent. Not only blunt force trauma but also rapid acceleration or deceleration (whiplash) can cause subdural hematoma, cerebral hemorrhages, cerebral contusions, subarachnoid hemorrhage, axonal injury, intracranial hemorrhage, intraocular hemorrhages, retinal lesions, hemorrhage of the optic nerve sheath, and blindness.[17] The brains of infants and small children are more vulnerable to acceleration/deceleration, which may result in irreversible brain damage, mental retardation, and blindness. But when there is no "blunt force trauma"—no impact to the head—there is no visible sign of the injury.

Injuries in automobile crashes are the leading cause of brain damage. Every fifteen seconds one person in the United States sustains traumatic brain injury. The consequences are devastating: memory loss, difficulty with judgment and concentration, speech impairment, extreme impulsivity, disinhibition, and seizures, many of which are fatal.[18] Brain-damaged patients often become impossible burdens on their families. The victim may sit benignly for some time and then suddenly explode in a raging tantrum, destroying furniture and other household items, then go dashing out into the night and disappear for days. There are not adequate facilities available to care for them. When the hospitals discharge them, they are often warehoused in convalescent homes. And, of course, the brain damage is irreversible. According to the Brain Injury Association of California, traumatic brain injury claims more than fifty-six thousand American lives annually.[19]

There are thousands of brain-damaged patients lying in hospitals with no hope of ever again having a normal life. Some babble in nonsense syllables. Some just stare at nothing. Some are almost normal, but when you engage them in conversation you soon discover that some of their brain function is gone. Some grin or laugh impulsively for no apparent reason. Will you choose to join them?

Even if you do not land in a hospital, a jail, or a morgue, loss of your driver's license and a heavy fine can make it very difficult for you to provide for your family and for yourself, and the record of your reckless driving will follow you for years, accessible to prospective employers, clients, and others upon whom you need to make a favorable impression.

GUNSLINGERS

Two cars collided at an intersection in Irvington, New Jersey, in June 1999. One of the cars, a Ford Mustang, rolled over. The drivers and the passengers of both cars got out and began to argue as to who had the right of way. Gunfire was exchanged and one bullet went through a parked car and struck a five-year-old boy in the face. He was taken to a hospital where he was listed as being in critical but stable condition. Police examined shell casings at the scene and said they believed at least two guns were fired during the shootout. The occupants of the two cars fled. A few days later police arrested three men and took them into custody. Police would not say who fired the first shot or whose bullet struck the five-year-old child. One man was held on $250,000 bail.[20]

An Arizona man was driving his truck in a suburb of Phoenix in April 1999. There were other people riding in his truck, including his three children. He was involved in a road rage altercation with the driver of a smaller pickup truck. The rage heated up as he pursued the other driver. Both vehicles pulled off the road. He confronted the other driver with a gun, according to police. There was a struggle. A shot rang out, and his seventeen-year-old son was struck and killed. Police said that it was not he but the other man who fired the fatal shot, that the other man had somehow taken possession of the gun. Nevertheless, the father was arrested and charged with first-degree murder. It was his decision to pursue the other driver and confront him with a gun that caused the death of his son, police said. Under Arizona's murder statute, any person committing a crime is culpable for a death that occurs as a result of his committing the crime. That man did not have to lose his son. He chose to put himself on a course of action that resulted in his son's death.[21]

ANGEL OF MERCY

In West Palm Beach, Florida, during a road rage altercation Leo Marx, MD, punched seventy-one-year-old Ralph Peck in the chest after the victim told Dr. Marx he had just had bypass surgery. According to the police report, the doctor "punched him in the face and Peck fell into the fetal position while Dr. Marx kicked him." Later, the judge, prosecutor, and Peck's lawyer all turned down a plea agreement after they learned that the doctor had been arrested again for allegedly punching a woman in the face and and poking his finger in her eye. Because Peck is over sixty-five, Dr. Marx faces a felony charge that could get him a sentence of five years in prison.[22]

To engage in combat with another car when you are alone is dangerous enough, but some people bring their families and children into it. Many drivers introduce a gun into a road rage altercation—which can be as dangerous to the man holding the gun as it is to the victims. We need to understand why people choose to engage in such self-destructive behavior. We need to peel away the outer layers and get to the heart of the matter.

NOTES

1. Elizabeth Evans, "Trucker's License Seized," *Dispatch/Sunday News* (York, PA), March 13, 2001, p. C-1; http://www.roadraging.org/

articles/showcase.asp?faq=ii&fldAuto=64; Mike Argento, "Road Rage Case Goes to Court." *York (PA) Daily Record*, September 30, 2000, p. 3, html://ydr.com/awards/1beath.shtml.

2. Michael Fumento, Atlantic Online (*Atlantic Monthly* digital ed.), August 1998, pp. 4 and 6. http://www.theatlantic.com/issues /98aug/roadrage.htm.

3. Kyoko Altman, U.S. News Story Page, CNN.com, http: //www.cnn.com/US/9707/18/aggressive.driving.

4. National Motorists Association (NMA), http://www .motorists.org/info/road_rage.html.

5. Jeff Collins, "Instead of Swerving Toward Road Rage, Turn the Other Cheek, *Orange County (CA) Register*, January 11, 1997, p. 1. See also Louis Mizell, Matthew Joint, and Dominic Connell, *Aggressive Driving: Three Studies*, prepared by the AAA Foundation for Traffic Safety, Washington, DC, March 1997, p. 5.

6. AAA Foundation Report on Aggressive Driving: http: //www.aaafoundation.org/pdg/roadragePR.pdf. See also PNN online: http://pnnonline.org/article.php?sid=4209.

7. National Highway Traffic Safety Administration, *National Automotive Sampling System: Crashworthiness Data Systems*, Washington, DC, US Department of Transportation, 1993–1995, pp. 7, 129.

8. Ibid., pp. 15, 18.

9. Ibid., pp. 6, 13.

10. AAA Foundation Report on Aggressive Driving: http://aaa foundation.org/pdff/roadragePR.pdf.

11. Steve Berry, "LAPD Officer Gets Five Years for Shooting Driver," *Los Angeles Times*, October 30, 2001, p. B-3.

12. Evelyn Larrubia and Nicholas Riccardi, "Court to Pay Inmates Millions," *Los Angeles Times*, August 15, 2001, p. A-1.

13. California Secretary of State Web site: http://www.ss.ca.gov.

14. Larrubia and Riccardi, "Court to Pay Inmates Millions," p. A-1.

15. National Automotive Sampling System, pp. 30–34.

16. Ibid.

17. National Institute of Neurological Disorders and Stroke, NINDS Traumatic Brain Injury Page: http://www.ninds.nih.gov/health_and_medical/disorders/tbi_doc.htm. See also Neurotrauma-Law Nexus, "Understanding Brain Injury," http://www.neurolaw.com/brain.html.

18. Ibid.

19. Ibid.

20. Todd Venezia, "Man Charged in Road Rage Shooting of Boy," June 22, 1999, http://www.apbnews.com/newscent.

21. Pete Brush, "Father Charged in Road Rage Killing of Son," April 19, 1999, http://www.apbnews.com/newsquest.

22. Malcolm Balfour, "Cardiologist Punches Bypass Patient in Road Rage," *New York Post.*

5

HOW ARE WE GOING TO FIX IT?

"Dealing with the Madman"

I have read most of the literature on road rage—the books, the articles, the Web sites, and the studies and surveys. I have watched the films, the videos, and the television documentaries, and I have attended classes on driving. Unfortunately, everything I have read addresses behavioral symptoms, not underlying causes, so I do not have any "authorities" to support the following concepts, only my own experience, observation, and thought.

In chapter 1 I listed the most common acts of rudeness that ignite the explosive anger we call road rage. When another driver tailgates you, passes you, cuts you off, flips you the bird, and shouts vile epithets at you, looking at you with ugly malice and loathing, and you are seized with a hot, adrenalin-fueled trance that pervades your mind and body, and you feel the raging need to dash forward and punish him—

that is the crucial turning point. That is the time to step back, mentally, and take a second look at what you're about to get into. Will you push the pedal to the floor and go roaring into a battle that could cause you to lose everything? Or will you ease off and distance yourself from the assailant? It is hardly necessary to say that it is better by far to distance yourself and forget it. If it feels ignominious and you still have an overpowering need to smash him, crush him, and see him squeal and beg, you can take consolation from the fact that a person so ugly and mean-spirited will almost certainly, sooner or later, find himself in jail or in a hospital.

We need to look deeper into ourselves. Inside most of us there is an intelligent, thinking human being, capable of doing wonderful things with his brain. There is also another entity, the prehistoric savage killer. He does not think outside the narrow corridor of war and battle. He is much older and more powerful than rational thought and he can be managed only by a powerful act of will. But he *can* be managed. If this is not true, we are doomed.

If it feels ignominious to withdraw from combat, it is well to remember that refusing to fight does not make you a wimp or a coward. Our species has been out of the Stone Age for only a very short time and the admiration of violence is still very much a part of our culture, a vestigial leftover from a time when we were little more than subhuman beasts. It takes more dignity to stay out of a fight than it does to grapple like a beast and bash another driver.

If it feels ignominious to move away from violence, it is well to remember that it takes more courage to refuse to engage in violence than to lose your life in battle. It takes more courage to live than to die. The brightest and the strongest people generally do not rush into a massacre to avenge a trivial insult from a stranger, just as a good general does not commit his army and all of his resources to attack a small family of aborigines.

We need to have the courage and the strength to look inward, ever aware of the savage inside and ready to hold him in check when he rises up to attack. Many people deny that they are animals, even though they can see that we have all of the organs and the biological functions of other animals, particularly the apes. Many people don't want to look at their simian cousins and acknowledge their kinship. When the savage rises up, they deny his existence and cast the blame elsewhere: "It was his fault! He was in my way! I had to teach him a lesson."

There is a general consensus among those who have studied road rage that there is no "typical" aggressive driver: the tendency is in all of us, latently or overtly. It is not some foreign virus that invades us and afflicts us with madness. It is an inseparable part of us, encoded in every cell of our bodies. We need to take responsibility for our acts; we need to heed Konrad Lorenz's advice and be aware that we are a part of the universe and that we obey the laws of nature. We need to be mindful of the fact that the energy that burgeons up when we are enraged can be diverted into creative work of great value that will enhance our lives and the lives of others.

6

PUBLIC PERCEPTIONS

"What the Cars Are Saying"

In 1997 the National Highway Traffic Safety Administration (NHTSA) commissioned the research firm of Schulman, Ronca, & Bucuvalas to conduct the National Survey of Speeding and Other Unsafe Driving Actions.[1] A national household sample was constructed by using random digit dialing and a total of six thousand telephone interviews were conducted. The persons interviewed were primarily people who drive almost every day. The survey found that two-thirds of all drivers drive a car; the second most common vehicle is the pickup truck. Twice as many men drive pickups as women. Men are, in almost all categories, more unsafe drivers than women.

Although the questionnaire was a lengthy one—taking about thirty minutes to complete—very little was said about the phenomenon of aggressive driving and virtually nothing was said about the dynamics of road rage combat, which, according to the government and the AAA Foundation for Traffic Safety, is the most common cause of crashes that result in death and disabling injuries. The authors of the NHTSA survey write: "Unfortunately there is no general agreement among traffic safety experts as to what constitutes aggressive driving. Consequently, the survey focuses more on specific unsafe driving acts rather than on aggressive driving."[2]

One question asked whether the interviewee believed that racing another car was dangerous. More than 90 percent answered in the affirmative. Another question asked whether the interviewee had ever engaged in racing with another car. Nearly all of those interviewed denied having raced with another car—all but 3 percent.

The survey also included questions about speeding, following too closely (tailgating), cutting in front of another car dangerously, and making "obscene" or insulting gestures. But these acts are treated as separate, unrelated behaviors, which they are not. There is no exploration of the dynamics of belligerent driving: how it starts, how it ends, and how it can be avoided. Perhaps this is because so little is known about the etiology of road rage, and because it is embarrassing. Almost all of us do it, but we do not like to admit that we are susceptible to such boorish, unfashionable conduct. What we do to another car while driving does not differ from what we do to our competitors in order to achieve career advancement or to win a desired mate from other suitors—except it is more primitive, more elemental, and more brutish.

What we do to our rivals in the office, in pursuit of a mate, or when cultivating the friendship of people of power and influence is more secretive and more devious. But nearly all of us do it, including the public figure who stands before the television cameras and zealously denounces dangerous driving—and then goes out on the freeway and does it himself. We don't like to talk about it, unless we are talking about somebody else's driving, not our own. I knew two men who never engaged in angry, aggressive driving and were never stopped by the police. Both were criminal psychopaths.

Six out of ten of the persons polled said they feel that speeding is a major threat to their safety and the safety of others. Two-thirds said that unsafe acts other than speeding were a major threat. The most common complaints were tailgating, "cutting very closely in front of me," passing in a dangerous manner, making an "obscene" gesture, weaving from lane to lane, running a red light, and ignoring a stop sign. Almost all of the drivers surveyed said they felt that "something should be done." The drivers were concerned about speeding on unsafe roads, particularly rural roads and residential streets.

One-third of the respondents said they felt that driving was more dangerous than it had been the previous year. The reasons they gave were heavier traffic, careless, inattentive drivers, more cars, faster drivers, increased speed limits, aggressive driving, young drivers, and drinking drivers. Unsafe speeds on roads and highways were the most commonly reported reasons. When asked about their own unsafe driving, three out of ten drivers reported entering an intersection as the light was turning red. Others reported failing to stop at a stop sign and driving 10 MPH over the speed limit. The least common self-reported acts of unsafe driving were driving under the influence of alcohol and aggressive driving. Men were more likely than women to commit acts of unsafe driving, but men's recklessness declines as age increases. Drivers sixteen to thirty years old perceived almost all acts of unsafe driving as less dangerous than older drivers did. Although many reported observing such acts as racing and making the insulting third-finger gesture, very few acknowledged having done it themselves or having retaliated.

There is a predictable lack of frankness on the part of the interviewees in this survey. Most people do not understand why they experience out-of-control rage and act on it. They do not want to talk about it but prefer to assign the blame elsewhere. Most people do not understand the other influences that surround them: the vehicle, the roads, and the lack of candor and ignorance of the dynamics of the car industry and of the funding of public roads and highways. The prospect of diminishing highway slaughter in the near future looks dim—but not hopeless.

The average unsafe driving score is nearly twice as high for drivers from New England as compared with drivers in the northwest and mountain states. Sixty-two percent of the drivers who had the highest unsafe driving scores had never been stopped by police.

Asked whether they were driving faster or slower than last year, 75 percent said they were driving about the same. Of drivers with less than a high school education, half said they were driving faster and half said they were driving slower. Of drivers with higher educational levels, those who said they were driving slower outnumbered those who said they were driving faster by a large margin.

Nearly one-third said they pass other cars more than other cars pass them, and 58 percent said other cars pass them more than they pass others. Twice as many of the drivers in the sixteen to twenty age group tend to pass as compared with those who tend to be passed. The tendency to pass drops as age increases. Those in the sixteen to forty-four age group reported that they enjoy the feeling of speed and get impatient with slower drivers. Males are more likely to pass, enjoy speed, and get impatient with slow drivers than females. Most drivers (77%) felt that speeding on urban residential streets is unsafe.

In the multiple-choice questions about the driver's reasons for speeding and unsafe driving, the answer most often given is "late/behind schedule." Other answers given (though by fewer people) include "unaware of speed," "traffic flow," and "emergency." There is no mention of anger.

More than half of those surveyed admitted to speeding and running a red light; 32 percent wove through traffic, switching lanes; 23 percent acknowledged having tailgated another car on a highway with only one lane in each direction; 20 percent made the third-finger gesture; and 10 percent drove on the shoulder to pass. Very few admitted to racing.

Very little relation was shown between unsafe driving score and educational attainment, but the mean safe driving score was highest for high school graduates, lower for those with some college, and still lower for college graduates, which supports Konrad Lorenz's observation that a high degree of aggression transposes into competitiveness, ambition, and achievement in a person who has the mental equipment to achieve[3]—college graduates were less likely to retaliate against unsafe drivers. There is also a direct correlation between income and unsafe driving: Those with the lowest incomes had the highest safe driving scores; those in the middle income category scored lower for safe driving, and those with incomes of $100,000 or more per year had the lowest safe driving scores of all. But we are not told whether this includes road rage driving. It could be that the high achiever who earns $100,000 or more drives faster because he knows he can afford to buy another car if he wrecks the one he is driving. The pauper cannot.

Most of those surveyed believed that there is too little enforcement on residential streets. Those who enjoy speeding want less enforcement. More than half said there was too little enforcement of tailgating and weaving. Drivers between the ages of sixteen and twenty-four were most likely to be stopped by police.

One out of four drivers has been in a crash in the past five years. Almost all drivers felt that unsafe driving and speeding by others were major threats to them and to their passengers. Three out of five drivers said they had been threatened by other drivers within the past year, but only one in ten acknowledged having responded to the threat by retaliating.

As for countermeasures, most drivers felt that the most effective measures to reduce speeding and unsafe driving were more police, more ticketing, larger fines, increased public awareness, and revoking licenses. Business as usual. One-third of those surveyed had never heard of photo enforcement. Once it was explained, most drivers felt it would serve as a deterrent to running stop signs and red lights, reduce speeding, reduce crashes, and get dangerous drivers off the road.

Sixty-one percent had never heard or seen a public service announcement about unsafe driving. Thirty-five percent had. Only 12 percent said they believed the public service announcements had a lot of effect and 28 percent said they had some effect.

About half said photo enforcement would have "a lot" of effect on unsafe driving practices. Slightly over 20 percent said they would have "some." Nearly all said it would be "a good idea" to use photo enforcement to identify drivers who are running red lights and stop signs, and those who were speeding. Those who thought photo enforcement was a bad idea said they feared the camera might be inaccurate, that person-to-person contact with the police officer would be better to assess the situation, and that the camera identifies the car, not the driver, and that the licensee must pay the fine no matter who was driving. More than two-thirds of all drivers felt that photo enforcement was a good idea. An even higher number of drivers favored photo enforcement in places where crashes frequently occurred and in school zones.

NOTES

1. National Highway Traffic Safety Administration, *National Survey of Speeding and Other Unsafe Driving Actions*, 3 vols. (Washington, DC: US Department of Transportation, 1998). Available online at http://www.nhtsa.dot.gov/people/injury/aggressive/unsafe (December 2, 2002).

2. Ibid., vol. 2, chap. 1, http://www.nhtsa.dot.gov/people/injury/aggressive/unsafe/att-beh/Chapt1-2.html#1 (December 2, 2002).

3. Konrad Lorenz, *On Aggression* (New York: MJK Books, 1963), p. 248. See also pp. 251 and 278.

7

NEW LEGISLATION AND PROGRAMS

"Some Immodest Proposals"

Whenever a problem becomes too large to ignore we make more laws, build more jails, impose more penalties, and hire more cops. Legislation to abate road rage was introduced in seventeen states in 1998 and in eighteen more states during the 2000 legislative session. Generally, these proposed statutes were perceived as superfluous and unworkable because of vague language that leaves too much latitude for interpretation by police and the courts. Focus groups of judges, police, prosecutors, public defenders, and defense attorneys expressed a belief that new legislation was not needed to address road rage driving.[1] The National Committee on Uniform Traffic Laws and Ordinances (NCUTLO) has called for strong and consistent enforcement of existing traffic laws as the best way to reduce road rage battles. This is not very encouraging.

There has been a general effort in state legislatures across the nation to enact separate statutes for (1) reckless driving, (2) aggressive driving, and (3) road rage. In one study, road rage is defined as "an event in which an angry driver intentionally injures or kills another motorist, passenger, or pedestrian; or attempts or threatens to kill or injure another driver, passenger, or pedestrian."[2] The new proposed statutes attempt to define these as separate offenses. Road rage incidents are defined as willful acts of a criminal nature. Nine states defined aggressive driving as a charge separate from other violations of traffic codes. Violent road rage behaviors are defined as felonies, while reckless driving remains a misdemeanor.

But intent, or state of mind, is difficult to prove, even when there is contact, and it is more difficult to prove when there is no contact. Judges are unpredictable. You may be convicted of a felony; otherwise, it will be a misdemeanor. The new proposed legislation approaches road rage in several ways: formulation of legal definitions; recommended penalties; and proposals to enhance enforcement and driver education programs.

A bill introduced in Illinois, HB 2509, provides separate charges for road rage and aggravated road rage. Several other states have proposed legislation that mandates additional penalties for aggressive driving. In Arizona, a new statute amends the reckless driving law by adding the new misdemeanor of aggressive driving, an offense in which the driver speeds and commits two other reckless driving offenses, such as following too closely, passing on the shoulder, or failing to obey a traffic control device. The Arizona law provides a fine of up to $2,500 and a possible jail term of up to six months. The law also compels those convicted of aggressive driving to avail themselves of a driver-training course and suffer the suspension of their driver's licenses for thirty days. Those who go out and do it again may face additional fines and a one-year suspension of their driver's licenses.[3]

Three bills introduced in New York State are interesting: AB 5168, AB 8817, and SB 7451. AB 10968 provides for a study and evaluation of the impact of driver education upon traffic infractions and road rage.

A Nevada law enacted in 1999 defines aggressive driving as "speeding and the commission of two or more offenses within one mile that poses an immediate hazard to another vehicle or person."

A Delaware statute sets forth the meaning of aggressive driving as a combination of unsafe driving behaviors. Those found guilty of three or more specified violations within the same incident are required to attend behavior modification sessions. Repeat offenders may have their licenses suspended.

Rhode Island's legislature has passed a law that outlines which acts fall under the definition of aggressive driving. Penalties are $250, $500, mandatory driver education, and suspension of driver's license.

Oklahoma now has a section in the vehicle code that defines aggressive driving as "actions that pose immediate hazards to any other person or vehicle." The penalties are approximately the same as in the other states.

Virginia has enacted legislation that requires driver's education to include aggressive driving, how to cope with anger, and how to cope with aggressive drivers.

Prohibition does not usually achieve the desired result. Despite the ghoulish penalties that await those convicted of murder, tens of thousands of people kill others each year in the United States. According to FBI statistics, eighteen thousand people were murdered in 1997.[4] One must be wary of statistics. This number does not include "voluntary homicide," attempted murder, aggravated assault, and the thousands of unsolved murders that occur in the United States each year. What is needed is universal education that will enable people to understand why we do what we do and how to manage our primal instincts, not just for graduate students but for everybody.

The National Highway Traffic Safety Administration (NHTSA) has a grant program that provides funding to states for programs to combat aggressive driving. The Federal Highway Administration also provides grants to implement programs that target aggressive drivers. The NHTSA is conducting several research studies to examine aggressive driving, and also plans to evaluate law enforcement's methods in dealing with the problem of aggressive drivers.[5]

The AAA Foundation for Traffic Safety has produced educational materials on road rage: a brochure called *Preventing Road Rage*, which explains how to avoid confrontation; a video, also titled *Preventing Road Rage*, which offers techniques to manage anger and avoid combat with an angry driver; and a CD-ROM that gives tips about road rage and a scenario in which a teen is threatened by an aggressive driver.

Several states have programs in place that address belligerent behavior on the roads. "Smooth Operator," a program funded by the NHTSA, originated in California and was adopted by Washington, DC, and the surrounding metropolitan area. A program called "STOP" in San Francisco is apparently nothing more than the seizure and impoundage of cars driven by unlicensed drivers.

"ADAPT" (Aggressive Drivers Are a Public Threat) is a Colorado program that relies on unmarked cars, motorcycles, and aircraft. The Delaware "Take It Easy" program uses unmarked cars and "nontraditional vehicles" in conjunction with marked patrol cars.

In Florida there is a program called "Where's Jockers?" operated under the aegis of the St. Petersburg Police Department, which uses a variety of nontraditional vehicles and a plainclothes officer with a radar unit to alert patrol vehicles in the area. The Washington, DC, area's "ADVANCE" (Aggressive Driver Video and Non-Contact Enforcement) program uses digital video cameras and lasers on the Beltway. Letters and photographs are mailed to aggressive driving offenders. The "3-D" (Drunk, Drugged, and Dangerous) program in Massachusetts uses video-equipped unmarked cars. Ohio's TRIAD (Targeting Reckless and Intimidating Aggressive Drivers) program uses thirteen aircraft. There are more programs with acronyms, all of which are essentially the same, except for a few that use lasers and other high-tech gadgetry.

Sometimes simpler methods work best. The *Nashville Tennesseean* has published a list of alternate routes to diminish the overload on highways and main roads. A multiplicity of hotlines allows drivers to report road ragers to law enforcement—but there are at least twenty-three of these numbers and drivers may be confused as to which number to call and eventually give up. Almost all of the proposed legislation calls for driver education, but we are left with the question: What will be the quality of the education? Most of the bills introduced in state legislatures during the past two years include higher fines, mandatory jail time, and loss of license. I do not doubt that these enhanced penalties diminish aggressive driving in some small measure, but until we understand the underlying causes and are willing to take bold, humanistic action to make our environment less dangerous, we will make little or no progress. It could get worse. Next to Boston, Minneapolis has the lowest incidence of traffic deaths. Why? Residents of Minneapolis are of the same species as the people of Los Angeles, but they have a very different attitude toward their neighbors and their community. There is a sense of collective and individual responsibility to make their city a clean, safe place; a good city to live in. If they can accomplish this, so can we. When we consider the monetary costs of road rage—to say nothing of the cost in human lives destroyed—investing in more intelligent programs and gifted people to implement them would pay out more than it costs.

Will tougher laws, increased penalties, more jail time, higher fines and insurance payments, more cops, and more technology put an end to road rage? No, they won't. These measures will deter some people, but not the hard-core bully. Even if aggressive driving were made a capital offense, some people would still do it. The Stone Age killer is hiding inside all of us. When he is behind the wheel on the highway, he becomes restless. The paleolithic warrior lashes out spontaneously without external stimulus. He also is stimulated by unintentional, perceived slights in the actions of others. His actions don't go through the frontal lobes. The Stone Age warrior does not evaluate his behavior or its consequences. He strikes swiftly, kills, destroys, and moves on in search of new challenges, new victims. He is waiting for you in the shopping mall, in the market, and on the road.

Second only to aggression, the "big one," the greatest source of road rage violence is overcrowding. Like other social animals, we have innate inhibitions that restrain us from killing each other. Unlike nonhuman animals we also have cultural inhibitions that deter us from killing members of our own species.[6] But when too many of us are crowded into too little space, these compensatory mechanisms break down and their energy is depleted.[7] As Konrad Lorenz has shown, we acquired the vicious aggression instinct for the purpose of spreading out the members of our species over a wider habitat, thinning out the density of the population to increase our chances of survival.[8]

Instead, we have allowed ourselves to be compressed into greater density, and we are living farther away from work and have to spend more time on the road to get there and back. We continue to overpopulate our cities and suburbs. We need fewer cars on our roads and more roads. We need safer cars and safer roads. We need safer streets so that people can walk without fear, without being robbed, beaten, or murdered. We need to create an environment that does not induce hate and other desperate states of mind. We need better public transportation: rail systems, buses, shuttle vans. We need better driver education that will truly and effectively motivate people to forgo freeway slaughter. Tens of thousands of deaths and millions of injuries are a problem too large to ignore. We have managed it ineptly, if at all.

After nearly a century of living with the automobile, we know what does not work. The primeval, savage aggressive instinct is not going to be effaced by imbecile platitudes about obedience and respect for authority. The only effective remedy—short of physical restraint—is fear, provided the fear is great enough to dissolve the aggression. We need television and films that show extremely graphic images of the aftermath of high-speed crashes, no matter how revolting, no matter how horrible. Drivers need to see these images as frequently as they see car commercials on television and the car combat in action films. They need to see it not just once, but repeatedly, on television, in motion pictures, in trailers shown in theaters, on billboards and buses, on newspapers and magazines. We need to retain the most talented filmmakers, people who understand and care about the menace of road rage and have a reverence for life. We cannot afford to go on doing what we have done in the past, which hasn't been very productive. The prospect of working on such films and spots would be an exciting challenge for filmmakers and artists. This is an approach that will save lives.

We are bombarded by messages and images on television and in motion pictures telling us what exhilarating fun it is to speed, race, and drive dangerously. Carmakers and their advertising agencies know that this resonates with the aggressive instinct, particularly in young men. They also know that their sense of invulnerability makes young people in their teens and early twenties more likely to risk their lives racing with another car.

There should be state statutes requiring convicted road ragers to take care of those victimized, as volunteers in hospitals and clinics, or to assist those who have lost the ability to walk or drive as a result of road rage.

Our educational institutions do not teach one of the most indispensable of all survival skills: coping with bullies.

Having to deal with a bully is one of the most universal human experiences, and few, if any, people get through life without being confronted and threatened by a bully. The art and science of warding off a bully, repeatedly making him miss when he attacks, wearing him down and rendering him powerless, or just eluding him is one of the most fascinating skills. It begins with disconnecting your fear, learning to be unafraid of the bully, meticulously scrutinizing his actions, studying him, and formulating strategies that he cannot overcome.

Dealing with the road rage bully is in no way different from dealing with a bully in any other setting, except one: He has a 3,000-pound weapon. But he can lose the right to drive it if he persists in bullying and endangering other motorists and their passengers. The brightest and the bravest people would enjoy the challenge of formulating strategies to deal with bullies, on or off the roadway. An indispensable part of this program would be to thoroughly indoctrinate the bully and convince him that it is inexpedient to assault others and can have disastrous consequences. It should leave the bully pleased with his accomplishment, not seething with vindictive anger. It should leave him proud of his accomplishment, just as a smoker or an alcoholic takes pride in having liberated himself from a self-destructive habit. It should leave him happier and more content. Unfortunately, there are many people who devoutly believe that the most moral and perfect world is one in which each person licks the boots of the stronger person above him and grinds his heel into the face of the weaker person below him. But if a thin, 150-pound matador can take down a 2,000-pound bull, certainly we can do the same with a belligerent road rage driver.

We are told that we are the beneficiaries of that great and glorious good: government with the consent of the governed. But consent is not good enough. We need *informed consent*. We need a better-informed, better-educated population. We need people who understand why we do what we do and how behavior can be changed without violating our human rights.

Very little can be accomplished without leadership, and bullies tend to have better leadership abilities than less aggressive people. We need to sort them out, remove the corrupt and incompetent, and then try to work with the best, always keeping them under stringent scrutiny. Bullies are not omnipotent, and road rage, although it is a complicated dilemma that emanates from our most primeval instincts, is not beyond our power to manage and can, in time, be reduced until it is of negligible dimensions. We can manage the road rage madman if we always remember and acknowledge that it's not just the other car; he resides inside all of us.

I have offered some concepts that are feasible if the right people can be retained to assemble them. We cannot examine road rage in a vacuum. It is an inseparable component in a very complicated organism, a component we share with many other animals. But unlike other animals, we have a large neocortex that gives us the capability to manage it and put the energy contained in it to good use if we do not allow the worst kind of people to hold power—as we have done in the past, more often than not.

Those who invented the automobile greatly enhanced the quality of our lives. Those who plan our roads, our highways, and our cities have made a mess of it. We have the power to make it better.

NOTES

1. Daniel B. Rathbone and Jorg. C. Huckabee; *Controlling Road Rage: a Literature Review and Pilot Study*, prepared for the AAA Foundation for Traffic Safety (Washington, DC: Intertrans Group, 1999), pp. 7–9.

2. Ibid., p. 3: http://www.aaafoundation.org.resourcesindex.cfm?button=roadrage.

3. Arizona Revised Statutes, tit. 28, chap. 3, art. 5. The full text of this statute is available online at http://www.azleg.state.az.us/ars/28 /00695.htm.

4. Murder Statistics Home: http://www.murdervictims.com /murder_statistics.htm.

5. —A new "tool kit" created in response to State and Congressional requests for materials to make people more aware of the growing problem of aggressive driving.

—Aggressive driving enforcement strategies for implementing best practices.

—Aggressive driving team work plan.

—A compilation of the Department of Transportation's aggressive driving–related projects and activities originating from NHTSA, the Federal Highway Administration, the Federal Railroad Administration, and an intermodel Aggressive Driving Team comprised of several modes within DOT.

—Stop Aggressive Driving, a program designed to reach as wide an audience as possible of "everyday people" including young professionals, blue-collar workers, and moms picking up their children at daycare. All kit materials are in English/Spanish format. The kit will be distributed to the media and law enforcement.

—Aggressive Driving and the Law, a symposium consisting of law enforcement, prosecutors, and members of the judiciary to solicit ideas for developing guidelines for charging, sentencing, and treatment of offenders.

(These and a long list of other studies and programs are available online at http://www.nhtsa.dot.gov/people/injury/aggressive/index .html.)

6. Rathbone and Huckabee, *Controlling Road Rage*, pp. 7–9.

7. Konrad Lorenz, *On Aggression* (New York: MJF Books, 1963 [in German], 1968 [in English]), p. 240.

8. Ibid., p. 254.

8

WARNING SIGNS

Spotting Trouble before It's Too Late

Look around you. These are some of the drivers and situations you need to recognize and avoid as soon as you see them. It's important to be alert and vigilant at all times so you can get out of harm's way before you're drawn into a dangerous situation.

THE LONE MARAUDER

Pay particular attention to the vehicle driven by a lone driver, unaccompanied by human passengers, cats, or dogs. When an angry driver is alone she will engage in assaultive acts that she would not do if others were in the car, watching her.[1] Usually, a driver does not flaunt her rage in front of her friends, family, or coworkers. We all give ourselves a bit more latitude when we are alone and unseen. But there are exceptions to every rule. A car filled with hyperactive young men between eighteen and thirty years of age, shouting and throwing things out on the street, should also be avoided. One should be particularly wary of the young driver who repeatedly guns his motor and whips his car from one lane to another with the outraged expression of a man rushing into a barroom fight to avenge some gesture of disrespect.

WEAPONS OF MASS DESTRUCTION

Pay attention to sport-utility vehicles (SUVs), trucks, or any vehicle that is larger, heavier, and higher than yours. The driver of a large vehicle often feels the urge to bash you if you are driving a small car. It has happened to me and I have seen it happen to others. There have been a number of cars that were beautifully designed works of art: the 1942 Lincoln Continental, the Packards of the 1930s, the 1956 Thunderbird, and the 1965 Mustang. The SUV is not a thing of beauty; it is a battle wagon. Some have bars on the front grille that look like a shark's teeth. It is heavier and higher than an ordinary passenger car. The SUV is one of the best-selling cars on the market today. Only a few years ago I would not have believed that Lincoln, Mercedes, and Lexus would build and market such machines, but they know what people want. They want to win, and they are willing to pay the exorbitant price of the SUV and the excessive cost of gas consumption. They want to beat up the little guys. They are best left alone.

I know of no scientific literature on SUVs and the mentality of their operators, but the Web is filled with complaints about aggressive drivers who operate SUVs. I have downloaded and printed out a hefty stack of these. There is hardly a word of praise for the SUV. A group of religious organizations has mounted a "What Would Jesus Drive?" media campaign to inform the public that SUVs are not only dangerous but also consume twice the amount of gas a smaller car would use and blow out twice as much air pollution, causing "a serious threat to human health." I watched *Firing Line* on CNN as the Christians unanimously denounced the SUV, with one exception. The ubiquitous Rev. Jerry Falwell, president of Liberty University, proudly said that he drove a Suburban, and that he does not believe science supports the existence of global warming. "If Jesus were here, he would drive one of the better vehicles," Falwell said. A member of the audience replied, "Jesus might return with two SUVs to carry all of his disciples." That, in itself, constitutes a kind of informal survey that may not have the precise controls of a study done by professional statisticians, but is nonetheless revealing. On one Web site the statement is made that "the SUV driver is the motorcyclist's worst nightmare." The article refers to SUVs as "machines of dominance."[2]

An article in the *San Francisco Business Times* states that "some SUV drivers assume a superior, invincible, entitled attitude—as though the added bulk allows them to speed around, weave through or nuzzle the bumpers of cars that thoughtlessly get in their way. Those of us who drive regular cars have all experienced it. Those big headlights bearing down at some triple-digit figure over the speed limit. . . . Combine road rage with congealed traffic with bloated, ego-inflating SUVs and you have a recipe for more angry, dangerous confrontations . . . [S]tudies show that an SUV usually (and often fatally) prevails in a collision with almost anything smaller."[3]

Another protester writes: "I am sick and tired of letting you and your SUVs push me around."

Another writer asserts: "There is plenty of evidence to support the fact that SUVs are killing others on the road at ever increasing numbers. . . . SUVs don't have the same crash requirements as cars.[4]

The Web site for the PBS show *Frontline* contains the following: "A Ford Explorer is 16 times as likely as the typical family car to kill the occupants of another vehicle in a crash."[5]

Another bulletin notes that each SUV sale brings about $20,000 profit to the manufacturer.[6]

There are also jokes about SUVs: "You can rate the prowess of an SUV by the number of VW Beetles stuck in its grille."

Enough.

It would be unjust, and also unrealistic not to mention that not all SUVs are malevolent. Many are occupied by benign parents carrying their children to a picnic or a ballgame. The problem is that, for many people, being in possession of that measure of power, weight, and mass tends to release excessive and dangerous aggression that otherwise would be held in check. Just as certain professions give their practitioners authority and power that tend to breed depravity, being in possession of a large, heavy machine often propels an angry driver into dangerous, unexamined violence and cruelty.

THE SODBUSTER

Beware the driver who so desperately needs to win a race that he drives on the shoulder at high speed to pass the vehicles moving at legal speeds. If he is that reckless and cares so little about his life, you can be sure he cares even less about yours.

When a driver is speeding on the shoulder to pass the other cars and then tries to get back on the freeway, other cars will often speed up to prevent him from getting back onto the pavement. This can have disastrous consequences. Sometimes the outlaw speeding on the shoulder will tumble into a ditch or crash into another vehicle. To avoid those risks, he may force his way back into moving traffic.

THE BOSS

One of the troublesome drivers you will see almost every time you drive in dense traffic is the person—usually a male, but not always—who looks at the driver in front of him and rotates his head, moving his face from side to side, with a look of exasperation and harsh condemnation, announcing his disgust, outrage, and his superiority. I have found no scientific literature that focuses on this driver, but he and his colleagues are out there in large numbers. He may be angry at you. He may be angry at another driver. More often than not he is reacting to an extremely trivial offense, a small mistake made without the intent to be rude or threatening. Some drivers do it constantly, even at a benign, courteous driver who has tried to make a gesture of kindness and generosity toward them. Some will do it just because you happen to be sitting in front of them at a red light. The Boss is not rational. He wants to judge and punish.

He wants to be *the boss*. He is usually driving a large car or an SUV or pickup, so if there is a crash he will have less damage than a small passenger car, and so that he can sit in an elevated position above you, like a magistrate. His demeanor is self-important. He wants to point the finger of moral condemnation. Yet this person would rather die than admit to the most minimal imperfection in his own behavior and his driving. He is always correct; the other driver is an idiot, a menace, a demon. We all need a demon and an idiot. It helps us to forget, and to pretend we don't know that the real demon is inside us.

The Boss wants to be a magistrate. This is the person who always moves into positions of power, authority, and leadership, which is one of the most comprehensive of all societal problems. He usually has no vision, no intelligent or responsible leadership to offer. If you ever have sat in a meeting of the city council or a state legislature or the United States Congress I'm sure you have observed the drab hollowness of "leaders," and their arrogance. Walt Whitman described them as "lizards."

The Boss may just drive on with a look of impotent outrage. But if you turn your head, look back, and laugh at him, or slow down in front of him, it's like igniting a spark in volatile, unstable gas. His compressed rage may suddenly explode into mindless violence. He may slam on his brakes, make a sudden U-turn, and come rushing at you, demanding that you pull off on the shoulder and do battle with him. I've seen it happen and I have seen the crumpled, blazing cars after the duel is over. When you see that face, slow down, change lanes, move away from him as inconspicuously and as quickly as possible.

I once knew a man who was always doing this, endlessly protesting the idiocy of other drivers in conversation as well as on the road. One night when my wife and I were at a banquet, he was seated across the table from me. I was becoming weary of his cheap-shot judgments of others. I said to him, "You must be the world's finest driver if you feel qualified to judge other people so harshly. How many awards have you won for your world-class driving?" Several people seated at the table laughed.

He froze. He stared at me ominously, motionless as a mummy.

"When you point the finger at another, there are three fingers pointing back at you," I told him. His face bulged with hard anger. He did not return to the task of eating his dinner but continued to stare at me.

"I'm going to call the mayor's office and ask the city council to allocate funds to build a monument with your name and face on it and, in big fat letters, the words, WORLD'S FINEST DRIVER. AN INSPIRATION TO OUR YOUTH." More laughter bubbled up from the guests sitting with us at the table as I spoke.

When the banquet was over and the guests were leaving he was waiting for me in the parking lot. There was a brief moment of conflict. The security guards and several other men seized us and ordered all of us to disband.

THE WARLORD

Another face to beware of is the driver, usually an older man, whose lips are clamped together like the gates of a fortress. His eyes are narrowed like the slits in a gun turret and his face seems to say: I will not give an inch. I will give you nothing. Get in my way and I'll bust up your car, and your face, too.

If you perform an act of courtesy—slow down and offer him an opportunity to change lanes with a friendly wave of your hand—his grim demeanor will not thaw in the slightest. He does not smile or laugh. He is not looking forward to a peaceful, relaxed, joyful day. He is looking for combat. He wants to defeat and smash a car and batter a weak, defenseless person. Best to move away from him and not attract his attention. You cannot always know all you need to know about a person from a quick glance at his face through the side window or the rearview mirror, but it is better to be safe than sorry.

THE COMMANDING GENERAL

Many drivers turn on their headlights when it is foggy, cloudy, or raining, or when visibility is impaired by dust or smoke. This is a good idea, and in some states it is required in the vehicle codes. And there are now cars that automatically turn on the headlights when you start the motor.

But there are many people who will put their high-beam lights on to punish you, even in bright sunlight, if they are annoyed by your failure to drive at 80 MPH. The driver who does this is saying: Make way for the big man, all you little people. The Commanding General is coming through. Get out of my way. Move it!

They're everywhere and they are extremely aggressive. You can see the potential for violence on their faces which expands into full-blown road rage at the slightest frustration or annoyance. Some will pull around and pass you. Others will remain behind you and flash their high beams, hoping to inflict sufficient pain on your eyes to force you to scurry out of their way. For the Commanding General this is a small victory. The Commanding General naively thinks his headlights will sweep all cars out of his path and open up traffic so he can speed to his destination, and then wait. When it doesn't happen and he finds himself surrounded by traffic, he can become extremely hostile. Best to leave him alone.

Some drivers retaliate by slowing down, pulling in behind the General, and turning on the high beams, to give him a taste of retinal pain. Frequently this triggers an all-out clash, leaving the expressway littered with pieces of the cars, tiny shards of shatterproof glass, oil, water, gas, cops, firemen, ambulances, and thousands of cars backed up, drivers watching in silent fascination as the dead and wounded are carried away.

THE REAR ADMIRAL

Watch out for the driver who pulls up behind you, so close she's almost touching the rear end of your car, even when you're stopped for a red light. If you move forward a few feet, she will move up again and stop, just a few inches from your rear bumper. You move up again. She follows, almost touching your car. One might expect that she would leave a little room rather than risk the ruin of her car, but she does not usually back off.

Once, when I was being tailgated by a much larger car and we were stopped at a red light, I got out of my car and shouted to the Rear Admiral, "Leave a little room between us. If you rear-end me that's wrong in all fifty states. You'll get a very expensive ticket, and your insurance payments will go up." I have done this several times. Sometimes it works; sometimes not.

Sometimes she will just ignore you and desist. Usually she will continue to tailgate you. Sometimes she will use colorful "adult" language and when the light turns green she will try to pass you, cut in front of you, and make colorful "adult" gestures, or try to force you off the road and wreck your car.

If you feel diminished by this statement of contempt and angered by her apparent intent to wreck you, and if you have a hot engine, you may elect to hit it, spinning your wheels, leaving her behind in your dust and smoke with her anger and humiliation. There are those who will pursue and stalk the bully and take their revenge, unable to disconnect their raging anger. But is it worth it to risk your life in such an insignificant dispute? Aren't there better things to do with your life? There will be another Rear Admiral, and another, and another, until you are too old and infirm to drive. Can you beat them all?

When you are tailgated by a large pickup or SUV while you

are driving a small compact car, you may be in great danger. Some SUVs are driven by benign soccer moms, but some are driven by people who have an irresistible need to create panic and terror in the minds of other drivers. Having a larger, heavier machine lowers the threshold for violence. When there is a fatal collision involving a truck and a passenger sedan, it is almost always the driver or passenger in the car who dies, not the driver of the truck or SUV.[7] If you are being followed dangerously close by one of these large tanks, it is best to get away from it as quickly as possible. The Rear Admiral tailgater is a menace to public safety. Being in front of an angry bully in an SUV is a dangerous position, but not necssarily hopeless if you are a skilled, experienced driver. A small compact car can make a tighter turn at higher speeds than a big pickup truck or an SUV because the compact has a shorter wheelbase and a lower center of gravity.[8] You can make a U-turn and speed away while the pickup is backing up, moving forward, and backing up again, trying to reverse its direction in order to search and destroy. It is easy to outmaneuver a raging, violent SUV. His anger diminishes his awareness of the precarious state of a vehicle with a high center of gravity and a high roll axis, trying to make a tight turn at high speed. Anyone driving one of those "tanks" must have a very precise awareness of its limitations.

THE EXECUTIVE

The Executive is usually a very ordinary, drab, lower-middle-class person, but he has an overpowering need to be boss. He moves with the quick, officious bearing of an office manager. If he is going slowly, blocking traffic for whatever reason, and you gently beep your horn, he ignores you. Some Executives will loudly command you to "stay there until I tell you to go!" even when there is no reason for you to sit behind him and wait. If you pull around him, pass him, and get in front of him he is likely to swiftly come after you in a sudden burst of pious, punitive rage, chase you, cut in front of your car, and force you to the curb before you have sufficient time to take evasive action. I have seen it happen many times. It has happened to me several times. The Executive wants to trap you between his car and the curb so he can intimidate you, bully you, scold you, lecture you, make you whimper and grovel. Then he departs, bulging with malicious pleasure and self-righteous satisfaction. He wants to be boss: a tough, punishing boss who takes swift, merciless action against his underlings when one of them steps out of line. He will become more aggressive if you appear frightened, because he will be less cautious and less restrained by fear. It is absolutely imperative that you show no fear or weakness in your facial demeanor, your voice, or your movements. Project the appearance of calm dignity and kindness.

If he believes that by reason of your race, youth, or poverty the police will do nothing to protect you, he will become even more aggressive. If he is unable to intimidate you, he may resort to violence if you do not appear to be physically formidable. Try to back out, pull around him, and leave.

If you are a woman or a small man faced with a much larger, more powerful man, you do not have the luxury of playing games with a bully. A man afflicted with road rage is as likely to beat a woman as he is to assault a man. Keep your windows closed and your doors locked. Turn on your alarm. Turn on your flashing emergency lights. This attracts witnesses. Lean on your horn. If he is on the driver's side, open the window on the other side and scream, shout, call for help. If he comes around to the passenger side, close the window and move to the driver's side, open the window, and shout and scream for help. Be sure to get his license plate number and make the obligatory police report. If you don't, he may tell the police that you were driving like a maniac, that it was you who caused the altercation, that he was being a good samaritan, trying to protect other drivers from you, and he probably will try to have you charged with hit-and-run.

HORATIO HORNBLOWER

The literature of road rage and the Internet are filled with anecdotes about Horatio Hornblower. This is the man who rattles your neurons and synapses with his horn at the slightest frustration or delay. If he is stopped behind you and you do not punch it with a rabbit start the instant the light turns green, he will trumpet his wrath at you. He is always leaning on his horn. Frequently, he is driving a car that is less than a year old but has already worn out five horns. He is angry. He is frustrated. This anger is compressed and contained inside him and is looking for an outlet. If he rear-ends you he will loudly cast the blame on you for whatever happens.

These people, in real life, are not Commanding Generals, Rear Admirals, or Executives. Generally, they are very average people of menial status trying in sad futility to rise above their obscurity.

MOTORCYCLES

Many drivers have an irrational hatred for motorcycles because they are able to pass cars in heavy traffic by going between lanes. Do not drive behind a motorcycle. If one appears in front of you, slow down. Give him plenty of space. If he loses control of his motorcycle and falls, you will probably kill him. That is a heavy burden to carry for the rest of your life. I saw it happen once. A motorcycle swerved in front of a speeding car and overturned. The driver was crushed under the car. After the car was removed he lay there, staring up at the sky with blind, blue eyes.

THE TRUCULENT TRUCK

One of the dangerous drivers you will see most often in heavy traffic is the man driving a truck. He is usually a man who does manual labor. He feels the imperative to win every skirmish. If you pass him, he may come after you, changing lanes, cutting off other drivers, accelerating like a football player trying to tackle his opponent. He may not quit until he passes you, or until he is left so far behind you that he has no choice but to abandon the contest.

MRS. MEATBALL

Look out for the driver who runs red lights and enters intersections when the light is yellow. She is one of the most frequent causes of crashes. She may be just a reckless driver who is late for work, but it has been my observation that more often than not she is racing with another car. If you pull out into the intersection as soon as the light turns green, she is likely to T-bone you, or you may broadside her, depending upon who arrives first. Always look both ways before you enter an intersection, no matter how much it may annoy drivers waiting behind you. Your car, your life, and that of your loved ones are more important than the annoyed driver behind you.

THE DUELIST

Avoid the driver who flips you the finger. If you don't want him to have the satisfaction of insulting you without getting spanked, pretend you didn't see it. Focus your eyes on something else and go cheerily on your way with a happy face. That may anger him as much as a verbal or physical counterassault, but he usually is not sure that you saw it and scorned him by ignoring it. Just move away from him and stay as far away as possible.

WHAT'S MY LANE?

Stay away from the car that repeatedly changes lanes without signaling first. Also beware of the driver who has that look of desperation that stems from being late for work or for an important appointment, or from being passed. Don't get into your car and drive when you are angry. Monitor your emotional state. If you have been having a fight with your spouse, try to resolve it before you get behind the wheel.

Don't try to punish other cars. Don't even think about punishing other cars. You might not be coming home again.

Don't drive when you are tired. You'll be amazed at how many dangerous mistakes you make—unless you're too tired to even notice. It takes only one to end your life. You are less likely to notice dangerous road conditions, dangerous weather conditions, and dangerous drivers if you are tired. A tired driver is a dangerous driver. Fatigue doesn't show up on an autopsy but there is little doubt that fatigue is one of the major causes of death on the highway.

Always look at drivers' faces. The physical structure of the face tells you little or nothing but the demeanor usually betrays what is going on inside: his emotional state, his propensity for violence.

All of this sounds rather depressing. There are so many people who cannot control their anger and aggression. And there are more than a few who are pathologically violent or insane. Morons, madmen, and crackpots. And there are some very good people out there, people of kind and generous spirit who are not afraid to help a stranger. It's not all bad, once you sort it out and come to know what to look for, and form the habit of always scanning the terrain around you. You take a risk every time you go out into the world, but what kind of a life would you live if you never took a risk?

NOTES

1. I have no scientific literature to support this statement but it is something I have observed almost daily for most of my life. Russell Geen and Edward Donnerstein, eds., *Human Aggression: Theories, Research, and Implications for Social Policy* (New York: Academic Press, 1998), pp. 40–41, 128–29.

2. "Beware of the Road Gods," Cyberprofile, rtb.home. texas.net/road gods3.htm.

3. Don Nelson, "New Meaning to the Term 'Road Hog,'" *San Francisco Business Times*, http://www.bizjournals.com (April 26, 1999).

4. "The SUV Fad: A Public Menace," http://www.geocities.com/ capitol_himm_lobby/1818/3_1suv.htm.

5. "Rollover: The Hidden History of the SUV," *Frontline*, http://www.pbs.org/wgbh/pages/frontline/shows/rollover/etc/before.html.

6. Our SUV Hate Page: http://members.tripod.com/lunas_2/SUV.html.

7. National Highway Traffic Safety Administration, *National Automotive Sampling System: Crashworthiness Data Systems* (Washington, DC: US Department of Transportation, 1998), p. 18.

8. Ibid., pp. 42–48.

9

OUTSIDE AGITATORS

Ambient Precursors of Aggression

To understand the dynamics of road rage, it is necessary to understand aggression. The next step is to identify the precursors that activate violent aggression so it can be reduced to manageable dimensions.

We have already discussed passing another car, intruding upon the driver's space, or "flipping the bird." Passing another car in a slow lane would seem to be an innocuous act, but nearly everybody reacts to it by speeding up, trying to overtake the passer and leave him behind. We are a competitive species and we feel soiled when we are surpassed. Passing, encroaching on the other driver's territory, or taunting him are the acts that usually start a contest. These can and usually will get you into a road rage duel.

We have discussed overcrowding as one of the eliciting precursors. Overcrowding may also be one of the most difficult to remedy.

TERROR ON THE HIGHWAY

ANONYMITY

Another condition likely to release violent aggression is anonymity. In a laboratory experiment, one group of university students was made anonymous by wearing large coats over their clothing and hoods over their heads, and they were not addressed by their names. Another group was not concealed behind hoods and coats. They wore large name tags. An assistant to the experimenter spoke in a rude, obnoxious manner. The students were told to deliver an electric shock to this person by pressing a button. Not surprisingly, the anonymous, hooded students whose faces were not seen were more aggressive, giving the assistant longer shocks.[1]

When there is an altercation on a road or highway, both drivers are anonymous. They may be seen, poorly and briefly, but usually only by strangers. Tinted windows further conceal the drivers. Anonymity, or *deindividuation* (not being recognized as an individual), removes the social controls that restrain aggression. Like the masked, unseen sniper or the person who is assimilated into a gang or a mob, particularly at night, the driver, hidden inside the steel shell of his car, is capable of aggressive acts he would not commit if he were in plain view and identifiable. A recent experiment disclosed that drivers of convertibles with their tops down were less belligerent than those with their tops in the closed position, obscuring their faces and concealing them from other motorists.[2] More people are driving alone than in the past. This enhances the sense of anonymity. Generally and collectively, we like violence and competition. It is in our nature to try to retake our position in front of another driver when he passes us. We live in a culture that worships athletes—boxers and other fighters, wrestlers, race car drivers, and football players—far more than it admires persons of creative and scientific genius. Motion pictures and television programs that feature warfare, explosions, gunfire, and the taking of human life are usually the most profitable for the producers and networks.

CULTURE

The culture of one region or city is not always the same as another, even in the same country. For example, when I visited Minneapolis–St. Paul, I was stuck by the remarkably clean streets and sidewalks. I noticed that whenever a scrap of paper appeared on the sidewalk, somebody quickly went out, even in freezing weather, and swept it up. There appears to be a sense of shared responsibility for the condition of the community—unlike Los Angeles, where it is common to see young people standing on the sidewalk drinking from large paper cups, then dropping them to the sidewalk, even when there is a garbage receptacle only a few steps away. It is interesting to note that Minneapolis is also one of three cities with the lowest incidence of aggressive driving and deaths caused by road rage in the United States.[3] Southern California, on the other hand, is among those areas with the highest number of road rage deaths.

"Cities that have more transportation options have fewer driving deaths," according to Barbara McCann of the Surface Transportation Policy Project, which probably explains why New York is also one of the three cities with the lowest percentage of driving fatalities.[4] One seldom has to wait more than a minute or two to board a bus or a subway train. Most of the cars on the streets of Manhattan are either taxis or vehicles engaged in some form of commerce or government function. They don't have time to fight. There are street altercations and traffic tie-ups in Manhattan, but nothing like Los Angeles. Everything moves at an extremely fast pace in Manhattan. Even people going out to or returning from lunch move at a fast walk. In cities where there is a good public transportation system you can say, "I just don't feel like driving today."

HEAT

Temperature is one of the conditions that have been seen as antecedents of aggression but the research is ambiguous.[5] Heat has been viewed as a precursor to aggression, but recent medical literature concludes that at high temperatures people become too lethargic to engage in combat. There is evidence that more violent crimes occur in the southern states, where the temperature is higher, but there are also many other variables, such as poverty and large populations of the disadvantaged.

What happened to the hostile, aggressive driver before she got into the car? Did she discover that her husband was having an affair? Did her daughter tell her that she was a worthless piece of garbage, after she labored for years to pay the child's way through college? Did a neighbor's dog defecate on her driveway? Did a bully insult and demean her before she got into her car—or on the road—before she came into your presence? To quote an old aphorism from the rural South: "He takes it out on his wife, his wife takes it out on the kids, and the kids kick the dog." Or perhaps he takes it out on you. It is reasonable to assume that discomfort can raise the likelihood of aggressive behavior, but not all belligerent drivers are deprived of air conditioning. In Southern California almost all cars are sold with air conditioning, but this can cause engine overheating and traffic problems in hot weather.

NOISE

The noise level on Los Angeles freeways is deafening. Noise is a stressor: the rumble of doom. It makes people paranoid, afraid, and angry. The noise is high in New York City, too, with its many horns and people shouting, "Hey! Come on! Move it!"

TICKETS

Most drivers are aware that the police issue thousands of traffic citations that are unfounded or, at best, frivolous: tickets for offenses that do not create a danger to other drivers or to pedestrians. Most of them cannot afford the fines, which have grown enormously. If you go to court to contest the ticket you will lose a day's earnings waiting for your turn to plead not guilty, a day's earnings your family can ill afford to lose. The government doesn't care. Great masses of people are processed by the traffic courts daily, pronounced guilty by bored, dull-witted judges, and fined—without any corroboration of the allegations.

Even those who bring witnesses, photographs, videotapes, audiotapes, and other evidence to refute the charges are routinely pronounced guilty and fined. The defendant leaves the courthouse feeling soiled, demeaned, robbed, impoverished, and powerless, with a brooding hatred of government. This, too, lowers the threshold. One would think that this would motivate people to behave better on the highway and not attract attention to themselves, but it doesn't always work that way. Anger is powerful.

Once, I went to traffic court to defend myself against two citations. The cop spoke. It was clear that he did not remember the event that gave rise to this landmark judicial proceeding—or that he was just lying. I spoke. As I began speaking, the judge turned and engaged in a lengthy conversation with the court clerk.

I waited. The judge finally concluded his discourse with the clerk and looked at me.

"Are you finished?" he asked.

"Yes." The judge pronounced me guilty of the charge of which I was not guilty and found me not guilty of the charge of which I was guilty. I asked a lawyer who was sitting in the courtroom, "Are the regular trial courts as incompetent as this?"

"Oh no," he replied, smiling. "Much worse."

I know a lawyer who found a parking ticket on his windshield and ignored it. When he received the letter threatening him with added fines and even more chilling penalties, he went to court, where he was pronounced guilty and ordered to pay up. He gave notice of his intent to appeal. All the state and federal appellate courts rejected his appeal, so he took it to the US Supreme Court where he prevailed! The Court held that he was not properly served! It was not cost-effective for the lawyer. It was time-consuming. But he was a stubborn man. We need more people like him.

The discovery of a parking citation under the windshield wiper is an experience that generates burning rage in many drivers. Sometimes this rage ascends to critical mass, resulting in acts of vandalism and raucous threats of violence. Los Angeles parking ticket writers and their vehicles have been decorated with feces, tomatoes, ketchup, eggs, and other delicacies. Parking fines run from $25 to $330 in Los Angeles. If you contest a citation you may be surprised to find that the officer who issued the summons is not present. I contested a parking ticket recently and appeared in municipal court with photographs to use during my cross-examination to prove the citation was false and absurd.

"Where is the officer?" I asked.

The judge, an elderly lady, replied, "The officer is not required to appear."

"What happened to my Sixth Amendment right to be confronted by my accuser?" I asked. "What happened to my right to due process?"

"We don't do that anymore," she answered.

In the fiscal year 1999–2000, Los Angeles motorists paid more than $113 million to the city in parking fines. I have seen many parking enforcement officers issue overtime tickets when there were still two or three minutes left on the meter. They know that the owner of the car usually won't return and catch them in the act.

GONE TO HIS REWARD

The message of organized religion is a dangerous one: the promise that when you die you don't really die, that your essence still exists and thinks—that someday we all will rise up from the grave and be reunited with our cars. Some of the experts inform us that religious faith makes us better drivers.[6] I don't think so. We need to communicate with our young people, talk to our teenage children, try to protect them from the pernicious influence of government and organized religion. Teach them to fear death because the gates of heaven are not waiting for them. Teach them to say no. Teach them that it takes more courage to live than to die. The belief in resurrection has a powerful grip on many people because they are terrified by the presentiment that in a few years they will not exist, and in a few years after that they will not even be remembered. Everybody wants to go to heaven, but nobody wants to die.

Economic insecurity, income disparities, and frustration—the inability to achieve a desired goal—also contribute to aggressive violence, according to a number of studies.[7] That goal may be the desire to get to work on time when confronted by a traffic jam. Our spartan, militaristic forebears believed that willingness to suffer pain and frustration made us better men and women. That may be true if the pain and frustration are not too great to transcend, and are not of endless duration. People who have never experienced pain or frustration tend to be without compassion. There is also clear and growing evidence that pain and suffering can make us worse rather than better, and certainly do not make us better drivers.[8] There also is evidence that people who have little or no skill in dealing with difficult, hostile interactions with others, and people with poor verbal skills, tend to "speak with their fists" or by ramming the offending person with their cars.[9] Before resorting to violence, they tend to "hold it in" until it discharges in explosive rage. There is nothing manly about enduring abuse without resistance and protest. Ramming the other car and killing its occupants is not the best remedy.

There is also the fact that we each have a script that is internalized in childhood.[10] If a person is reared in a cruel, violent environment, where he sees the perpetrator getting what he wants and suffering no consequences, there is a lower threshold for aggression.

NARCISSISM

For years the apostles of New Age pop psychology have told us of the great efficacy of self-esteem as a panacea for all that ails. It may be useful in some cases where one has extremely low self-esteem. It may form an awareness that life is too precious to be put at risk in a trivial traffic dispute with a stranger, but it may also devalue the other person's life.[11]

A person with high self-esteem is more likely to be oblivious to the rights, feelings, and property of others, and to feel no contrition when trampling over others. A narcissist often reacts impulsively and aggressively to any person or condition that he perceives as a threat to his high self-esteem.

James Dean was not a person of low self-esteem. Neither is Jack Nicholson. People of low self-esteem are not likely to rise to the level of international celebrity.

The psychologist Michael Mantell writes that "in the majority of workplace homicide cases we have studied the root cause of these incidents starts and ends with the perpetrators and their total lack of self-esteem."[12] So perhaps a lack of self-esteem is as dangerous as an excess of it.

Self-control is more important than self-esteem, and the failure of self-control may be the broadest cause of crime. Recently I saw a pickup truck driven by a young man who was rudely changing lanes without first giving a signal, cutting off other motorists, nearly causing a serious accident. He accelerated and sped away, grinning. On the tailgate of his truck was a bumper sticker that declared in large black letters:

YES, I DO OWN THE ROAD
IF YOU DON'T LIKE MY DRIVING
CALL 800-F——K YOU

ALTERED STATES

There is a paucity of research on the causal relationship between psychoactive drugs and human aggression, and very little experimental evidence.[13] Publications, both scientific and mainstream, have been tainted by the artificial line between legal prescription drugs and illegal, proscribed drugs, a line drawn by people with extremely questionable motives. In the daily press, on television, and in medical journals we see the phrase "alcohol or drugs," creating the deception that alcohol is not a drug. Of all psychoactive substances, alcohol is clearly the greatest progenitor of violence.[14] More than half of all crimes in the United States are committed while the perpetrator is under the influence of alcohol. As an old Texas farmer once told me, "Any man that gets his courage out of a bottle better put that bottle down and leave it be."

The involvement of alcohol is more frequent than any other drug in crashes of passenger cars operated by drivers between the ages of twenty-five and thirty-four. The highest involvement of alcohol for drivers in crashes of light trucks is in the age group between thirty-five and forty-four.[15] Drivers between the ages of twenty-five and thirty-four have the highest rate of alcohol consumption, followed by the twenty-one to twenty-four age group, and then, slightly lower, drivers between the ages of thirty-five and forty-four.[16] Drivers of light trucks involved in crashes have, on average, twice the alcohol level as drivers of passenger cars. One-third of all pedestrians over fifteen killed by motor vehicles were intoxicated.

In May 1999 Rep. Lucille Roybal-Allard (D-Calif.) urged the government to include antialcohol messages in its billion-dollar youth antidrug media campaign. The alcohol industry launched a massive counterattack to persuade the federal gov-

A young woman (foreground) lies on the ground after falling from a car as it tumbled through the air. *(Photo by Shirley Eberle)*

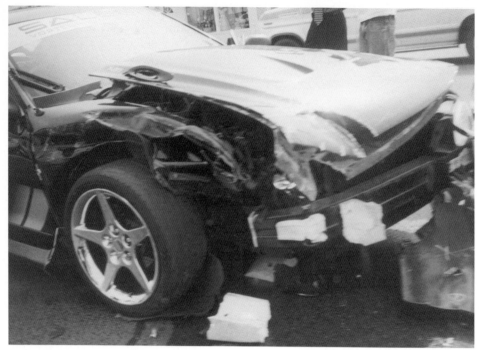

The rewards of wild driving. The driver of this car tried to make a speedy U-turn on a crowded street. *(Photo by Paul Eberle)*

A billboard high above a Los Angeles building sends a message to all: it's about fighting and flying and the thrill of car war. *(Photo by Paul Eberle)*

The challenge. This is how many road rage duels begin. *(Photo by Paul Eberle)*

A car displays the scars of road rage combat. *(Photo by Paul Eberle)*

The conclusion of a road rage joust, in a Los Angeles suburb. *(Photo by Paul Eberle)*

This is a roll cage of the type welded into stock racing cars. It protects the driver from being crushed in a high-speed crash. *(Photo by Paul Eberle)*

Pickups capsize more easily than ordinary cars when making high-speed turns. *(Photo by Shirley Eberle)*

The Ventura Freeway, one of Los Angeles' main highways where road rage duels occur almost daily. *(Photo by Shirley Eberle)*

The rewards of making a left turn into oncoming traffic. *(Photo by Shirley Eberle)*

Billowing smoke in the aftermath of a multiple-car collision. (*Photo by Shirley Eberle*)

When Dr. Jekyll gets behind the wheel he is transformed into Mr. Hyde. (*Courtesy of Joseph J. Roberts*)

ernment not to include alcohol, zealously asserting that alcohol is not a drug but a "legal product."[17] Apparently the lobby succeeded. Alcohol still is not included in most antidrug messages on television.

Recent studies have shown that marijuana inhibits aggression.[18] It makes the user more contemplative. It is believed to be efficacious in the treatment of glaucoma, epilepsy, high blood pressure, and other diseases. Its effects have been described, even in medical literature, as "enhanced perception, relaxation, and a sense of well-being." Habitual users say it augments the enjoyment of sunshine, flowers, and music—that "you become a part of it" and perceive nuances that you normally would not notice. Marijuana is an enhancer. It amplifies and intensifies whatever is going on inside the user. That's why some people experience horror and cannot do it, while others dislike being without it. Driving a car after smoking marijuana, however, is not recommended because it is imperative to be focused.

There is little or no evidence of aggression by persons under the influence of LSD,[19] but no one would recommend driving a car after ingesting it. Several years ago I was riding from Carson City, Nevada, to Los Angeles in a new Cadillac Seville, driven by a man who had taken LSD just before beginning the four-hundred-mile journey across the desert. It was a smooth ride. We were humming along at about 70 MPH and I could see that he was fully in control of the car. But he repeatedly told me: "There's a mountain up ahead. How are we going to get around that mountain?" There was no mountain.

Violent activities caused by PCP are infrequent, and data on the relationship between PCP and aggression are inconclusive. Those who use PCP say that it may generate the desire to "act out" but diminish the coordination and focus needed to act aggressively.

There is an abundance of academic literature that concludes that there is a relationship between amphetamine use and aggression. There are other studies that indicate no basis for such a conclusion, that amphetamines may actually reduce aggression, that other factors have been overlooked, and that amphetamine use causes violence only in overdoses large enough to cause psychosis or in the presence of preexisting psychosis. Some authors maintain that amphetamines may reduce the likelihood of aggressive behavior[20] and that, despite the arousal effect, these stimulants have only a minimal effect on aggression.

I was driving on the Hollywood Freeway toward my suburban home when I observed wrecked cars and trucks on the freeway at intervals of less than one-quarter of a mile. Then I saw a large, green, diesel tractor-trailer ramming into cars, one after another. Suddenly, the truck appeared behind me, ramming a small Honda occupied by an elderly couple. I hit the gas and got away from the truck as quickly as possible. When I arrived at home I saw it again on television: the huge, green, diesel tractor-trailer rig, crushing and demolishing everything in its path. Then I saw my minivan and my head, tilting, looking back at the enormous truck looming over me. Then I saw the van changing lanes and accelerating in great haste; I could not see the driver's face. The television news announcer reported that when the police took him into custody they found methamphetamine in his truck. Was he loaded on meth? Was he angered by something that happened to him that day, or by a continuum of disappointment and frustration? Or did he have high self-esteem?

Depressants, such as Valium and other benzodiazepine drugs, are generally presumed to be inhibitors of aggression. There is little or no evidence of increased hostility and aggression since these agents first appeared forty years ago.[21] A person taking benzodiazepene or barbiturate drugs is less likely to engage in highway hostilities, but all sedatives have serious withdrawal symptoms and if a person overdoses on them, she may not be able to control a car. Most psychopharmacologists agree that opiates like morphine, codeine, and heroin decrease aggression, though there are others who disagree.

At the very least, 30 million people have used cocaine in the United States.[22] William S. Burroughs described cocaine as "the most exhilarating of all drugs." Some psychopharmacologists believe that cocaine use facilitates aggression, but a number of correlational studies found no relationship between cocaine use and violent behavior. It is a powerful central nervous system stimulant, but the "high" dissipates in a very short time, leaving the user somewhat depressed and lethargic. Habitual users of cocaine tend to overdose and find it difficult not to take "one more" line, and then another, because the rush attenuates so quickly. Cocaine users tend to become verbally aggressive and overbearing, but one would have to have a copious supply to sustain a serious, combative mode without other provocative stimuli. Why would anyone spend that much money for a form of entertainment that provides no music, no laughter, tells no story, and offers no enlightenment?

Despite the official edicts, "say no," and "zero tolerance," respectable prescription drugs may be more dangerous than the illegal ones that are proscribed by law, particularly if a person is taking several prescription drugs simultaneously.

Driving while sedated is dangerous. A recent study shows that over-the-counter antihistamines that contain diphenhydramine may impair driving ability almost as much as alcohol.[23] According to William C. Dement, MD, founder and director of the Stanford University Sleep Research Center, excessive loss of sleep contributes to one-third of all accidents and has been proven to increase a tendency toward anger and violence.[24] Americans are working longer hours and sleeping less. A poll by the National Sleep Foundation concluded that 38 percent of Americans work sixty or more hours a week and get about six hours of sleep. Some of them sleep behind the wheel.

TELEVISION

Automobile makers and their advertising agencies cater to the aggressive instinct in their advertising—particularly on television. We see the luxurious new XL3 Thunderbutt Terminator sedan going over a mountain road at great speed, an illusion generated by computer and an impossible feat, unless you wish to end your life in a blaze of burning, exploding gasoline and crushed metal, bones, and flesh. The actors who appear in these car commercials are smiling as they travel at breathtaking speeds. People emulate the rakish young actor in the television commercial, driving the shiny new car with the bleached blonde at his side, speeding over the mountain road as the off-screen announcer exults: "Test-drive the new 370-horsepower Dolt! Today!" The young person equates it with manhood, excitement, adventure, and romance.

Pushy Charlie, the pudgy office bureaucrat, becomes the omnipotent young actor in the TV spot. He becomes outraged when a slower car thwarts his desire to be the latest action movie star, driving at an impossibly dangerous speed. He feels cheated. His day is ruined. He leans on his horn and screams. One television car commercial shows a shiny new car moving at a high velocity while an off-screen voice says, "Too sexy for the slow lane!"

Almost all television dramas and movies contain violence and an abundance of aggressive driving, performed by professional stunt drivers and enhanced by computer graphics. Turn the dial of your television almost any time of the day or night and you will see a high-speed chase. One of the cars spins out of control, goes over a cliff, tumbles, crashes, burns, and explodes—and the principal actor steps out, unharmed, his makeup freshly applied. His glamorous blonde companion also emerges, unscathed, as they pursue the bad guys on foot, dodging bullets from dozens of automatic weapons and ducking when the car explodes.

This is a very dangerous message. An experienced driver knows that it is not a realistic representation, but an inexperienced young driver is likely to take it at face value, push the gas pedal to the floor, and go racing to an early death. There is also a high probability that he will take others with him. It is not the *violence* on television and in motion pictures that is dangerous; it is the perception that you can engage in such reckless, self-destructive behavior and emerge without a bruise or a scratch. Like most of the information we receive on television it does not tell the whole story. People—particularly young people—need to know the consequences of reckless behavior.

ACTION FILMS

Action films are popular with young people. Some of these films are little more than ninety minutes of high-speed car chases and crashes, interrupted by gunfights; hand-to-hand, unarmed combat; murders; and bombings. These films have about as much resemblance to reality as a comic strip. They *are* comic strips. In the real world the good guys don't always win and the bad guys aren't usually taken out. There may be a few disturbed folk who will try to emulate the dashing young actor, unaware that it is not the actor who is driving the car. There are also people who go berserk after eating certain foods. But would it make any sense to ban cabbage and bananas? The solution is to treat the patient, not the stimulus.

A notable exception is David Cronenberg's film *Crash*, which, although it is extemely violent, addresses the psychological merger and mutual absorption of the human being and the machine. The crashes are very real, as are the injuries, the scars, and the prostheses. It's a serious film, not a comic strip. Martin Scorsese called it one of the best films of the past decade.

These "action" epics do glamorize speeding and reckless driving, but in a study, young men and boys who were shown the serious injuries and heard the screams of pain resulting from violence became less aggressive.[25]

Automobile makers and their ad agencies also appeal to the aggressive driving instinct by giving their cars names like Cutlass, Le Sabre, Rapier, Sting Ray, Blazer, Charger, Speedster, Avenger, Probe, Toronado, Jaguar, Cougar, Panther, Cobra, Thunderbird, Bronco, Intrepid, Grand Prix, Firebird, Barracuda, Viper, the Vanquish, and any number of other names that depict carnivorous beasts and violent forces of nature.

For years, public figures, posturing for votes and money and pretending to be motivated by a desire to protect us from violence and sex, have been piously demanding that the portrayal of sex and violence on television and in motion pictures be carefully controlled. People who advocate censorship of the arts and literature are, for the most part, people who do not like art and literature, do not comprehend the most sophicticated art and literature, and know little or nothing about the arts, or the importance of the arts. Television does not induce or create inside us what is already there. It is our responsibility, not the government's, to exercise some judgment as to what television films our children watch and to dissuade them from wasting their time watching films that are nothing but gratuitous violence. It would be impossible to design a controlled experiment to determine whether violent films and television cause aggressive behavior because there is no control group. Nearly everybody has watched them. Media violence is not one of the important causes of antisocial behavior, only a possible stimulus. But book burners are not interested in empirical evidence. They don't understand the importance of evidence. They don't understand the importance of free speech and freedom of expression in the arts and sciences. They don't want to understand. They want to make laws. They want to judge. They want to punish. They want to ban. They want to control. They want to be boss. They want to regulate and censor.

Censorship is the death of civilization, of science, and of art. Censorship must be eradicated. We do not need regulation of words and pictures. We need *more* words and pictures—pictures that show people, particularly the young, what is likely to happen to them if they repeatedly engage in reckless, aggressive driving.

They need to see the crushed cars with brain tissue splattered on the seat covers, the blood and viscera, the burned and slaughtered, the dead bodies lying on the pavement, the others being pulled from the wreckage. This will undoubtedly bring out the "decency" vultures, stridently squawking that young people should not see such disturbing images. But they *must* see them. The best interests of a child are not served by keeping him in ignorance of the dangers that await him in the real world. It has been my perception that politicians and other self-anointed public figures who rabble-rouse for the abatement of sex and violence on television and in movies are usually trying to divert our attention from their uncaring incompetence, their misconduct, their cynicism, and their failure to address the conditions that are the real antecedents of violence and despair.

AUTO RACING

Auto racing is an extremely popular spectator sport and an immensely profitable industry in the United States and Europe. The legendary figures of car racing are folk heroes. Auto racing generates more than a billion dollars annually in America alone.[26] We have found no controlled study that correlates the Indy 500 with aggressive driving, but when a young man goes to the track or watches a race on television he occasionally sees a car crash against the wall at a speed of about 100 MPH and disintegrate. Then he sees the driver walk away from the wreckage with only minor injuries, sometimes none. Most people know that these are not ordinary cars, but many do not know that the car was built to disintegrate on impact at that speed, thus absorbing some of the energy, and that the car has been fitted with a very strong steel roll cage that protects the driver from being crushed. He is also wearing fireproof underwear, padding, a five-point harness, and a very strong crash helmet.

But the young spectator sees the driver making a pit stop, surrounded by a crew of men who speedily cater to his every need as he sits in his elevated position like a medieval knight and waits, impatient to get back into the fray. After the race is over, the driver is surrounded by attractive young women climbing over one another to get his attention. He watches all of this and dreams of being the next Mario Andretti. Then, when the young spectator is driving on the highway and he is unable to maintain his excessive speed because another person is prudently driving at the posted speed limit, he becomes enraged. His fantasy—his vision of who he is—has been blown. No longer is he Mario Andretti; now he is just a crabby, obnoxious nerd. His day is ruined. He flashes his brights. He sounds his horn. He rides your bumper. If you continue to frustrate him by acting properly on the road, he is likely to go crazy, if he isn't already. When he guns his motor and passes you, be totally attentive. Be ready for anything, a gun, a broadside, a burrito, a knish, a golf club.

In Los Angeles and neighboring counties, unauthorized, outlaw street racing takes place at night in several locations at any given time. These festivities occur on roads that are deserted at night: long, wide, straight roads that service industrial areas and warehouses during the daytime. Spectators and participants say the police shut them down, only to find that they resurface at another location. Sometimes the police seize and hold the cars for thirty days. These are tricked-out stock cars that are capable of great speed and acceleration. According to police there has been extremely reckless driving, assaults, and murders at these renegade contests, all of which is not too different from the "authorized" stock car races at regular racetracks. One night a Los Angeles television newswoman and her camera crew visited one of these unauthorized racetracks and interviewed one of the drivers, a short, stocky young man in his twenties. Asked about his racing experiences, he told the television reporter that he had steel rods in his legs and metal plates where his hips and other bones had been smashed.

"Are you going to quit racing?" the reporter asked.

He answered, "No, as long as I can get in the car and drive I'm gonna keep on racing."[27]

TERROR ON THE HIGHWAY

On October 7, 2001, the media reported that the city of Ontario, California, a medium-sized city a few miles east of Los Angeles, announced that its police would not only arrest the drivers in these outlaw stock car races, but would also take spectators into custody and charge them with a misdemeanor. If you happened to be walking in the proximity of one of these events your name could be put into law enforcement databases as a convicted spectator. I do not understand how a casual passerby who stops to look could be accused of aiding and abetting, but that, apparently, is what the city's government intends to do.

MUSIC AND THE SAVAGE BEAST

I have been unable to find any evidence that consumption of pornography increases the propensity for aggressive driving. As for music, that is a more complicated equation. For most people soft, melodic, pastoral music—or even happy pop-rock music—tends to calm the savage beast inside. Carlos Santana has said that "there is something about music that makes your hair stand up." He also said that "music rearranges your molecular structure." Music can get you higher than any drug, and the euphoria stays with you long after the stereo is turned off. We see young people—and even some older persons—bouncing on their car seats to the music of their favorite artists. They are not in a fighting mode. Music dissolves the need for violence—but not for everybody.

There are people who are tone deaf. They have no receptors to process music and they perceive it as noise. It's sad, because music resonates with, combines with, and enhances our deepest, most beautiful experiences. There are certain types of music that are loud and chaotic, dissonant and atonal, like "gangsta rap," but when one hears gangsta rap one generally sees people dancing, not fighting. Music has been known to trigger aggression. When Stravinsky's *Sacre du Printemps* was first performed in Paris, the audience rioted. Vaslav Nijinsky, the principal dancer and choreographer, jumped from the stage and began pounding the hecklers with his fists. Since then we have become accustomed to Stravinsky and recognize him for the genius that he was. And, one hopes, we have come to understand that a work of art can be, at times, loud and chaotic, dissonant and abrasive, even shocking, and at the same time, important, ennobling, and uplifting.

In recent years there has been less music and more talk shows on commercial radio stations. When we turn the dial, hoping to hear some happy, mellow music, we instead hear an abrasive talk-show host, a loud know-it-all, braying his ignorance in a tone of authoritative certainty: "Everybody knows that there is no racial injustice in the United States!"

In the past, radio announcers were selected for their rich, mellow, bass voices. Now, many talk stations are using shouters with harsh, abrasive, high-pitched voices. This kind of talk show may be interesting and sometimes informative, but not particularly conducive to a peaceful, nonaggressive state of mind. We need more music and laughter! Shared laughter diminishes the potential for aggression and forms a bond among those who share it, even though it may be ephemeral. A good laugh, next to music, love, and sex, is the highest experience of which we are capable. There are some who would rather die than have a good laugh. They laugh when they see cruelty, agony, violent death, and tragedy. It gives them a sense of power and self-congratulation. That is not a good laugh. Those people are part of the problem.

We still don't know much about aggressive driving. We need more research.

Of all the conditions and influences in the environment that make road rage more likely to occur, these greatly exceed all of the others: striking, kicking, or otherwise damaging another car. That will bring the driver out, wielding his fists or a weapon. When you damage another person's car it provokes the same reaction as kicking his spouse or his child, which shows how property oriented we are.

Other primary causes of road rage violence are tailgating, cutting off another vehicle, blocking another car, racing with another car and passing it, flipping the bird, and trying to force another car off the road. The most powerful triggers of violence are actions that threaten to destroy the other driver and his car, terrify him, belittle him, and challenge him to a duel.

In this chapter I have examined some of the external stressors that initiate violence. I have tried to cover all of the usual suspects. But there are more.

NOTES

1. Brad J. Bushman and Craig A. Anderson, "Methodology in the Study of Aggression: Integrating Experimental and Nonexperimental Findings," in *Human Aggression: Theories, Research, and Implications for Social Policy*, ed. Russell Geen and Edward Donnerstein (New York: Academic Press, 1998), pp. 23–24.

2. Ibid., p. 41.

3. Joelle Babula, "Drivers's Rage Is All the Rage," *Las Vegas Review-Journal*, March 26, 2000, p. 2.

4. Ibid.

5. Russell Geen and Edward Donnerstein, *Human Aggression: Theories, Research, and Implications for Social Policy* (New York: Academic Press, 1998), p. 249.

6. James, Leon and Diane Nahl, *Christ Against Road Rage*, http://dyc@aloha.net, and http://aloho .net/dye/yarr/ christ.html.

7. Geen and Donnerstein, *Human Aggression*, pp. 57–58.

8. Ibid.

9. Lydia Dotto, "The Seven Second Solution," *Equinox* (February/March 2000): 32+.

10. Stuart P. Taylor and Michael R. Hulzinger, "Psychoactive Drugs and Human Aggression," in Geen and Donnerstein, *Human Aggression*, p. 141.

11. Ibid., p. 139.

12. Michael Mantell with Steve Albrecht, *Ticking Bombs* (New York/Burr Ridge, IL: Irwin Professional Publishing, 1994).

13. Taylor and Hulsinger, "Psychoactive Drugs and Human Aggression," p. 141.

14. Ibid., p. 160.

15. National Highway Traffic Safety Administration, *National Survey of Speeding and Other Unsafe Driving Actions* (Washington, DC: US Department of Transportation, 1998), vol. 2, pp. 112, 113.

16. Ibid.

17. Sonia Nazario, "Industry Opposes Push for Anti-Alcohol Campaign," *Los Angeles Times*, May 13, 1999, p. A-19.

18. Taylor and Hulsinger, "Psychoactive Drugs and Human Aggression," pp. 146–47.

19. Ibid., p. 147.

20. Ibid., p. 143.

21. Ibid.

22. Ibid., pp. 152–55.

23. Johns Hopkins University, "Asthma and Allergy," http://www.hopkins=allergy.org/news/articles/2000/aaai/driving .html. See also *Honolulu Star-Bulletin*, Thursday, April 1, 1999.

24. *Time*, December 8, 1997.

25. Stacy L. Smith and Edward Donnerstein, "Harmful Effects of Exposure to Media Violence: Learning of Aggression, Emotional Desensitization and Fear," in Geen and Donnerstein, *Human Aggression*, pp. 188, 189, 192.

26. "Auto Racing: Speed Sells," http://www.businessweek.com /1997/32/63639109.htm.

27. CBS News, May 25, 2001.

10

DENSITY

Too Many Cars—
Not Enough Roads

O ver the past two decades, drivers in the
United States have been shooting, ramming, killing, and maiming each other
at a steadily increasing rate. Road rage is not
new, but if, as the statistics indicate, acts of violent, aggressive driving have increased by 50
percent since 1990 and continue to grow each
year, it could get much worse. Those numbers,
although they are the newest available, are more
than two years old.

Not much work has been done to explore
the phenomenon of road rage, its causes, and
how it can be abated. Maybe we really don't
want to know because it reveals too much about
ourselves, who we really are, and what we do
when nobody is looking. We like to look outward at the violent behavior of others, the
ruined cars, the ruined human bodies, but we
don't like to look inward at the primeval beast

that exists inside all of us. Perhaps we don't want to confess how much we hunger for deadly combat.

The reasons are not hard to find if we are willing to look. Between 1980 and 1997, there has been a 68 percent increase in the number of vehicle miles driven on public roads, while the increase in miles of roadway created was only 1 percent.[1] There are more cars on the road, and the number of cars is steadily increasing. The population of California has doubled since 1960. It is now over 32 million. Developers are going forward with plans to build twenty thousand new homes adjacent to the San Fernando Valley, which is the bedroom of Los Angeles commuters. Its population already exceeds 1 million. Traffic planners anticipate 2.7 million new residents in the near future.[2] The ten-lane Ventura Freeway already is choked with stop-and-go traffic belching out tons of toxic emissions. What next?

More women are working. The number of female drivers has doubled and the number of women involved in car crashes has increased. More men than women are involved in traffic fatalities, but women have more collisions.[3]

If a married woman wants to pursue a career, no unreasonable obstacle should be placed in her path. But the gap between income and cost of living has become so broad that most women who would prefer to stay home and parent their children no longer have that option. For the average couple, one paycheck is not nearly enough to support a family. In the Los Angeles area nearly a million people are working at jobs that pay the state's minimum wage: in 2001, $5.75 an hour. A small apartment in an unfashionable neighborhood can rent for about $1,200 a month, but the renter must pay a deposit of approximately $1,400 before she can move in. All of this generates anger and despair, lowering the threshold for a sudden blowout of rage.

There are so many people who live and work in abominable conditions, so many who feel they are not valued by anyone, so many who think their deaths would cause no sorrow for anybody, so many people who believe they have little or nothing to lose. This lowers the threshold. There is more divorce, more stress, more problems with childcare, less parenting, and families spend less time together. There was a time when families spent time together. Some worked together in cottage industries or farms as apprentice and journeyman. There was a continuum of teaching the precepts of civilized conduct from parent to child to grandchild. It may have been less than perfect, but there were rules of civilized behavior that were generally observed. We seem to have lost that process, which may partly explain why so many young people behave in a manner that indicates they are unaware of the consequences of violence: that it is terribly painful to be shot, stabbed, or injured in a car crash. They appear to also be ignorant of the long-term consequences to themselves and the community at large. Maybe they don't care. The absence of parenting causes serious deficiencies in a young person. That also lowers the threshold for aggression. But most couples cannot subsist on one paycheck. There are many men—and some women—who work at two jobs, which causes great fatigue, stress, elevated blood pressure, and the inability to stay awake while driving. Driving after not getting enough sleep is as dangerous as driving under the influence of alcohol. But many people have no other option but to choose between danger and indigence, the loss of family, home, everything they have. I must confess that I have more than once fallen asleep at the wheel while moving at a velocity of 80 MPH. Like so many others, I desperately needed the money to pay the rent.

If you want to understand why this condition exists,

remember when you were in kindergarten, and two bullies were playing in the sandbox and they would not let anyone else play. They didn't want to share. They wanted to reserve it all for themselves and keep the little guys out. We need to understand that there is enough sand for all of us. I told this to a young German businessman who was only about forty years old and very successful. He told me, "Democracy is immoral. We need losers. There's no fun in being a winner if we don't have losers to look down on."

"Adolf is alive and well," I replied. He suddenly went blank and drifted away.

It's not just overcrowding. There are fewer jobs than there were twenty years ago, and there is a sense of insecurity that causes people to become obsequious and ruthlessly overcompetitive, producing less and spending more time fighting among themselves to hold on to a paltry job. And there is a growing gap between the underclass and those who have attained a precarious foothold in the suburban paradise of the petit bourgeois, to say nothing of the real high rollers in their private jets. There is a widening gap in opportunity and quality of life between the gifted and the average, general-purpose peons. For the first time in our history there are almost 12 million people who are homeless in the United States. Some sleep in their cars. Some sleep in trucks, warehouses, public parks, or on the streets and alleys, in cardboard condominiums. All of this lowers the threshold.

Another part of the mix is that millions of immigrants have crossed the borders and entered the United States, greatly aggravating the overpopulation and overcrowding. According to the US Department of Transportation, 3.5 million commercial trucks come into the United States from Mexico each year and 0.5 percent are inspected for safety violations. Arizona and

Texas do not inspect incoming trucks from Mexico at all.[4] Many of them have dangerously worn-out tires and brakes.

We have enough problems with our own trucks. Congress has restricted the length of the large tractor-semitrailer rigs and their weight to eighty thousand pounds. But many states allow the operation of a tractor pulling two forty-eight-foot trailers with a total length of 110 feet and a total weight of 140,000 pounds. Some companies add a third trailer. Aside from the damage this extraordinary weight does to highways, there are serious hazards for drivers and passengers in the cars that share the highway with these behemoths. Large trucks, although they comprise only 3 percent of total registered vehicles, are involved in 13 percent of all crashes resulting in fatalities. In 98 percent of the car-truck crashes, the driver or a passenger of the car dies. Large tractor-trailer combinations are difficult to control. Triple-trailer combinations are even more unstable and tend to whip and sway almost constantly. They take longer to stop. They also reduce visibility for drivers of cars because they tower over them. During peak traffic hours we see hundreds of these giants on the freeways, looming over the cars, reducing visibility, poking along in stop-and-go traffic, belching out clouds of diesel smoke. When they leave the highway and travel on urban streets they require two or three lanes to turn.[5]

Many truckers drive too many hours without sleep. This is dangerous. Many truckers openly discuss their use of amphetamines (speed) in order to stay awake, but longtime amphetamine users will tell you that speed rots the brain, the teeth, the bones, and other useful body parts.

In some parts of Los Angeles County the freeways are as many as twelve, even fourteen, lanes wide. Yet during peak traffic hours—which is now most of the day—we see a massive confluence of cars and trucks at a standstill, moving a few yards, then stopping again. The smoke and other emissions continue to flood the air we breathe. The media refer to Los Angeles as "America's second-largest city," but that is not precisely correct. The entire southwest corner of California is one enormous example of urban sprawl, almost uninterrupted by rural terrain, forests, and open fields. Los Angeles, San Bernardino, Riverside, Orange, and San Diego Counties form what is probably the biggest urban sprawl on the planet.

"The stress that people are under at their employment causes them to drive in a manner that normally they would not have under a less stressful situation," Maryland State Police Officer Craig Miller said at the scene of a wreck.[6]

Only a few years ago we saw the Avon Lady and the Fuller Brush Man walking from door to door with smiling faces, and people invited them into their homes. We don't see that anymore. When I was a seventeen-year-old insomniac, I walked the streets of Manhattan from the Battery to Harlem without fear. Nobody would do that now. The streets are no longer safe because of the many indigent, desperate people living on them.

We all know about the celebrated studies of animal behavior with rats and primates in which it was found that violence and aggression increased in direct proportion to the degree of overcrowding. In California, government and media have projected an increase in population to 50 million within the next twenty years. We, too, are animals.

The last state to feel the discomfort of overcrowding on the highway was Montana, a very large state with a population of less than 1 million. Until 1999 there was no speed limit. Elderly grandmothers sailed down the highway at 100 MPH, or even faster. Now, they have a speed limit of 75 MPH, but if you actually drive on the highway at that speed you will become the focus of great wrath, wailing, and gnashing of teeth. In such a setting the checkered flag would be more appropriate than red and green traffic control lights.

Every time you drive, there are thousands of drivers in close proximity to you who are only one paycheck away from oblivion. You are surrounded by drivers who have already cashed and spent that final paycheck and are living in subhuman conditions. Some sleep in their cars. There are thousands of drivers out there who, because they are unskilled, are no longer needed by our technological civilization. They know they are rejects. Some of them become dangerous obsessive fanatics.

Some of the worst road rage violence occurs in traffic jams, where there is no escape route. It is in this kind of gridlock situation that one driver gets out of his car and attacks another, or both drivers get out of their cars and fight, sometimes with weapons, sometimes with fists and feet. Sometimes the car is used as the mechanized assault unit. When the traffic jam dissipates and the vehicles are able to move again, the high-speed duels begin. Malthus warned us of the dangers of overcrowding two centuries ago. Nonetheless, we go on breeding and killing at an alarming rate, while our leaders flash their plastic smiles at the cameras, enumerate the cosmic benefits they have bestowed upon us, and tell us how much we love them, how happy we are, what we like, and what we don't like.

One day in 2001, traffic was backed up for miles on one of the Los Angeles County freeways. Two men got out of their cars and began fighting with their fists, then kicking and wrestling. One was a very large man wearing no shirt, displaying his huge bulging arm muscles and his tattoos. The other was a small, spare man. As they hurled their fists at each other, the larger man took a savage beating before the eyes of his wife and children. Blood was flowing from his nostrils and his mouth. The smaller man knocked him down twice, then lifted him up and bashed him again. The larger man tried to wrestle, burying his face in the smaller man's chest to protect it from further damage, but the smaller man continued to pound him. The television news anchors cried out elatedly, "Wow! Look at that!"

"The one with the shirt is winning!" the blonde anchor-woman shrilled exuberantly.

"He's beating the stuffing out of the big guy!" the male anchor exulted. The police arrived and took the combatants into custody. Then we were presented with a talking cat endorsing a familiar brand of cat food.

Hardly a day goes by without a high-speed chase or a road rage duel on the five o'clock news. Sometimes two or more are in progress at the same time. The television news producers know that it gets ratings. Sometimes a particularly spectacular high-speed chase occupies the entire television news hour as the cameras follow the speeding cars across the city. Why bother with foreign policy? Why bother with Congress, the economy, the election? The producers know we like to see a race or a battle. When there is a particularly gory crash on a freeway, traffic is backed up for many miles because people stop and gaze raptly at the crumpled, burning cars, the dead bodies lying on the ground, and the survivors being removed from the wreckage.

One day in May 1999 the five o'clock news opened with the exclamatory caption, superimposed across the screen in large, bold letters: "LIVE ACTION BREAKING NEWS." It was a police pursuit, but the vehicle they were chasing was a large, unwieldy motor home. The motor home occupied about three lanes of a five-lane half of the divided freeway. It was sur-rounded by police cars. The police ordered the driver to stop, but he ignored them and drove on. Over a million people watched until the driver died in a hail of police bullets. The station's audience was more than twice its normal size. The air was filled with police and media helicopters. Traffic was stalled, bumper to bumper, for dozens of miles, but it was not much worse than the typical daily five o'clock freeway overload.

For decades, people have asked in perplexed tones why it is that Los Angeles, one of the largest urban sprawls on the planet, has no interurban rail system like the subways of New York City and Washington, DC. Certainly it would take an immense load off the public roads and freeways, eliminate tons of toxic air pollution, and save many lives.

Most of the people living in Los Angeles today do not know that the city once had the largest, most efficient electric interurban system in the world, the Pacific Electric Railway. One thousand miles of trolley lines not only covered Los Angeles, but extended into San Bernardino, Riverside, and Orange Counties. What was once an arid desert with a few small towns was transformed into the great metropolis that is Southern California. The Pacific Electric operated six thousand speedy, comfortable coaches daily. They were called the Red Cars. The system was in place for half a century, joining forty-five cities.[7]

In the late 1950s the Pacific Electric system was gradually dismantled. The last of the Red Cars was taken out of service on April 1, 1963. There was a frantic freeway contruction program in motion. The freeways were so overloaded that they were obsolete before they were completed. It would have been easy to make space for an electric rail system on the freeways, as was done by designers in Chicago and other cities, and to maintain the existing rail system, replacing obsolete tracks and cars with new, high-speed technology, saving the people of California enormous taxes, air pollution, and the daily exasperation of driving in stop-and-go, bumper-to-bumper traffic.

But the career politicians were not interested. The developers, manufacturers, lawmakers, and other profiteers benefited hugely, but the quality of life for the average person declined. Those who are old enough to remember will tell you that before the 1950s, Los Angeles was one of the most beautiful cities in the world. Since then, it has grown like a weed patch, with little or no intelligent planning: four thousand square miles of ugly strip malls; ghettos; cheap, dirty, high-density apartment complexes; used-car lots; wrecking yards; and choked freeways, to say nothing of the foul air and the decaying inner city.

I believe that a part of the problem is the ugliness of the surroundings in which we drive. This and overcrowding and foul air do not combine to form a joyful state of mind.

On television Tom Bradley, the former mayor of Los Angeles, said that it was the world's largest purveyors of gasoline, cars, and tires who inconspicuously acquired the Pacific Electric, dismantled it, and sold the rights-of-way. "That was forty years ago and I don't think there are a thousand people in L.A. who know about it," the mayor said.

When I first arrived in Los Angeles, the smog was so dense, we could not see the trees only one block away from our house.

In the 1980s construction of a new subway from downtown Los Angeles to Hollywood was begun. Since then, billions have been spent on this project. There is a very large body of newspaper stories alleging huge cost overruns, some of them rather frivolous. Only five miles of subway had been completed in 2000. Since then, another short segment ending in North Hollywood has been completed. Where did the money go?

California State Senator John Burton, smiling at the cameras, recently announced a plan to issue $16 billion in bonds to repair the state's obsolete transportation system.[8] The bond issue bill does not specify what will be done with the $16 billion.

I asked my friend Walter, an elderly lawyer, "Will we ever get an adequate rail system in L.A.?"

"By that time we'll be too old to work," he said.

But our transportation system is already too old to work.

In 1968, when my wife, Shirley, and I were newspaper reporters, we were told that the city of Los Angeles was planning to create a vast network of bicycle paths, which would make it possible for people to ride their bicycles to work. We were excited and told the editor we wanted to cover the story. Bicycle paths would have reduced the foul exhaust emissions from cars and diminished the overcrowding on the freeways. They would have provided people who labor at sedentary jobs an opportunity to engage in vigorous exercise, which would greatly lengthen their life expectancy. We made an appointment and visited one of the large municipal buildings, where we saw a room full of engineers sitting at drawing boards, designing the proposed bicycle path system. One of the engineers enthusiastically showed me maps of the elaborate network of bicycle paths that were to cover Los Angeles County, explaining as he pointed at the proposed routes. About three years later I saw the same engineer. He remembered me. I asked him, "What happened to the bicycle paths?"

"They vanished, like the Pacific Electric rail system," he said. "Bicycle paths don't sell gasoline. But they don't make smog. And you'll live longer if you ride a bike to work instead of sitting on your butt in a car."

For decades, we have seen and heard brief stories in the media about the possibility of converting from air-polluting, gas-burning cars to automobiles powered by electricity. Foul air is almost certainly another of the many stressors that assail us when we drive in cities like Los Angeles. I once conducted a lengthy interview with Los Angeles Chief Coroner Thomas Nuguchi. He told me that when he performs an autopsy he immediately knows whether the person had been a resident of Los Angeles by the color of his lungs. Electric cars would be a quantum leap from the primitive, smoke-blowing gas burners we now drive, but whenever the electric car is mentioned on the media we are shown ugly little machines that look like inverted bathtubs, and we are told by the manufacturers and the media that we still do not have the technology to produce an electric car that would have a range of more than one hundred miles, and that we would have to stop and wait for hours while the batteries are recharged. The talking heads of the media, reading from the TelePrompTer, invariably treat the electric car as a joke, something that is not feasible and never will be. In August 1999 I watched a panel discussion of automobile manufacturing executives and members of government regulatory bodies on the automobile and air quality on C-SPAN. One of the members of the panel said, "The electric car has been a miserable failure." The others obediently echoed this statement like true believers responding to celestial voices. I find it difficult to believe that people who can put human beings on the moon and retrieve them could not design a very satisfactory electric-powered car. But these electric prototypes always vanish, along with the bicycle paths and the electric rail systems. Whose agenda is being served?

For millennia, the world's most learned men told us that nobody would ever construct a flying machine, that it was not feasible, that all efforts to build a flying machine had been a "miserable failure."

In September 1976 the US House of Representatives voted 307 to 101 to override President Ford's veto of a $160-million program to develop an efficient electric car in five years (HR 8800). Contracts were to be let for twenty-five hundred cars. The Energy Research and Development Administration projected 10 to 20 million vehicles in the near future. Plans for a network of one hundred fast-charge stations for battery-operated cars in Los Angeles were discussed by the commissioners of the Department of Water and Power.

But there was a catch. The Electric and Hybrid Vehicle Research, Development, and Demonstration Act of 1976 became Public Law 94-413. This law authorized funding. But the actual provision of money for its implementation required separate legislation.[9] That was twenty-three years ago. What happened to the money? Where is the electric car?

In 1982 the General Accounting Office announced that the program to develop electric vehicles had been a failure and should be dropped.[10] Whose failure?

In 2000 it was announced that the US Navy was planning to build a new fleet of destroyers propelled by "efficient electric motors," which would generate enough wattage to also operate "futuristic weapons such as lasers or electromagnetic launchers."[11] According to then navy secretary Richard Danzig the new electric-propelled ships would be simpler and more streamlined in their operation and would require a much smaller crew. He called the switch from internal combustion engines to electricity a change equal in importance to the change from sails to steam. The new electric propulsion technology was already being used in ships much larger than a naval destroyer, ships with a displacement of one hundred thousand tons. If an electric-powered engine can propel a one-hundred-thousand-ton ship, why would it not be able to drive a one-ton car?

In May 2000 a panel of engineers was commissioned to

study the feasability of the electric passenger car. Predictibly, they painted a dark, pessimistic picture of the future of the electric car, saying that batteries that would appeal to motorists were still five years away. They sharply criticized California's mandate requiring that large numbers of pollution-free cars be sold beginning in 2002. But the California Air Resources Board issued a report that said the mandate is achievable because electric car batteries have already advanced substantially and the cost is steadily declining. About twenty-three hundred battery-only cars were already on the roads of California in 2000. General Motors, Ford, Chrysler, Toyota, and Nissan mounted a powerful lobbying campaign to eliminate the mandate. Environmentalists and proponents of alternative energy said that the market for the electric car could be strong and that the auto industry was stifling it.[12] But the times are changing. If you drive the freeways of Los Angeles you will see signs telling motorists:

ELECTRIC CAR BATTERY
RECHARGE STATION
ONE MILE

We are beginning to see advertising for the Honda Insight, a hybrid that runs on electricity and a small gasoline-burning motor. It is self-charging. Even the brakes act as generators. It travels about seventy miles per gallon. We are also seeing news reports not only about electric but also hydrogen-powered cars, fuel cells, methanol, and even compressed air.

When extreme traffic density and high speed combine with poor planning, a typical result is what has been happening on California Highway 46, the highway where James Dean, the film actor, died in a shattering head-on collision on September

30, 1955.[13] There were thirty-one fatalities on this highway between 1992 and 1999, and many before 1992. Five of them occurred in one month (May 1999), most of them on a twenty-two-mile segment near Paso Robles. The traffic is dense on weekends and holidays. The cars usually are full. Local residents call it "Blood Alley." Funding for roads and highways has gone mostly to improving the huge interstate expressways and very little to the obsolete, narrow highways where most of the fatalities occur.

Highway 46 is a very straight, flat strip of cement. Many drivers travel as fast as 70 or 80 MPH on their way to Bakersfield or Fresno. But it is narrow. James Dean was driving too fast to stop if another car turned in front of him. Some witnesses said he was driving at least 100 MPH in a car that had a top speed of 130 MPH. One terrified woman who was nearly hit by Dean's Porsche said she saw him grinning. It was twilight and his silver-gray Porsche Spyder was hard to see. A Ford entered an intersection, moving at a velocity of about 55 MPH. The two cars collided, head-on. James Dean's Porsche and the Ford appeared to merge in a crumpled bolus of sheet metal. The Porsche tumbled and struck the ground several times, then came to rest. James Dean's arms were broken in several places. His neck was broken. One mangled arm and his head hung grotesquely from the window. He hoarsely exhaled his last breath and expired into oblivion. His recently completed movie, *East of Eden*, was opening at a nearby drive-in theater. He was twenty-four years old.

Racing and passing at high speeds on a crowded two-lane undivided highway can be detrimental to your health. Very little has been done to correct this condition, while the population of the surrounding area has grown 120 percent in recent years. The California Highway Patrol has received a federal grant for more patrols on this dangerous stretch of highway and there are plans to widen it in about five years.

Overcrowding is extremely dangerous and it is one of the greatest causes of road rage. But it must be understood that overcrowding is only one of the external conditions that are the precursors—not the source—of violent aggression, although they are closely interrelated.

NOTES

1. Dominic Connell and Matthew Joint, *Aggressive Driving: Three Studies* (Washington, DC: American Automobile Association Foundation for Traffic Safety, 1997), p. 2.

2. Lisa Mascaro, "Looming Traffic Crisis," *Los Angeles Daily News*, August 4, 2002, p. 1.

3. *Los Angeles Times*, February 10, 1998.

4. Robert Kuttner, "Big Trucks, Big Trouble," *Los Angeles Times*, October 25, 1999.

5. Tom Lankard and John Lehrer, "Photo Cop: Think Twice before Racing a Red Light," *Westways*, October 1999, pp. 46–49.

6. "Road Rage Runs Rampant in High Stress U.S. Society," CNN, http://www.cnn.com/US/9707/18/aggressive.driving /index.html (July 18, 1997).

7. Spencer Crump, *Ride the Big Red Cars: The Pacific Electric Story* (Glendale, CA: Trans-Anglo Books, 1970). See also Spencer Crump, *Ride the Big Red Cars: How Trolleys Helped Build Southern California* (San Diego: Lucent Books, 1966).

8. Carl Ingram, "$16 Billion in Transit Bonds Urged," *Los Angeles Times*, February 19, 1999.

9. Letter to former US senator Alan Cranston (D-CA) from Vincent J. Esposito, director, Division of Transportation, Energy Conservation, United States Energy Research and Development Administration dated May 6, 1977 (sent at my request). See also

Bernard Asbell, "Emission Standards: The Roadblock Ahead," *Los Angeles Times*, sec. 8, Opinion, November 21, 1976, p. 1. Also *Congressional Quarterly*, September 4, 1976, pp. 2447–49, and *Congressional Quarterly*, September 18, 1976, p. 2504.

10. http://proquest.umi.com/pqdweb?TS=...=1&Did=0000 00047714&Mid=1&Fmt=3. See also John O'Dell, "More Cars Rated 'Green' in Survey," *Los Angeles Times*, February 20, 2003, p. C-3.

11. Robert Suro, "Navy Plans High-powered New Destroyer; Compulsion Progress Compared to Jump from Sail to Steam," *Washington Post*, January 7, 2000.

12. *Los Angeles Times*, May 2, 2000, p. A-22.

13. Walter G. Olesky, *The Importance of James Dean* (San Diego: Lucent Books, 2001), p. 83.

11

THE CAR AS SACRED ICON

"Do Not Kick the Holy Virgin"

Recently I saw an interview that was filmed in 1955. An extremely old man was telling a television network newswoman about his youth as the scion of one of America's most aristocratic families: "When I was a boy we were the only family in town that owned an automobile. Now, everybody owns an automobile. But we were all somehow happier in those days."

I'm not sure that we were all somehow happier when only one man in town owned an automobile. But in 1908 Henry Ford built an assembly plant that produced the Model T, a car that was sold for about eighty dollars. He sold more than 15 million of them and changed the face of America. The cars were primitive and there were those luddites who, delighted at seeing one stalled on the side of the road, shouted, "Get a horse!" A few of them still remain with us and preach against technology, but few take them seriously.

Then came the Model A, and the assembly-line workers were driven to work faster and produce more cars for millions of customers. Henry Ford gave us mobility, freedom, empowerment, glamour, autonomy, adventure, and a sense of national exhilaration and optimism. No longer was the automobile something only the aristocracy could hope to own; the horny-handed sons of toil bought millions of Ford's cars. The wealthy bought Packards and La Salles. In the agricultural heartland of America, there was the popular aphorism:

> The little Ford was made of tin
> But tin was made to pack things in.

In America the car is more than an artifact: It is a religion. The sacrosanct position of the car in our culture is another component of road rage that cannot be ignored. This is the reality that must be understood before we can comprehend the elements of road rage. The car is the precious family jewel, the coat of arms, the banner that must not suffer defeat. We view the car as something inseparable from the self, like the tortoise and its shell. It is an extension of the home. When you damage or attempt to damage another person's car, you will elicit the same response you would see if you damaged his home, spouse, or child. The car is a shrine, a temple, an object of mystical veneration. There are drive-in chapels where couples can be married in their cars or attend religious observances on a Sunday and be redeemed in their cars. Children have been conceived in cars. Both adults and infants have been baptized in their cars, received confirmation in their cars, and some have been given the last rites inside their automobiles. A few years ago a California woman, executing her last will and testament, enjoined her attorneys, executors, and successors to see to it that when she passed on to that great car wash in the sky, her remains were to be buried in her car—or more precisely, her Cadillac was to be buried with her remains in it. In America the issuance of a driver's license and taking possession of one's first car is a sacrament, a rite of passage, a mitzvah.

A person who does not wash his car is viewed as ritually impure. I was once employed at a radio station with a very successful disc jockey, a large, portly man who never washed his car. Such a menial task was beneath his dignity. It was a very large Cadillac, covered with dust and deceased insects. The office staff looked upon his car with pious, brooding horror, as one would view an affront to the supreme being. One day, they decided it was imperative to act, for fear that this outrage might bring down the wrath of Jehovah upon all of us.

They washed half of his car. Someone drew a line with his finger in the dust, bisecting the giant Cadillac, and they washed only on one side of the line. When the announcer looked out and saw what had been done to his car, he looked at me with a cynical smile and said, "Do they think that's funny?"

"Maybe they think they've saved us from eternal damnation," I offered.

"Why don't they get a life?" he asked sourly.

I tried to explain that in their minds he had committed a sacrilege—that the car was a holy icon and not to wash it was a mortal sin. A car wash is a temple, a sanctuary, an informal meeting place where you can engage in conversation with others and find a mate. Washing the car is a ritual of absolution. When it emerges from the tunnel, immaculate and glistening, your past sins are washed away and you are ready to go out and commit bigger and better sins.

Like the portly radio announcer, I, too, neglected to have my car washed. There were always too many other things I was expected to do, and not enough time. The advertising director, the accountant, and the general manager, who were always very correct, watched me furtively behind dark, enigmatic eyes, the way one might look at a man who had failed to have his child baptized, and said in hushed tones, "Better get that car washed, Paul."

*   *   *

Sharie McGarry and Sonny Knight met at the AutoSpa Car Wash in California. He was the manager, a handsome man, about forty years old. She was a customer, a young woman with blonde hair and a radiant smile. She became enamored of Knight and began visiting the car wash as many as five times a week, hoping to get his attention. She also came in the morning to see if he arrived alone, and at closing time to see whether he left alone or with another person. "I didn't know whether he was married or gay," she recalled. On Tuesday, November 30, 1999, they were married—at the car wash. It was an extravagant wedding with 130 guests. The bride was dressed in a white gown, a cowboy hat and white boots with rhinestones. The groom also wore a cowboy hat. The owners of the car wash arranged the wedding. One of them said that the car wash was "not the most appropriate place but they had such a wonderful experience meeting here." The groom said it was the perfect place. The bride said that the car wash "is what means the most to us." This story was published on the front page of the *Los Angeles Daily News*.[1]

If you want to assess the position of the car wash in our civilization you might rent the motion picture *Car Wash*. It is not a technical manual on the cleansing of cars, but it is a very interesting and entertaining exposition of the important place of the car wash in our collective mind.

I have heard the young car worshipers talking about their cars:

"That's a virgin. She's never been passed."

"That used to be a radical car but it got beat."

"I saw two cars race and one of them crashed and burned and exploded with the driver inside. It was really cool. It was like an out-of-body experience."

"That's Louie. He's a Ford lover."

Often, a person is identified by the color and make of his car:

"That's Jim, the white Chevy Malibu."

"That's Ray, the blue Buick Regal."

"Do you know Brad, the green Ford Mustang?"

Even Ken and Barbie have a car.

When a young man gets a better-paying job, sells his old Ford, and gets a new Lexus or a BMW, everyone's perception of him changes: sometimes for the better, sometimes not. Recently, an acquaintance of ours was able to buy a nearly new Cadillac Eldorado at a bargain price from a wealthy friend who had too many cars and just wanted to get rid of it. He paid his friend for the Cadillac, drove it home, and parked it in front of his house as he had always done with his previous cars. A neighbor came to the door, a man in his late forties, and pressed the doorbell. The couple who had acquired the Cadillac opened the door and said, "Good morning" to this neighbor, who had always been friendly to them.

"I see you got a Cadillac," he said.

"Yeah."

"Where'd ya get it?" he asked.

"We bought it last week."

The neighbor stared at the Cadillac, then turned to the young couple and said, "Well, I don't like it but I guess there's nothin' I can do about it." He looked at them with dark inscrutable hate and left.

It is not uncommon for a person who has just brought home a new car to find it vandalized by a neighbor, particularly if the neighbor believes he is of higher standing in the community than the person who has acquired a newer and more expensive car than his own—which tells us what a large symbol of rank and status the car is in our national consciousness. As my friend Frank once said, "The automobile is the heartbeat of America."

If you want to get a sense of the primacy of the car in our culture you might look through a catalog or an encyclopedia of the pop music of the last eighty years, or go online, and try to count the massive body of car songs: young men—and some women—singing hymns of worship to their cars, accompanied by background singers responding with their antiphon: "Yeah yeah yeah yeah."

If you have any lingering doubts about the sanctity of the car in the collective mind of America, consider the recent death of Dale Earnhardt, the legendary NASCAR racing driver who was killed on February 18, 2001, during the final turn of the last lap of the Daytona 500, when his car crashed into the outside wall at a speed of nearly 200 MPH. According to spectators, some of whom commented that he preferred to risk death than be passed, he lost control when he was bumped by a car that was behind him. The horrifying spectacle was seen by at least two hundred thousand people in person and, later, on television by millions.

Earnhardt's death received more newspaper and television coverage than the deaths of former presidents and Nobel Prize winners. The media threnody continued, day after day, with endless replays of the crash. Full-page accounts were published in newspapers. Some papers filled several pages with various aspects of the story and large photographs of Earnhardt with his cocky smile and fatherly demeanor. There were many photographs of his weeping admirers. His victories and accomplishments filled the columns of newspapers from top to bottom. He earned $41,640,462 driving and winning races, and several times that amount with his corporation, which built and raced other cars driven by a three-driver team including his son, Dale Earnhardt Jr.[2]

He was not an ostentatious man. He enjoyed the elemental pleasures of life. He loved his family, his home, fishing, driving, speeding, racing, and winning. He didn't need the money. He had everything he needed. But he wanted one more race. And then another. He once said, "Any time there's a race, I want in it."

When the news of the crash was announced on dozens of television sets at a nearby Wal-Mart, there was a stunned silence. Women screamed and men wept. By the end of the day almost all of the Earnhardt memorabilia were sold out. Shirts, hats, toy cars, racing jackets, T-shirts, seat cushions. By Monday the shelves were bare. Many people placed these items against a fence outside the building that contained Earnhardt's offices, a museum, and a garage where racing cars were built. These offerings formed a line about 120 feet long. An unknown poet wrote these lines and posted them on the wall:

> Now he drives in heaven, racing for the Lord.
> I only hope that God didn't put him in a Ford.[3]

Dale Earnhardt's death raised another issue that has been a source of contention in auto racing for some time. Earnhardt refused to wear the head and neck restraint system (HANS), a newly designed harness that can save a driver's life and prevent head and neck injury. The HANS is credited with saving at least one race car driver. Three NASCAR drivers who were killed in 1999 were not wearing it. A head-on crash at high speed usually causes neck and basal skull injuries, but when a car hits a solid wall, causing an instant deceleration from 200 MPH to zero, the spinal column in the neck snaps, along with the arteries and blood vessels, causing an immediate bleedout.

Earnhardt spent his childhood in a small North Carolina town where the streets were named after cars and engines. He married a beautiful young woman, Teresa Houston, whom he fell in love with, he said, when he learned that she fixed her own car. He was the first driver to earn $30 million driving race cars and the first race car driver to have his likeness emblazoned on a Wheaties box.[4] He frequently used his bumper to knock other cars out of the way. His hard-charging style earned him the nickname "The Intimidator." A NASCAR driver once said, "He could do things with a car that you didn't think anybody could do." Another said he believed that Earnhardt possessed supernatural powers, the ability to see what was not visible to others. Unlike the younger, more glamorous drivers, Earnhardt was a man with whom the racing fans could identify. He drove a pickup with a gun rack, liked fishing, and raised chickens. Fans wore his racing jackets and hats.

Bumping and banging other cars on public roads is a serious violation of the criminal and vehicle codes, but in professional racing venues like the Daytona 500 it is a matter of course. It is not unusual to see the winning car covered with tire marks, dents, scratches, and paint from contact with the other contenders' cars.

Stock car racing is to road rage what Major League Baseball is to sandlot baseball. It has become a huge industry with television ratings that are second only to the NFL among spectator sports. There is CART (Championship Auto Racing Teams), IRL (Indy Racing League), F-1 (Formula One), and NASCAR (National Association of Stock Car Auto Racing).

Auto racing had its origins in the rural South, where moonshiners designed modified cars to outrun the federal agents who came to collect taxes, make arrests, and seize the product of home-based distilleries that were cottage industries not licensed or inspected by the government.

It has come a long way. NASCAR is now a $2.5-billion industry. Its licensed product sales alone were estimated at $1.3 billion in 1999.[5] All three major networks plus three cable channels now broadcast Winston Cup races live.[6] In 1998 eighteen of the twenty most-attended sporting events were stock car races. Some of the tracks have the capacity to seat an audience of 170,000.[7] NASCAR alone controls eight major tracks, including Daytona. New tracks are being built or planned in Kansas City, Chicago, and New York. These are more than stadiums and arenas; these are temples where we go to worship the car in a frenzy of religious hysteria and receive absolution in displays of almost unlimited danger, violence, and self-immolation. The contestants are more than just drivers. The best are seen as men, and a few women, with preternatural, mystical powers: messiahs and gods.

Dale Earnhardt's on-track earnings were over $40 million but his off-track income was of approximately the same magnitude as that of Michael Jordan. RJR Nabisco, Eastman Kodak, Texaco, Procter & Gamble, and others spend tens of millions to be closely identified with leading drivers. In 1998 corporations paid $476 million to NASCAR for promotion.[8] Insiders have no doubt that NASCAR events will surpass the Superbowl in audience size and cash flow. NASCAR's greatest challenge has been the task of managing itself in the face of such enormous and rapid growth. All of this reflects the enormity of our spellbound fascination with fast cars.

Before the advent of the car, allusions to cows, horses, and other animals were pervasive in our language:

> You can lead a horse to water but you can't make him drink.
> Stubborn as a mule.
> Where's Floyd? He went out back and the hogs ate him.

Now our language is filled with phrases that stem from the car and its parts:

Quit spinnin' your wheels.	Don't be in a hurry.
Don't strip your gears.	Don't panic.
She boiled over on him.	She got angry at him. This is an allusion to a car radiator, overheated and spurting boiling water in all directions.
She told him to hit it.	Told him to leave, move out.
Keep on truckin'.	Persevere.
Don't get all revved up.	Have patience.
Don't blow a gasket.	Don't have an aneurysm.
He's not firing on all eight cylinders.	He's mentally deficient.
He's just running on fumes.	He's exhausted his energy.
She walked out in an eight-cylinder huff.	She walked out in a huff.

He's gonna bend your frame.	He will do great bodily harm.
When the rubber hits the road.	When we make the transition from rhetoric to reality; when the chips are down.
He's burning rubber.	Starting out from a stop at a high rate of acceleration; the wheels spin, the friction generates heat and burns the tires. Also, "He's in a hurry."
In the fast lane.	Being in a dangerous, highly competitive occupation.
Full bore.	At great speed; full throttle.
He T-boned him.	One car broadsided the other at a ninety degree angle.
He's losing it.	At first this meant that a fast driver was losing control of his car but now it has come to mean that he has lost control of his anger, grief, or fear.
Put the pedal to the metal.	Hurry.
Open it up.	Full throttle.
Mad car disease.	Road rage.
A loose nut behind the wheel.	A dangerous, unpredictable driver.

Some of the shibboleths of the age of the horse are an almost exact match to those of the age of the car:

TERROR ON THE HIGHWAY

Before the Car (BC)	After the Advent of the Car (AAC)
Useless as teats on a bull.	Useless as a fifth wheel.
He holds the reins.	He's in the driver's seat.
Get on your horse.	Put it in gear and hit it.
He's on his high horse.	He thinks he's hell on wheels.
Heaving like an old horse.	He's running on empty.
She lassoed him and tied him up and put her brand on him.	She repoed him and impounded him.
That old mare ain't what she used to be.	That old Subaru's got a lot of miles on it.
That filly is kickin' up her heels.	She's all jacked up.
He's feeling his oats.	He's running on high octane.
He's goin' at a full gallop.	He's roddin' it.
We ain't goin' anywhere 'till that horse gets up.	We ain't goin' anywhere 'till you get it out of reverse.
He's the big bull in the barn.	He's a big wheel.
Don't look a gift horse in the mouth.	Don't kick the tires. Or— Don't lift the hood.
Hold yer horses.	Throttle down.
If a man shall steal an ox . . . he shall restore five oxen for an ox.	Any person who takes possession of an automobile with the intent to permanently

deprive the owner of said
automobile shall be guilty of
grand theft, auto, a felony.

Even professional athletic teams have names like the Oilers
and the Pistons. Young men who like to build and race cars are
commonly called "greasers." When referring to a superior artifact people often say, "That's the Cadillac of shoes" or "That's
the Cadillac of mattresses."

The bodies of many street rods and stock car racers are decorated with extraordinary art that is at least as good as the pop
art hanging in fashionable art galleries. Among the most
famous of the "hot rod artists" was Ed "Big Daddy" Roth, who
has been described as a surrealist similar to Salvador Dali.
Another is Robert Williams, who now exhibits his work in Los
Angeles and New York. When you look at his work you cannot
but see the car as a work of art.

The automobile is built on the same principle as that of the
human body. There is a skeletal framework and a system of
cables that carries the driver's commands to the moving parts.
The vital internal organs are put in place and connected. A skin
is formed around this structure. It has a voice. It roars, grunts,
whines, hums, groans, gurgles, howls, and screams. It breathes,
ingests, and excretes. It is fearless, a trait we admire and envy.
Many people think of the car as an organic being and form surprisingly strong emotional bonds with their cars. For some, it is
the only emotional bond they've ever had. The car feels like a
womb that houses and protects its occupant, a mother who carries him from one place to another in order to nurture him and
provide for his needs. It raises him above the common.

Many men will kill or risk being killed if you damage their
cars in some small way. I've seen it happen. I have stood and
watched as the police drew their chalk line around the lifeless

remains of the fallen man. This frequently happens when a car crosses a sidewalk, forcing a pedestrian to stop or jump out of the way to avoid being hit. The enraged pedestrian lashes out and kicks the car. Then the driver gets out of his car.

My wife and I were walking on Vine Street in Hollywood when we saw a van come out of an alley, nearly striking a pedestrian. The driver had failed to stop and look both ways. He just hit it. The pedestrian had to leap to avoid being injured. He was so angered that he kicked the van. The driver got out and approached him, hungry for battle. The pedestrian drew a small handgun and fired two rounds into the driver's chest, killing him instantly. The police and the paramedics arrived and covered the dead man with a sheet. Then the media arrived. Each of the television crews asked the paramedics to uncover the cadaver so they could photograph it. He was uncovered and then covered again several times before his body was finally carried away.

You can kick a statue of Jesus or the Virgin Mary and face less wrath than you would by kicking a car.

In several species of birds, sexual selection by the female is influenced by the size, color, and beauty of the male bird's wing feathers. Many human females are strongly stimulated by the size, color, and beauty of a man's car. Men know that a man's car is a powerful part of his sexual attractiveness. A television commercial shows a young man riding in a small economy car with a beautiful woman. When she sees another young man getting into an expensive, high-powered car she abandons her date with the cheap car, flashes a seductive smile, and gets into the expensive, hot car with the other man. This little drama has been resurrected over and over again for decades on television by various automobile manufacturers. It does not require a genius to decipher the message: If you do not buy the new Thunderbutt Terminator XL3MS you will be doomed to a life of celibacy.

Ray was a university student and a member of a prestigious fraternity. I knew him slightly. I had met him a few times and seen him in various restaurants, but we were not closely acquainted. When Ray bought his new Corvette he felt like a young man who had been knighted, buckled on his armor, his sword, and the Maltese Cross. He drove to the home of his girlfriend, Donna. Like her father and her brothers she was a devout car worshiper. She looked at the glistening new car and shrieked with religious fervor, "A Vette! Is it yours?"

"Yep," he smiled.

"When did you get it?"

"Today. Get in."

Ray and Donna went to dinner. When they left the restaurant she said eagerly, "Let's take it out and open it up!"

A dusty-looking man in a dusty car cut in front of him with a look of hatred toward the handsome young man with the handsome new car and the beautiful young woman at his side. Unwilling to suffer this affront to his beautiful new car and the disgrace of being passed by such a lowlife in an ugly old junker, Ray floored it and went in pursuit, but the other car went down the off-ramp and soon was nearly a half mile away. Ray followed at high speeds over narrow surface streets, gaining on the other car until he was close enough to take him. He was on a curved street and his right front tire caught the curb, causing the Corvette to jump across the parking strip and crash into a giant maple tree almost eight feet in diameter. He was moving at a velocity of about 80 MPH when he hit the giant tree. The tree shrugged. We arrived at the scene of this crash only a few minutes later. It was a hot summer night and this was a place where it normally would have been quiet and dark, except for a street light shining through the maple leaves, and the usual bugs. There was a crowd of people standing and staring. The headlights of several cars lit up the street like the stage of a theater. The fragments of the Corvette were scattered over the surrounding area: a wheel, a bucket seat, an engine. The shards of the fiberglass body were everywhere. The girl was lying in a pool of blood, facedown.

A physician who lived in one of the nearby houses examined her and said, "She's dead. There's nothing I can do for her." Ray was lying on top of a piece of the frame, screaming and gasping in even, orderly repetition. A paramedic asked him, "Does it hurt?"

"You're damn right it hurts!" he shouted, continuing to scream. Gradually his screams lapsed into silence, as did his alpha waves. Their passing was briefly noted in the morning newspaper because Ray's father was a wealthy, prominent doctor. It happens all the time. Yet we worship the car with mystical adoration. It has changed the face of our world.

We've paid a high price for it: close to 3 million dead, more than all the people killed in all the wars we've fought. The dead and the disabled have never been accurately counted.

According to the US Department of Transportation, for every person killed in a car crash at least one hundred are injured.[9] Some recover; some are irreversibly damaged.

NOTES

1. Brava Mistry, "Soap Opera Romance," *Los Angeles Daily News*, December 1, 1999, p. A-1.

2. Rick Bragg, "The Last Cowboy," *New York Times*, August 8, 2001.

3. Brian Schmitz, *Los Angeles Times*, February 21, 2001, pp. D-1, D-2, D-7, D-14.

4. Ibid.

5. Cory Bronson, *Sporting Goods Business*, January 4, 2000. See also Shav Glick, "Polls Aside, NASCAR Calls Business Great," *Los Angeles Times*, January 21, 2000.

6. Peter Siegel, *Forbes*, October 11, 1999.

7. *Newark Star-Ledger*, November 11, 1999.

8. Lee Walczak, "Auto Racing: Speed Sells," http://www.bus .nessweek.com/1997/32/63539109.htm.

9. AAA Foundation for Traffic Study, "'Road Rage' on the Rise, AAA Foundation Reports," Aggressive Driving Study, Washington, DC, 1996.

12

ROAD RAGE PSYCHOLOGY

The Roads Scholars

A scientific study of road rage is long overdue. Several psychologists and at least one psychiatrist have begun to dissect it, catalog its constituent parts, and analyze them.

A useful and intelligent analysis can be found in *Steering Clear of Highway Madness: A Driver's Guide to Curbing Stress and Strain,* by John Larson, MD.[1] Larson is a professor at Yale University Medical School. At his Institute of Stress Medicine he teaches an antistress, heart-attack-prevention program. He has found that there is a high correlation between road rage and heart attacks. He writes that chronic rage and frustration behind the wheel of a car can and does induce heart attacks. After interviewing more than one thousand heart attack patients he found that 80 percent of them had a long history of violent anger behind the wheel.

He cites a study by his colleagues, Friedman and Rosenman, both cardiologists, which discovered in heart attack patients a pattern of overcompetitiveness, excessive aggressiveness, and an exaggerated sense of urgency.[2] He classifies these men as "Type A" and notes that they have almost three times the frequency of heart attacks as non-Type-A people. Larson cites another study by Dr. Dean Ornish, which concluded that partially clogged arteries can begin to open as a result of stress reduction and anger management.[3]

Larson further states that stress is not just external irritation; it is also the body's internal response to external stressors, the outpouring of adrenalin into the bloodstream. It is easier to change the internal response than the external provocations, but we need to learn to live with both in a way that does not generate violence.

Larson has isolated and classified five types of drivers: (1) the speeder; (2) the competitor; (3) the passive aggressor, who habitually thwarts the other driver's effort to pass him; (4) the narcissist; and (5) the vigilante, who feels the compulsion to punish other drivers.[4] These classifications are useful. Nearly all of us engage in this kind of behavior, some more often than others.

Time urgency, Larson writes, is a medical condition: "This comes about through the action of stress hormones in the body. As a person hurries and continues in a state of hyperarousal and vigilance, his stress hormones gradually deplete the neurotransmitters in his brain." Stress hormones exhaust your body's endocrine glands and create abnormally high levels of cholesterol, which can cause heart attacks, diabetes, hypertension, and strokes. *Neurotransmitters* are chemicals that modify or cause transmission of nerve impulses between synapses. Neurotransmitter molecules bind to specific receptors. Neurotransmitters include acetylcholine, chloride, gamma-aminobutyric acid, nor-epinephrine, and many other chemicals.[5]

Larson enthusiastically proffers a program in which the state would furnish all drivers with five "driver safety report cards." On one side would be the address of the state Department of Motor Vehicles. On the other side would be spaces for people to report an act of dangerous or irresponsible driving, with a description of the car, its license number, color, make, and model, which they could mail to the police.[6] Such a suggestion is sensible and in some cases it could be useful, but if the reports would be anonymous, they would be dangerous. Anonymity breeds fabrication and spiteful behavior. It is possible that snitch cards might bring a few dangerous drivers to the attention of the police, but there is an equally high probability that the extremely angry, malicious driver would use them to irresponsibly and falsely accuse someone who is not an aggressive driver, and these reports may remain in the database. It is well to remember that the worst forms of government have always encouraged people to inform on their neighbors.

I think surveillance cameras are a better idea, so long as they are not used to violate our Fourth Amendment right to be secure against unreasonable search and seizure, our right to privacy, and our Sixth Amendment right to be confronted by our accuser. Hopefully, surveillance cameras would be used only to record the movements of a vehicle and a brief shot of the driver's face, but their use to identify passengers riding in the car and any other disclosure of the driver's private conduct should be prohibited.

Larson proposes another program for self-improvement: the use of three-by-five cards to "memorize and practice alternative new beliefs to replace the old ones."[7] The driver identifies an incident and the internal reactions that provoke anger and writes them on the card, estimating the degree of anger on a scale of one to ten. Then, using the cards, the driver memorizes the beliefs and their alternatives, then practices replacing the old road rage beliefs with the new, more reasonable ones. It is a sensible concept that could yield good results, with or without the cards—if people can be motivated to do it.

But will they, in a culture that honors violence and views courtesy as a sign of weakness? Will people be motivated to engage in such a civilized, rational program of self-examination in a culture that glorifies combat and consecrates one-upmanship and personal power? What of the shouting bully in his three-piece suit, talking on his wireless telephone in his expensive car, tailgating an elderly couple? Will he go to a stationery store, buy the cards, write down his negative thoughts, and share them with his peers? Will *he* embark on a program of self-assessment?

Larson's work deserves thoughtful discussion and debate, but some concern arises as to whether enough people will be able to put their pent-up anger aside and try such a rational program, or even understand it. I tried to tell an acquaintance that it is better to go home angry than to go home in a wooden box. He didn't seem to understand. He was still thinking about the ecstatic rush of beating and humiliating the other car. Most people want to be heard but do not listen. This is a dangerous flaw that is sometimes fatal.

Psychologist Leon James, PhD, and his collaborator, Diane Nahl, PhD, are prolific experts on road rage. They have a Web site containing articles, letters, and stories from readers, James's testimony before Congress, poems, songs, cartoons, and media interviews.[8] James is a professor of psychology at the University of Hawaii who, according to his Web site, has been teaching courses in traffic psychology for fifteen years. "Since 1962," he writes, "my research has focused on the application of behavioral science to cognitive and motivational processes." James defines himself as the "founder of driving psychology."

On his Web site he announced his forthcoming book on road rage,[9] modestly stating that "there is no authoritative book on road rage and how to deal with it, nor does any other author we are aware of have the authority, expertise, or the data to write such a book."

He warns that "venting your anger is harmful to your health," but other psychologists and psychiatrists have concluded that the absence of any outlet to vent your anger, or the lack of any skills for dealing with your anger appropriately is detrimental to your health and lowers the threshold for dangerously violent behavior.

James states that it would not be practicable to classify road rage as a mental illness, but he advocates the deployment of a national program of lifelong driver education. There are 191 million licensed drivers in the United States, which has a total population of 281 million. There are 226 million registered vehicles.[10] This would require a very large body of instructors and an enormous payroll, for which we all would bear the expense. There is already driver's education in public schools and there are private driving schools. Most states have "driving school" or "traffic school" for drivers who have been cited by police for infractions of the vehicle codes. If you attend traffic school you can have a citation expunged from your driving record. Traffic schools are usually conducted in high school classrooms on evenings and weekends. I have sat in on these classes for years in the process of researching this subject. They don't usually deal with anger or road rage, just a recitation of the vehicle codes with no on-road training. We need teachers who not only explain but also generate curiosity, a hunger for knowledge, and a love of exploring the mysteries of the universe and of our daily lives. Those are hard to find. A 1978 government study in De Kalb County, Georgia, found no reduction of crashes or traffic violations by students who took a driver's ed course compared to those who didn't.[11]

One of James's principal constructs is Quality Driving Circles (QDCs), in which drivers meet in small groups and discuss their driving experiences. Each group would have access to data from other QDCs. These would include checklists, tests, and inventories. It doesn't sound like a lot of fun, but it is an interesting concept. If millions of people could be persuaded to participate in such a program, some gifted person might come up with the magic breakthrough that would eliminate road rage.

"The dynamic power of groups to influence individual behavior is well known to social scientists," James writes. "We should be using this power for reeducating aggressive and emotionally impaired drivers."

I have some misgivings as to using the power of groups to shape the behavior of the individual. Wouldn't it be better to influence the individual to be self-motivated to change his behavior for the better while driving? Wouldn't the change be longer lasting if it came from inside rather than from others?

QDCs are an interesting idea and I would like to see them proliferate. But most people have too little leisure time already. They have more immediate issues in their lives, such as paying the rent, fixing the car, and making enough money to survive and keep the family together. Will QDCs attract enough people to thrive? QDCs might flourish if they were made compulsory, but most people do not want to be told—or to confess—that their driving skills are less than adequate, even though they urgently need to take a good look at what they've been doing behind the wheel.

Another of Dr. James's programs is "self-witnessing,"[12] in which drivers vocalize their reactions and emotions into a tape recorder while driving and, later on, listen to them or share them in a group setting. This could dislodge the lies and self-deception we all use to maintain our equanimity and get on with our lives. We need to find the strength to know ourselves and live our lives on a foundation of reality. But holding up a mirror to angry, rigid people and making them look at all the ugliness, malice, lies, and hypocrisy does not always produce the desired result.

Audiotape has its usefulness, but I think it might be more effective to show the driver a videotape of her driving, so she can see the movements of the car and also see her face as she deals with traffic. The driver could be placed in a car with a hidden video camera so that she can be shown her reactions while driving alone.

James has divided belligerent driving into five "zones": (1) the unfriendly zone (unfriendly thoughts and words confined to the inside of the car); (2) the hostile zone (visibly communicating one's displeasure and desire to punish); (3) the violent zone (an act of hostility in fantasy or in deed); (4) epic road rage (thinking about what one would like to do to the other driver without acting out); and (5) the major mayhem zone (uncontained, epic road rage). He also has drawn diagrams of road rage incidents, showing, step by step, how the rage escalates.

James divides driving behavior into three levels: oppositional driving, defensive driving, and supportive driving.[13]

I have tried to practice "supportive driving" for years with mixed results. When you slow down to make room for another driver to merge with traffic and enter the freeway in front of you, some drivers will smile and nod appreciatively. Most will make no acknowledgment of your act of courtesy. Some will quickly enter the space you have made for them with angrily clamped lips, fuming with rage. Who knows where the anger comes from. Possibly a previous incident in which the driver came out on the bottom, a lifelong habit of perpetual anger, or a lifetime of being shunned and ostracized.

Some drivers will respond to your magnanimous wave of the hand with a contemptuous, ridiculing smile and shake their heads with a look of weary exasperation. Sometimes the other driver will jump out of his car, screaming at a deafening volume and say, "What's the idea of making that hand jive at me? Are you tryin' to get smart with me?" Sometimes when you make room to let another car into your lane, a second car will rush in behind it, causing you to slam your brakes or causing a fender bender. The same is true of intersections with four-way stop lights. Nevertheless, it is better to be courteous and helpful than to charge forward to keep the other driver out and defeat him. Often he will not accept defeat.

Even though some drivers won't appreciate your efforts to be supportive and helpful, that isn't a reason not to do it. The most irascible road rager may, and often does, feel some contrition and sees your courtesy as more admirable than fighting—and may emulate your good manners.

I think James's advocacy of constant self-examination is an excellent idea that we all need to practice, not only on the road but in all situations. I have some concern as to how many people will do it.

James and Nahl also have published a document on the Internet titled *Christ against Road Rage: Principles of Christian Driving Psychology*, which enjoins readers to use the Bible as a guide or model for driving: "What we need to understand about driving psychology and its relation to the Gospels."[14]

Arnold Nerenberg, PhD, a California psychologist, provides individual therapy by telephone to a client while he or she is driving, for an extra fee. Nerenberg accompanies his client in the car and throws screaming tantrums, mimicking the driver's out-of-control anger in order to enlighten him or her.[15] Nerenberg has published a thirty-page booklet called *Road Rage*, which he dedicates to his publicist. In this and other publications he sagely defines road rage as "a mental disorder of an adjustment reaction type."

Nerenberg has been featured in mass-market newspapers and magazines, has appeared on many national television programs, and has testified before a congressional subcommittee. He maintains a Web site on which he modestly bills himself as the "WORLD'S ROAD RAGE THERAPIST," "THE LEADING PRACTITIONER," and "THE RECOGNIZED AUTHORITY" on road rage.

He advocates the use of a universal hand signal of apology to defuse volatile situations arising from driver mistakes. But any hand signal can be misinterpreted by a bully as a taunt or an insult. I once tried to defuse a potentially violent situation with a friendly wave of my hand, inviting the other driver to take the right of way and pass. He accused me of displaying the ornithic middle finger. He wanted to fight. There are always those who do not want harmony and reconciliation; they want to beat the stuffing out of the other driver. They appear to be unable to entertain themselves in any other fashion. Nevertheless, we see many acts of kindness and generosity and we should try to do the same, for our own safety and as an example others will hopefully follow.

According to a 1997 article in the *New York Times* there is a very active lobbying movement among a faction of psychologists who want road rage to be included in the *Diagnostic and Statistical Manual of Mental Disorders* (*DSM*), the Bible of the American Psychiatric Association.[16] This would mean that psychologists would be able to bill for treatment of road rage as a mental disorder. In order to be labeled in the *DSM*, a "disorder" must be supported by a substantial body of research literature indicating that it exists, and by a zealous lobby of mental health professionals.[17] Nerenberg defines road rage as "a maladaptive reaction to an identifiable psycho-social stressor that interferes with social functioning."

Road rage appears to be on its way to induction into the *DSM*. Several other candidates are not far behind: PMS, jury duty disorder, lottery stress disorder, airplane stress disorder, and Internet addiction disorder.

In its current edition, the *DSM-IV* lists more than three hundred mental disorders. Eighteen years ago there were only 106. In the mid-nineteenth century, only lunacy and idiocy were recognized by the federal government. There are already enough "disorders" listed in the *DSM* to cover all the behaviors that are commonly defined as road rage, but these psychologists want to consolidate it into one bigger and better "disorder." There are other behaviors that could be subsumed under the big tent. Recently, in Washington, DC, a man became enraged when the driver behind him persistently leaned on her horn. He stopped in the middle of the street, dragged the other driver from her car, and strangled her. This act, without the umbrella of road rage, would be the manifestation of an isolated, orphan disorder with its own name, perhaps the road rage anoxia syndrome. Fortunately the strangled woman was rescued by spectators.

There is no scientific definition of road rage. Inference and anecdote do not constitute science. Scientific conclusions result from carefully designed tests.

Nerenberg has stated that if you show anger toward another driver, stare, shout, sound your horn in anger, tailgate, or raise the bellicose third finger two or more times a year, you have been seized by a mental disorder.

According to Dominic Connell and Matthew Joint, authors of the AAA Foundation for Traffic Safety Studies on aggressive driving, "There has been a lack of well-reasoned explanations for rage and, in the main, only the most simplistic explanations for road rage."[18] Some of the psychological literature on road rage informs us that instincts like rage, fear, and lust are generated in the limbic system, and that not much is known about the limbic system.

Some of the psychologists who have studied road rage tell us to smile, to sing, to think pleasant thoughts, and to not annoy or challenge the other drivers. All of these can be helpful, but they don't always work. Anger is powerful. It is the most difficult instinct to control. It blots out rational thought. It blots out everything, even the most precious things in our lives. It feeds upon itself and grows until it reaches critical mass. In this chapter it has not been my intent to demean psychology or psychologists but rather to alert the reader to the fact that not all psychologists are the same. Some are more helpful than others.

One of the shibboleths of the road rage and anger management psychologists is "emotional intelligence," which is the title of a 1995 book written by Daniel Goleman, PhD.[19] Although it is not about road rage per se, road rage and anger management gurus have nibbled at his work and assimilated it into theirs.

His message, as it is generally understood, is that emotional intelligence can be more important than IQ in the struggle for advancement in the workplace and in other settings. Goleman believes there is a kind of intelligence other than abstract and concrete intelligence: the ability to deal with one's emotions and those of other people. It includes self-awareness, impulse control, and empathy. In other words, nice guys finish first. Well, maybe—and then again, maybe not.

TERROR ON THE HIGHWAY

Whether or not you believe that social skills and understanding other people's feelings are more important than IQ, this book has struck a very strong, sympathetic chord in the psychological community and with the laity. We do not like to accept our limitations or the probability that IQ is genetically determined. The massive self-improvement fad of the 1970s is by no means fading away; most bookstores still have large sections devoted to it.

This is not new. It goes back to the 1920s, when the psychologist Edward Thorndike invented the term "social intelligence," which became chic in the academic community for years. The term "emotional intelligence" was coined by other psychologists about twelve years ago.

It is known that when we are confronted with a rattlesnake or a mad, life-threatening road rager with a gun, the message goes directly to the limbic system before the thinking frontal lobes of the brain are notified. In such situations there isn't time for meaningful dialogue and a thoughtful decision-making process. There isn't time to form a committee and discuss it. You've got to move with lightning speed or your remains will be found and transported to a suitable place and released to your next of kin.

Fear, anger, lust, pleasure, and displeasure come from the limbic system. Goleman's program is to teach people in mutually hostile confrontations to find other options and solutions rather than acting out anger; to cooperate rather than to do battle; to develop social skills rather than to intimidate and bully; to understand that disputes can be negotiated; and to realize that one has a range of choices in dealing with a dangerous person or situation.

Goleman advocates retaining psychologists as "coaches" to teach and apply the wisdom of emotional intelligence to corporate executives, teaching middle management executives to sit down together, negotiate their disputes, and explore various solutions. While not about road rage per se, this book is useful in dealing with road rage and can be applied to road rage counseling.

In his final chapter Goleman describes classes in "self science," in which children bring their emotional life into the classroom dialogue and share it with their teacher and their contemporaries: ostracism, anger, envy, fear of not being popular, not being liked, not being wanted. These programs are also called "life skills" and "social and emotional learning."[20] Goleman states that there are several such projects already in place that have yielded encouraging results. But these are experimental projects conducted by the people who designed them. The next step, Goleman writes, is to generalize these programs and have them taught by ordinary teachers. Goleman projects a future in which children will learn to resolve disputes without violence.

Some theorists believe that threats to identity play a crucial role in intractable conflicts. Terrell A. Northrup, an assistant professor of international relations at Syracuse University and associate director of the Program on the Analysis and Resolution of Conflicts, writes that identity is more than a psychological sense of self; it is "a sense of self in relation to the world . . . a system of beliefs or a way of construing the world that makes life predictable rather than random."[21] She writes: "It may include self-definition of individuals or groups at many levels."[22] She also states that identity is a dynamic which underlies escalation and rigidification of conflict:

> In a sense, if one's core sense of self, the identity, is threatened by the demands, behavior, or identity of another person, then psychic or even physical annihilation will seem to be imminent.[23]

Northrup's article does not address road rage, but it would be helpful to those who teach or counsel drivers about road rage.

There are several university professors who have published articles and studies on aggressive driving and who have joined the ranks of the "roads scholars." There are institutes, think tanks, government agencies, and private organizations with roads scholars on the premises. Most of their work focuses on exploring anomalies in the frontal lobes of the brain, the part of the brain that normally puts the brakes on impulsive violence. Bruce Pappas, a behavioral neuroscientist at Carleton University in Ottawa, has stated that "the ability to behave in an appropriate social manner is very dependent on the integrity on the frontal lobes."[24] Psychologist Adrian Raine has discovered frontal lobe differences in the brains of murderers that are unlike those of "normal" people.[25] It would be interesting if we could get ultrasound and MRI pictures of the brains of road ragers who kill. We might discover that they, too, have anomalies in their brains. If so, these people would need more intensive therapy and scrutiny.

Ernest Barrett, a psychologist at the University of Texas Medical Branch reportedly has discovered differences in the frontal lobes of people who are unable to restrain their impulsive aggression.[26] Many people interpret nonaggressive speech and behavior as malicious, demeaning, and threatening. They respond with rage inappropriate to the perceived offense. Some are actively searching for a pretext to assault another car and engage its driver in combat, to intimidate the driver and experience the euphoria of the victorious warrior. Philip Klassen, a psychiatrist at the Centre for Addiction, writes that it is poor problem solvers who explode into violence. "The anger builds up because they have no other way of dealing with conflict," according to York University psychologist James Alcock.[27]

Matthew Joint and Dominic Connell found a strong correlation between murder statistics and road death numbers after reviewing statistics of law enforcement agencies, which means that in places and time frames where there is a substantial increase in murders there is likely to be a simultaneous increase in road rage homicide, presumably because the same influences and precursors are present.[28] Barbara McCann of the Surface Transportation Policy Project has said that "when we started the research on aggressive driving I was surprised by how little real data there is out there."[29] Julie Rochman of the Institute for Highway Safety states: "It's bogus, this science of road rage."[30]

Certainly there are variations and anomalies in the brains of all human beings. We are not identical. But that does not address the central truth at the heart of the matter.

The scientific study of road rage is long overdue and useful. The work now being done in this field will be helpful to future scientists, but it treats almost entirely of symptoms. The road rage psychologists have been offering their wares for years. States have passed tougher laws with stiffer penalties. Yet the number of road rage incidents has not decreased in the slightest but has continued to increase at a rate of slightly over 7 percent per year. We need to go beyond listing the symptoms. The next step is to look deeper and to cause others to look deeper. Most people are in denial. They do not want to speak or be spoken to about their embarrassing misconduct. In Detroit a driver tried to lecture another driver on his bad driving habits. The other motorist attacked him with a club.[31] Most people don't want to be told of their problematic behavior. They assign the blame to others. They don't want to know the truth about themselves and about all of us. As long as this condition exists, we are, collectively, a long way from understanding the underlying secrets of road rage and controlling it.

TERROR ON THE HIGHWAY

I think that, for starters, this could be done with film and video. Films could be designed that would terrify motorists so powerfully that they would drive like frightened elderly ladies. We could get the police and the highway patrol to help and participate. We could show people a prison and what goes on there, show them the newcomers and those who have been there for thirty years or more. The off-screen narrator could say, "It's always the other guy, right? Wrong. If you drive like that and continue to drive like that you will be the other guy, the person on the surgical table, trying to hang on to life; the person in a prison cell with nothing to look forward to but years of the same." We should film the survivors, the widows, children, and parents of those killed in road rage altercations and of those incarcerated for road rage homicide. It will be necessary to get the attention of everybody, including the least intelligent and the most aggressive, to powerfully motivate them to desist in their road raging. More people have been killed in car crashes than in all of our wars, and millions have been injured, some with minor injuries, others with irreversible disabling injuries. It's not going to go away. It's going to get worse, unless we stop it.

NOTES

1. John A. Larson, *Steering Clear of Highway Madness: A Driver's Guide to Curbing Stress and Strain* (Wilsonville, OR: Bookpartners, Inc., 1996).

2. Ibid., p. 7. See also Meyer Friedman and D. Ulmer, *Treating Type A Behavior and Your Heart* (New York: Alfred A. Knopf, 1985).

3. Dean Ornish, *Stress, Diet, and Your Heart* (New York: Holt, Rinehart, & Winston, 1985). See also Dean Ornish, *Reversing Heart Disease* (New York: Random House, 1990).

4. Larson, *Steering Clear of Highway Madness*, p. 40.

5. Ibid., p. 52. See also *Mosby's Medical Dictionary* (St. Louis: C. V. Mosby, 1983), p. 738.

6. Larson, *Steering Clear of Highway Madness*, p. 141.

7. Ibid., p. 56.

8. See http://www.drdriving.org. http://www.drivers.com /issues/road rage.

9. Leon James and Diane Nahl, *Road Rage and Aggressive Driving: Steering Clear of Highway Warfare* (Amherst, NY: Prometheus Books, 2000).

10. Federal Highway Administration, "Our Nation's Highways— 2000: Selected Facts and Figures," pub. no. FAWA=PL=01=1012.

11. http://www.drivers.com/issues/road rage.

12. James and Nahl, *Road Rage and Aggressive Driving*, pp. 116, 189, 202–204.

13. Ibid., p. 117.

14. Leon James and Diane Nahl, *Christ Against Road Rage: Principles of Christian Driving Psychology*, http://www.drdriving .org/articles/christ.htm.

15. Bob Greene, "Putting Road Rage Perpetrators on the Couch," *Chicago Tribune*, December 3, 1996, p. A1. See also *World Press Review* (November 1997).

16. Joe Sharkey, "You're Not Bad, You're Sick: It's in the Book," *New York Times*, September 8, 1997.

17. Ibid.

18. Dominic Connell and Matthew Joint, *Aggressive Driving: Three Studies* (Washington, DC: AAA Foundation for Traffic Safety, 1997), p. 29.

19. Daniel Goleman, *Emotional Intelligence: Why It Can Matter More Than I.Q.* (New York: Bantam Books, 1995).

20. Ibid., pp. 28, 195.

21. Terrell A. Northrup, "The Dynamic of Identity in Personal Conflict," pp. 55–82, in *Intractable Conflicts and Their Transformation*, ed. L. Kriesberg, T. Northrup, and S. Thorson (Syracuse, NY: Syracuse University Press, 1989), p. 55.

22. Ibid., p. 63.

23. Ibid., p. 65.

24. Lynda Dotto, "The Seven Second Solution," *Equinox* (February/March 2000): 32.

25. Ibid.

26. Ibid.

27. Ibid.

28. Ibid.

29. Joelle Babula, *Las Vegas Review-Journal*, March 26, 2000, p. 26.

30. Gerry Byrne, *New Scientist*, December 9, 2000, p. 13.

31. *Detroit News*, May 24, 2000.

13

DOs and DON'Ts

Avoiding the Land Mines

Authors, psychologists, and public and private agencies have published lists of dangerous road rage driving behaviors, the "Dos and Don'ts" of driving. Drivers would be wise to read and memorize them. I have added a few that the experts overlooked, and I have disputed a few with which I disagree, having driven more than 2 million miles during my lifetime and having spent about forty thousand hours behind the wheel of a moving car. I have seen the freshly killed men, women, and children on the ground being covered and carried away to the ambulance. I have seen the brain tissue, the blood and viscera splattered over the interior of the cars. I have seen cars and trucks immolated in blazing gasoline fires, once with the driver still inside. I have seen the grief of the survivors. I have broken all the traffic laws except homicide and vehicular assault. I have made all the foolish mistakes that inexperienced drivers make in the process of learning to navigate the battle-grounds of the road and highway systems. I will share with you what I have learned. These are the acts that are likely to incite road rage.

TAILGATING

Driving so close to the car in front of you that you are almost touching its rear bumper. Often, an exceptionally angry tail-gater will actually strike the bumper of the car in front of him. This is done when the tailgater is angry at the tailgatee for driving too slowly, preventing him from going forward at a high rate of speed. He may be doing it because he is angry; some do it because it feels good. When you look back at a tail-gater, what you see is usually a very ordinary suit or a pair of overalls. Just your typical Pushy Charlie. It is not unusual to see a white statue of Jesus standing on his dashboard and a bumper sticker proclaiming that he and God are buddies. He wants to push it to the floor and pass all the other cars. It's his way of trying to beat back the doubts that assail him.

Tailgating is usually accompanied by excessive, persistent use of the horn, shouting, screaming, and, at night, blinding the tailgatee by putting on the high-beam headlights. An orthodox tailgater becomes so enraged when he cannot pass the slow driver in front of him or persuade him to speed up that he is likely to twitch, jerk, grimace, wave his fist, flip the bird, shriek epithets, fling his arms and head, and rev up his engine. Tailgating is not recommended.

Not all tailgaters are the same. Some are afflicted with the bully syndrome. Others suffer from another disorder: Get-there-itis, which occurs when the driver gets a late start, feels a desperate need to arrive in Connecticut before nine o'clock, and can't get through the traffic jam. If you suffer from get-there-itis, think about this: Would you rather arrive late, or wake up in a hospital after being involved in a serious accident? Road rage occurs in all kinds of differing configurations. If you have a large, heavy vehicle and you are tailgating a small, compact car, you are in less danger, less likely to be killed, and probably less angry, since you can do almost anything you want to your adversary. If you are driving a large, heavy machine with a high center of gravity and you are being tailgated by a small compact car, you have the power. You can try to ignore it. You can even back up and crush it. But if you are the tailgatee and you are driving a small, compact car, being tailgated by a much larger, heavier machine, you have good reason to be afraid and angry.

Typically, the worst tailgaters, and the most belligerent drivers, drive SUVs and pickup trucks—especially the large ones with the huge wheels. When you see a large pickup be vigilant. But there are exceptions to every rule. You really cannot learn much about a person you know nothing about just by briefly looking at him and his vehicle.

A few years ago when my wife and I were on the staff of a newspaper, we were acquainted with a young woman, about twenty-seven years old, who owned a very small British sports car. She was driving back from lunch when a Chrysler began tailgating her. It was one of those huge chrome barges that were made in the seventies. The driver followed her so closely that he actually touched her car, shattering her tail light. She turned and screamed back at him, "Please! Stop it! Back off!" He grinned and continued to tailgate her. She speeded up. He speeded up, still tailgating her, still grinning. The light turned red. She stopped. He didn't. His car rode up over hers, crushing her to death. Naturally, he told the police it was her fault. He was still shouting and babbling when they took him away. I was in the room when they told her mother what had happened and I listened to her screams and sobs. Tailgating can, and often does, lead to brutal violence. I have seen it happen a few times.

I once saw a young man in a Buick tailgating a very old couple who were stopped at an intersection, trying to make a left turn. They were frightened. They hesitated. The bully was impatient. He did not want to wait. He wanted them to make a quick left turn into oncoming traffic, which is dangerous, but he didn't care. The young man moved up to the elderly couple's car until his bumper was touching their rear bumper. Then he put his car in low gear and pushed the elderly couple out into oncoming traffic, where they could easily have been killed, so that he would not have to sit behind them and wait. The elderly couple was terrified. The Buick and his girlfriend laughed. A gang of bikers roared up to the intersection and dismounted from their Harleys. Several of them restrained the bully while their companions directed traffic, allowing the elderly couple to proceed safely. Then they rode off into the night. One of them looked back at the girlfriend and said, "You're gonna be old someday, too."

Once, we were being tailgated by a young man driving a car that was old and tarnished, but large. He was angry and looking for a fight. He needed to prove his manhood. Ours was a very small car. I knew we were in great danger. Rather than joust with the young man while my wife and other family members were in the car, I pulled off onto the shoulder of the freeway and stopped in order to let him pass. He started to pull up behind us, screaming epithets—until he saw the police car approaching. He departed. The cop got out of his car.

"What's going on?" he asked, taking out his book of traffic citations.

"That guy was tailgating me," I told him. "He wouldn't back off and I was afraid we'd get killed, so I just pulled off the road."

"See yer license. Take it outa yer wallet. See yer registration." The cop looked at my license and registration, clipped it to his clipboard, and began writing.

"What's that?" I asked. He did not reply. I waited. Finally he spoke.

"You have been cited for driving on the shoulder. Sign yer name here."

"But I wasn't driving on the shoulder! I was stopped! That's what the shoulder is for!" I protested.

"Well if ya wanna go ta court we'd be more than happy to go with ya." He smiled, a cold, malicious semismile.

"How happy is 'more than happy'?" I asked. He bristled.

"Are you tryin' ta get smart with me?" he asked menacingly.

We went to court, flanked by two eyewitnesses and told the judge what had happened. He listened absently and then spoke:

"Find ya guilty of driving on the shoulder of a freeway. Fifty dollars or ten days."

BLOCKING ANOTHER CAR FROM PASSING OR TAILGATING IN REVERSE

Some psychologists call it "being passive-aggressive." It is one of the most sadistic and provocative acts in the entire repertoire of road rage. If you are driving an old, low-powered car and the car behind you is a late model, high-powered car capable of accelerating much faster than yours, you are not powerless. You have the power to thwart him and block him from passing. If the other driver changes lanes and tries to pass you and you change lanes in unison with him, remaining in front of him, it usually generates a degree of anger that is difficult to measure in words. If you do it a second and a third time when he tries to pass, you are raising the level of his rage exponentially, compressing it and igniting it. The war is on. It is likely to escalate into a high-speed duel, ending in an arrest or a crash, a death or disfiguration.

In heavy traffic a high-speed duel is not feasible, so perhaps overcrowding has its benefits as well as its disadvantages. When a driver is being blocked from passing and manages to get around the passive-aggressive blocker and leave her behind, the passive-aggressive blocker will become as angry as the tailgater was when he was being blocked. She will pursue the tailgater, fueled by a powerful mixture of gasoline, oxygen, adrenalin, and mindless rage, determined to regain her dominant position in front. This can lead to contusions, lacerations, hematoma, edema, abrasions, lumps, bruises, and worse.

Ron, an acquaintance of mine, was in a hurry to go home when a sadistic driver amused himself by doing this to him. Each time Ron changed lanes and tried to pass, the other driver changed lanes and remained in front of him, riding the brakes and slowing him down. Ron saw the driver, a middle-aged man, slightly overweight, with an acerbic face that said: I'm tough. Anyone that messes with me comes out on the bottom.

Since he does not believe in the resurrection of the dead, Ron did not ram the other car or race with him. He did pursue him to his destination, at a safe distance, unnoticed by the other driver. He wrote down the car's license plate number and a description of the car. When traffic was at a standstill he photographed the driver's face. During the ensuing days and weeks, with patient perseverance he was able to access the man's name, address, and place of employment. Then he stalked him for weeks, following his movements, learning where he spent his evenings, where and when he would be alone and vulnerable. During this period he looked grim, strained, and preoccupied. Then, one day, he looked elated, like a man who had had a great weight lifted from him, a man who had been liberated by the completion of a dangerous and onerous task. I don't know how this story ended. It's just as well.

Remember Natalie Davis, the young Virginia woman discussed in chapter 2? She was driving with her two small children and four other family members when she was blocked by a car stopped on a narrow road with several teenage girls surrounding it. She asked the teenagers to move their car. They refused. When she managed to maneuver her car around the other car that made them angry. They followed her and one of the teenage girls, a sixteen-year-old, grabbed her by her hair, pulled her from her car, and pounded her head into the pavement while another girl stomped on her head.

She died. The county prosecutor said the two teenage girls would face murder charges, and the state would seek to try the sixteen-year-old as an adult. Like so many combative drivers, they did not think; they just threw away their lives.

If you are driving in heavy or moderately heavy traffic, or even in light, high-speed traffic, look out for SUVs and those huge pickup trucks with huge wheels. Also watch for big vans, motor homes, and other large vehicles. They have a very high center of gravity and a high roll axis. They are heavy, just made for crushing and demolishing smaller vehicles. If one looms behind your car, flashes his lights, and sounds his horn, get out of the way. He holds the power. Change lanes, ride your brake pedal, and get far enough behind him to be out of his reach. Not all people who buy those large vehicles are men who like to demolish other people's cars, but some are motivated by that desire.

During the daytime, Milton Milktoast, mild-mannered middle-management man, sits unobtrusively at his desk, blending inconspicuously with hundreds of suits and desks. But when he gets behind the wheel of his SUV, his mild-mannered suit and tie fall away, revealing his alter ego: Superman! He goes forth at great speed and personal risk in pursuit of wrongdoers to bring them to justice. Once, a car salesman showed me one of those SUVs and said, "Those are for fighters, not lovers." But, again, not all SUV riders are intent on bashing smaller vehicles. To a considerable extent they have displaced the old station wagons as the automobile of choice for soccer moms and dads.

In places like Southern California, where the freeways are overloaded, you will notice that some of the drivers use their headlights in the daytime. Think before you rise up in anger because many of them are designed to automatically turn on the headlights when the ignition switch is turned on. But some drivers will approach your car from behind and turn on the high beams, which causes ocular pain. That is their way of saying: I'm here. Get out of my way. Best to stay out of their proximity. It may be momentarily gratifying to punish, torment, and humiliate them, but think before you act. Is it worth risking your life?

CHANGING LANES AND CUTTING IN FRONT OF ANOTHER CAR

Even if you give other cars plenty of room, some drivers react with anger, trumpeting their rage at you and making ugly, ribald gestures. But when you cut in front of another driver too close, you will have set off a chain reaction of savage anger, a race, and he will probably try to pass you and retaliate by cutting in front of you with the one-finger salute.

Many drivers now carry some kind of weapon while driving. I have contacted virtually every law enforcement agency in California, trying to find out how many out of one hundred drivers are carrying a gun. The answer is always the same: Nobody knows. We do know how many are licensed to carry, but those in possession of illegal weapons do not usually announce it to the community or the media. Some say as many as one out of five. Many drivers who don't carry a concealed gun have other weapons in the car. Don't challenge them. It's not worth it. Always carry a camera in your vehicle while driving—preferably two. Then, if you are rear-ended or sideswiped, you can photograph the two cars, yours and his, showing how they are positioned. You can also photograph the other car's license plate and its driver. If the other driver assaults you and tries to take away your camera, you will have to quickly get back into your car and make your getaway.

FLIPPING THE BIRD

Brandishing the erect third finger is a very provocative act because of the underlying sexual inference it communicates to the other driver. You are symbolically impaling him and violating him. You are making the unspoken admonition that you are more masculine than he is. You are boasting that it is you who are in possession of the phallus and that it is he who will be penetrated and entered. You are likely to be rewarded with an act of displeasure, resulting in great harm to your car or to your person. To many, if not most, drivers, brandishing the erect third finger is an abomination that cannot be endured without redress.

RACING OR PURSUING ANOTHER CAR IN ANGER

Racing is in our nature. We have enjoyed racing since before the dawn of history. Everybody wants to be the frontrunner. The spectators at a race love to watch. They eagerly tender their money to the ticket seller and they involuntarily jump, scream, and cheer when the car they like takes the lead.

It is extremely dangerous to race on a public road or a highway. It is also expedient to consider the fact that the driver you are chasing is charting the course and may be leading you into a trap. High speed is the most frequent cause of death on the road. We all know that. But sometimes, when a driver is passed—particularly when he has already taken the challenge and begun to race with the other car—something snaps and the restraints that normally suppress violence are gone.

SPEEDING UP OR SLOWING DOWN TO PREVENT ANOTHER CAR FROM CHANGING LANES

This is not one of the major precursors to violence, but it is sufficient to provoke some drivers to be seized with paralytic rage, pursue you with hot, tormented eyes, and seek revenge.

MAKING EYE CONTACT

"Don't make eye contact with an aggressive driver" is an admonition given by all the roads scholars. The reason generally given or implied is that if you look at an enraged driver you attract his wrath, by making eye contact you invite aggression by providing him with a conduit to discharge his anger. It's like the angry man in a bar or a public place who sees you staring at him and says, "What the hell are you looking at, punk?"

This is not particularly good advice. When you are in the proximity of an enraged driver you need to know where he is and what he is doing. People have been shot because they were not looking and paying attention. It is best not to stare at her too flagrantly, but a person seized with rage is unpredictable; she may raise a firearm and pull the trigger, or she may just go home.

Sometimes you can look straight ahead and watch her out of the corner of your eye, but that is not always sufficient to protect your life, your family, and your car. You may be able to scan across the surrounding area so that you make eye contact with her for less than a second. But if she knows you are aware of her presence and her state of mind and are avoiding her gaze, she may perceive that as an act of fear.

Fear is your greatest enemy. Fear is provocative. The appearance of fear and weakness is exhilarating for some people. It is not necessary to look at the other driver with the eyes of a mad killer. Just look at her with a face that says: I'm not looking for a fight but I'm not afraid of you.

I have a friend who drives racing cars. I presented him with the premise that one should never make eye contact with an aggressive driver and asked if he agreed with the experts. He thought about it for a moment and said, "That's an option you don't always have. If a madman gets out of his car and comes at you and you can see that he intends to break you up in little pieces, you've got to look into his eyes with such power that you can see everything that's going on inside him but you're putting out so much power that he can't see into you at all." This is a bit vague, but certainly intimidation is the operative dynamic in such situations. If the road rage aggressor has, in her own mind at least, gone beyond the point of no return, beyond the possibility of reconciliation, it is imperative to show no fear.

Not everybody has that kind of powerful presence. Not everyone is capable of projecting that kind of power. But it is imperative not to appear to be frightened. If a raging, bellicose bully thinks she has terrified you she will be far more likely to assault you than she would if you appear to be unimpressed with her bravado and unafraid of her. If you find it necessary to look at her, do it with the demeanor of a person who is totally unintimidated, not belligerent but unimpressed. This will arm you against many aggressive drivers. When this happens it is best to hastily depart and lock your doors. If you are trapped between her car and the curb, back up, move forward, turn, just keep moving.

GETTING OUT OF YOUR CAR AND ENGAGING IN A SHOVING MATCH OR A FISTFIGHT

This is definitely a bad idea. Do not get out of your car. You do not know what the other driver has in his car. You do not know what he has in his pocket, in his jacket, or under his belt. If he has you trapped in a cul-de-sac or a parking lot, keep calm. Many drivers carry some kind of weapon in their cars: a knife, a gun, a pipe, a club, a wrench, a steel bar. If the other driver succeeds in pulling you out of your car, you really have no other choice but to defend yourself by appropriate and legal means.

But, again, do not voluntarily get out of your car. If another driver tries to pull you out of your car, he is leaving his face, head, and other body parts unprotected and you can provide him with enlightenment. Once I saw two cars pull over on the shoulder of a freeway. One driver tried to pull the other out of his car, grasping his coat. The other driver remained in his car, leaned back, put his feet on his assailant's chest, and pushed swiftly with his legs while breaking the aggressor's grip on his coat. The man was catapulted out onto the freeway where he fell under the wheels of a tanker truck. I have no idea what was the final denouement of this drama. I was trapped in an impenetrable gridlock of cars and trucks. All the drivers were slowing down to get a look. The police were urgently waving the drivers on, trying to keep them moving.

CARRYING A WEAPON IN YOUR CAR

Almost everybody carries some item that could be used for self-defense: a pipe, a hammer, a wrench, pepper spray, mace. If you don't, you are at a disadvantage when the mad road warrior comes into your space. There are laws against carrying a concealed weapon that carry severe penalties. You can be tried and dispatched to the county jail or state prison. If you punch the attacker it may be ruled as only a misdemeanor or justifiable self-defense, but if you use a weapon you could be charged with a felony.

SHOUTING EPITHETS AT THE OTHER DRIVER

This can trigger extreme violence. Some drivers will ignore it. Others will pursue you for hours.

In Milwaukee, two cars pulled up to an intersection, side by side, waiting for the red light to turn green. The drivers began exchanging insults. One car was being driven by an eighteen-year-old man. He was alone. The other car, occupied by two men, pursued him until it was alongside him. A man sitting in the other car fired seven rounds, killing the boy.[1] Two drivers exchanging epithets is an extremely common occurrence. But in this case the shooter received a sentence of forty years. If you cannot endure insults from other drivers, you had better think about what's at stake before you decide to mete out punishment. If he draws a weapon you had better be an extraordinarily clever and skilled driver.

A neighbor of ours was sitting on his front lawn when a truck went by, going much too fast for such a narrow, residential street lined with homes, families, and children. He shouted, "Hey! Slow down!" The truck stopped and backed up. The driver looked at our neighbor and said, "Hey dude, you got a problem?"

"Yeah," he answered. "We have children here. You're going too fast to stop if one of them ran out in the street."

Epithets were exchanged and the third fingers were hoisted, an act of war. It was at this stage that things got out of hand.

"You had a little problem. Now you got a big problem," the truck driver said.

Our neighbor cursed him as he drove away. He should have known better but he just relaxed, lying in the sun, thinking it was over. A few minutes later the truck returned with four men in it. They got out and gave him a brutal beating which made it necessary for him to spend several days in a hospital and then a month at home, recovering from his injuries. It would have been more expedient for him to simply get the truck's license plate number and report it to the police, asking them to surveil that street.

LEADING THE OTHER CAR TO YOUR NEST

Never lead an agitated driver to your home, your office, your place of employment, or any other place you frequent. As long as she is following you, go around the block and keep going around and around the block until she abandons the chase and goes away. Choose narrow, residential streets where she cannot pass you. Watch her in your rearview mirror. If she raises a firearm, get down as low as you can and depart as quickly as you can to a more public place where there will be witnesses and possibly police.

My friend Mark was driving to work in stop-and-go traffic when another driver began to tailgate him and sound his horn in long, repetitive blasts. There was no way Mark could accommodate the horn blower because the cars in front of him were all stuck in the same massive, inert traffic jam. As the cars began to move again, the horn blower continued to ride Mark's rear bumper and trumpet his horn, accompanied by the raised avian third finger, summoning him to a duel. As Mark drew near the off-ramp, which was only a short distance from his place of employment, he found an opening, changed lanes, gunned his motor, left the horn blower behind, and sped away. The horn blower followed him with implacable, reptilian eyes. Mark quickly parked his car in the parking lot and went into the building. He looked out the large plate glass window and saw the horn blower entering the parking lot, where he stopped, searching for Mark with the hard, blank face of a fighter about to enter the ring, waited for a few minutes, then made a U-turn and drove away.

At five o'clock, when all of the employees were leaving one by one, Mark looked and saw Horatio Hornblower parked in the lot, waiting for him. Same car, same hard, blank predatory face. He saw Mark's car but he did not see Mark, who was sitting in his office, calling the police. It was getting dark. Mark waited. When the police car arrived Mark flipped the switch, turning on the 200-watt lights that lit up the parking lot and the horn blower like bright sunlight. The police detained him and took him into their custody.

The next day, and for several days afterward, Mark drove his wife's car, which was of a different make and color, hoping the horn blower would not find him in the crowded morning traffic. He need not have bothered; the man never returned. But it is better to be safe than sorry.

BLOCKING THE PASSING LANE

This is extremely frustrating to a speeder. It is less likely to result in deadly combat than tailgating or cutting off another car and giving him a "brake job," but it is a frequent cause of road rage. Best to just pull over and let the faster car pass.

FLOORING IT

Do not floorboard your gas pedal and bolt forward as soon as the light turns green, particularly at night. Look both ways before you proceed. Cars that run red lights are sometimes just in a hurry and late for an appointment, but some are racing, pursuing another car with raging anger, willing to risk death rather than be passed. Drivers who run red lights are one of the most common causes of fatal car crashes. If you accelerate too soon and too fast you are likedy to get broadsided. I was permanently cured of dashing forward as the light turned green when I did exactly that several years ago and escaped annihilation only by inches when a drunk driver in a large car went through the intersection at high speed long after the light had changed.

FIGHTING OVER A PARKING SPACE

Many people have been killed in disputes over parking spaces. Frequently, a driver will approach a driver who is already entering a parking space and try to frighten him away, saying in a menacing voice, "What are ya doing in my parking space?"

It is ignominious to surrender your parking space to a person who has arrived on the scene long after you were already halfway into the space. But you don't know how crazy he is, or how angry, or if he is armed. If you can keep him talking long enough, you may be able to dissipate his anger. That's one strategy. Another may be to just let him have the space and end the confrontation.

If the other driver believes that you are insane he may decide that it is best to leave *you* alone. Once, when I was backing into a parking space on Hollywood Boulevard, I saw a huge man driving a large car, a block away, looking over his shoulder at me with black, inscrutable hate in his eyes. He made a right turn, drove around the block and stopped his van alongside mine.

"That's my parking spot!" he demanded with deep, baritone firmness and certitude. I looked at him with the transcendental smile of a swami, a baba, or a car salesman.

"Peace be upon you," I spoke in the unearthly, ethereal tone of a holy man. "We at the Ashram of the Holy Thralawaffle believe that all men must live in peace, my child. We must be as brothers in order that we may enter the Kingdom of Thralawaffle where all shall be as one. The Illuminated One speaks to all of those who seek enlightenment. All shall be revealed, my child. You must sit and chant with me. I will be your mahatma. I will be your archetype. First, you must learn the mantra of the Swami Mahabagabagananda. I will teach it to you. It goes like this. Repeat after me. Oom balabalabala. . . ."

As I chanted my mantra he stared.

"Could you make a small contribution to the Ashram?" I asked. "Just a dollar or two? It will help us continue our work, teaching others to follow the True Path of Bwang Ching Dung."

He left.

This is not recommended. Very few people are that verbal and very few can think that fast on their feet. Better to just leave and end it.

Another way of dealing with the parking space bandit is to pretend you weren't able to hear what he said and cheerfully say, "Hi! How are you doing?" And then walk away.

On another occasion, when I was working at a newspaper, there was a parking problem. The builders and planners had not provided enough parking spaces. The high-rise buildings and shopping malls charged exorbitant fees for parking in their underground parking structures and there were few spaces on the street.

Our newspaper had about fifty employees—and only twelve spaces where cars could park. One morning someone vacated one of the spaces and a large car quickly zoomed in from the street and occupied the space. The driver was a man none of us had ever seen before. My friend Jim walked over to the car and asked the driver, "Are you here on business with the *Daily Bulletin?*"

The man did not answer. He was a very large man, tall and thick. Jim repeated the question: "Are you here on business with the *Daily Bulletin?*"

The big man ignored him and got out of his car. But when he tried to close the door, Jim put his boot between the door and the jamb, grabbing the door with his hands.

"This is a private parking lot," Jim said. "And we don't have enough spaces for our own people. You'll have to leave."

"I'll park here," the man said, quickly slammed the door, and locked it. We watched furtively as he walked to a high-rise building and got into the elevator. Jim flagged down a police car and told him what had happened. The officer called a tow truck, which soon arrived, and the car was towed away. When the big man returned his car was nowhere to be seen. He was beyond angry. He was seized with a degree of paralytic anger that rendered him speechless. He went to the door of the *Daily Bulletin* and demanded that he be allowed to enter and search for the culprit, Jim, who had already departed. The receptionist explained that he would have to get a policeman with a search warrant before he could enter. He left. When he returned, Jim was nowhere to be seen. The man asked me, "Did you see somebody messing with my car this morning?"

"What car?"

"The one that was right here in this space."

"What did he look like?" I asked.

"Skinny, medium height. He was wearing a hat."

"That narrows it down to about 500 million people," I smiled. "How did this happen?"

"I was parking my car and this punk told me I couldn't park here and I told him I was gonna park it whether he liked it or not."

"When you invade the other guy's nest and occupy his territory you are putting yourself in jeopardy," I said cheerily.

"I can handle it," he said. "I'm gonna take him outa that building and beat him so bad he'll wish he'd never been born."

I don't know how he handled it, but he did not return to the offices of the *Daily Bulletin*. Occasionally we saw him drive by, looking for Jim, but he did not stop to exchange greetings. He had no sense of humor.

TAKING TWO PARKING SPACES

Some people do it because they are inexperienced, clumsy drivers. Others do it out of malice. Once I saw a car occupying two spaces in a crowded parking lot. There was no other unoccupied space in the lot. Angry drivers were cursing the offending car. I waited until a car pulled out and quickly drove into the empty space. When I returned in the evening the parking lot was almost empty. I saw the car that had occupied two spaces. It had been torched. There was nothing left but a burned-out shell covered with ashes and dust. Someone had placed a note on what was left of the front seat:

DEATH TO ALL TWO-SPACE PARKERS

As a natural consequence of the growing number and density of vehicles and the insufficiency of adequate parking facilities, parking lot rage has joined road rage as a new collective pathology. Many drivers do not understand that a parking lot is not a public road and that pedestrians have the right of way. Drivers race with one another for a parking space and sometimes it's a tie, resulting in damage to both cars. Of the millions of accident insurance claims filed in 1997 about 30 percent were for accidents at speeds lower than 20 MPH. Police have no authority to enforce traffic codes on private property and do not become involved unless there is a homicide, assault, or hit-and-run.

FIGHTING OVER A GAS PUMP AND OTHER SILLY THINGS

I have a friend who worked at a gas station for two years. He told me that there were violent, brutal fights almost every week at the gas station. I have seen this happen several times. During peak traffic hours, the gas stations are crowded and having to wait is frustrating. Two cars race to a gas pump. Both arrive together, each blocking the other from using the pump. Angry words are exchanged. Then fists fly.

DRIVING NEAR A BIG RIG SEMI TRUCK

According to a publication of the State Farm Mutual Automobile Insurance Company, there are 250,000 crashes between cars and trucks each year.[2] Many are caused by aggressive acts on the part of the truck driver, enabled by the fact that he has the advantage of size, weight, and mass. A large truck has two blind spots where the driver can't see you: one on the side and one in the rear. If you are unable to pass the truck, just slow down, stay as far behind the truck as you can, and wait until you can pass. If a truck capsizes and falls on your car it will flatten it, and it will very likely flatten you, too. You don't need that. Do not duel with a large truck. If it's a tie, you will lose. The same is true of railroad crossings.

SPEEDING ON A NARROW RESIDENTIAL STREET

No matter what an upscale neighborhood you live in, you will often see belligerent young drivers racing by at 45 or 50 MPH. This often generates great anger and vindictiveness on the part of the people living on that street, and an angry confrontation.

ERRATICALLY CHANGING LANES

Resist the urge to repeatedly change lanes without signaling. When traffic is heavy and your lane comes to a standstill, there is a great temptation to change lanes when the lane next to yours is moving. But almost invariably your new lane will come to a stop and all those cars you passed will be passing yours, causing you to lose all the points you scored. Chances are you'll get there just as fast if you stay in one lane rather than risk a fender bender. Even if you arrive at your off-ramp ten seconds ahead of the other car, is it worth your life?

RUNNING A STOPLIGHT OR A STOP SIGN IN ORDER TO WIN A RACE

This is one of the most dangerous things you can do. It is bad enough to be hit from the front or the rear, but if you are broadsided at high speed, you are likely to be splattered. This is an excellent way to end your life prematurely. Many drivers speed through an intersection when the light is about to turn red in order to win a race. If another car collides with you it will happen too quickly for you to take evasive action, and you will be hit on the side where you have the least protection, just a door.

Also beware of pedestrian crossings—particularly the ones that have no stop sign or blinking red light. There is a real danger that you will maim or kill a pedestrian. Some drivers rage at pedestrians because they do not want to stop to let them cross the street. Some drivers also hate bicycles because it is sometimes necessary to slow down to avoid hitting them. It's better to lose a few seconds than to face charges of manslaughter. Juries do not like drivers who kill children and teenagers on bicycles.

BOLTING IN FRONT OF ANOTHER CAR

One extremely common provocation that psychologists often overlook is the act of bolting from a stop sign, a driveway, or the shoulder of the road just as a car is approaching. If you've done a lot of driving it probably has happened to you: You're driving along at 50 or 60 MPH on a deserted road. There is nobody in front of you for at least a mile or more and there is no vehicle behind you as far as the eye can see. Suddenly, you see a car on the shoulder, about to go forward onto the highway. Naturally, you believe he will pull onto the highway and accelerate long before you arrive, and you will not be forced to brake. Or you think he is waiting for you to pass so he can pull in behind you. But he does neither. He waits until you are right on top of him, only a few yards away, and he pulls out in front of you. When this happens you have to think fast to avoid an accident. He may be hoping that you will stomp your brakes too hard, causing them to lock, and you will skid, overturn, and crash, or swing around him across the oncoming lane into a head-on collision. He may be intent on suicide. He may be nothing more than an inexperienced, inept driver. But I have seen this happen many times and I have seen the malice on the face of the interceptor. It triggers great anger in the other driver, and if the other driver has a larger, heavier vehicle than his and there is no way to go around him, he really has no other option but to accelerate and demolish the intruder and may take great satisfaction from doing so. And he will probably come out with less damage than the other car, but not always. It's best to try to get around him without a mishap, but sometimes these suicidal kamikaze drivers wait until you are so close that you have no chance to elude them. I have no scientific study to corroborate this premise, but it has repeatedly been my observation that the driver who does this is usually a person so consumed with anger and despair that he wants to destroy himself and take you and your car with him. Sometimes it is just an inept beginner who forgets to look before entering traffic. There are always those among us who cannot do anything right. We should try not to hurt them. Sometimes the worst situations are caused by someone who means no harm. Sometimes it's a drunkard. This is one of the most common and frequent annoyances you will encounter while driving in traffic. Some suffer from get-there-itis, the fear and abhorrence of being late. Some enjoy the display of skill they exhibit when dashing through traffic like a hockey player. Some enjoy the defiant act of flying in the face of other drivers, usurping the right of way, causing them to panic and slam the brakes, and you can see the vague smile on the driver's face. Others do it to discharge some of their anger and smile maliciously—unless they are hit by a speeding car and no longer have the ability to smile.

LOSING CONTROL

Control your anger. Remember: it takes more strength and dignity to control it than to let it overpower you and cause you to do something abominably stupid, like throwing your life away in a road rage duel. A person who cannot control her anger is destined to be a loser. Divert that energy into something more rewarding. Anger management is very "in" these days. Los Angeles County has a pool of about one hundred anger management therapists to whom the courts refer thousands of people who have been foolish enough to let their anger get out of control.

Anger management is a very substantial growth industry that has already generated a considerable literature. Some anger management therapists invite the driving public to send in their horror stories, then provide them with strategies for dealing with their anger. A number of prominent researchers and therapists have expressed skepticism as to whether anger management therapy, as it is now practiced, has any efficacy at all. The shooters in the Columbine High School massacre in Colorado passed anger management courses, but it did not prevent them from slaughtering their classmates. The few researchers who have studied the effectiveness of anger management courses have found that they are "not very effective," and that they have produced only "mixed results."[3] Certainly it is a welcome departure from the government's obsession with incarceration as a panacea for all of society's various manifestations of disobedience, and the enormous growth of the prison population.

But we need to look at the quality of the instruction and therapy. There are people who could design an anger management program that would be highly effective, but they would have to disclose to us information about ourselves that many people don't want to hear. Most people don't want to acknowledge that they have behaved like idiots. Most people do not want to acknowledge that they have voted for idiots. Maybe we don't really want to give up the mindless catharsis of freeway violence.

Nevertheless, anger management is a concept whose time has come. Some of the worst explosions of anger have erupted in the workplace, as was the case at the Connecticut lottery office and in Orange, California, where a fired California Department of Transportation worker shot six of his former coworkers, killing four. If we cannot agree about anything else, there certainly is a general consensus that there is more anger than there was twenty years ago. The anger management industry continues to grow and prosper.

The Anger Institute in Chicago offers ninety-minute workshops for companies at a cost of $1,000. A Manhattan firm earns as much as $10,000 for a day of lectures and group sessions. Theater at Work, a Minneapolis company, performs short plays for groups of employees, followed by discussion led by a facilitator. Many Fortune 500 companies have availed themselves of these anger management sermons. There is big money in anger management.

Another company markets humorous bumperstickers and signs to display to road ragers. Laughter sometimes defuses anger. It's a very clever and charming concept, but it doesn't always work. There are people who would rather die than laugh. They want to smash, burn, rape, kill, and torture. They are best left alone. If you try to humor them and make them laugh, you may be playing a dangerous game.

Anger management is a step in the right direction. An intelligent alternative to incarceration is, hopefully, the remedy of the future. Incarceration as it is now practiced destroys the human spirit. It certainly does not rehabilitate. We need to understand not only our aggression but all of our natural instincts. There has always been a movement against self-knowledge. Primitive men and women who believe in the natural depravity of *Homo sapiens* have always fought against the dissemination of knowledge. They are not extinct. As freedom of speech expands, programs like anger management may be useful if they are done well by gifted teachers.

But it's not for everybody. Those who have been the victims of road rage and other forms of mindless violence will welcome the effort to manage anger, as will those who are genuinely troubled by their own aggressiveness. A person with an excessively high degree of aggression will generally view intelligent self-examination as effete and contemptible. He wants to fight. He wants to kill. He will have to be managed in a different way.

*   *   *

All of these admonitions pertain to symptoms, not the real underlying cause. Until now we have been identifying and discussing the acts that are likely to incite road rage aggression, the theories, advice, and publications of the experts. We need to look at road rage aggression, what it really is, where it comes from, and how and why we acquired it.

NOTES

1. Weekly Reader Corporation, art. no A53215116.

2. State Farm Automobile Insurance Company publishes a semiannual newsletter that is mailed to all of its clients. This one was published in the summer of 2001.

3. Pat Morrison, "Three Lessons from the Master of Anger Management," *Los Angeles Times*, September 19, 1999, p. 14. See also the Domestic Violence Center at http://www.dvc.org.nz/anger.html /#angertop.

14

REINVENTING
THE CITY

Leave Your Guns at Home

S tanding on the freeway, looking at the wreckage left in the wake of a particularly gory road rage crash, I heard a police officer say, "Sometimes I think it would be nice if we could just let those people kill themselves off and then we'd be rid of them."

But *we* are those people: the commuter, the teenager, the cop, the senator, the judge, the clergyman, and the psychologist, too. All of us. Most of us are worth saving.

California is in need of $110 billion in road improvements, according to the *Los Angeles Daily News*. These are not spectacularly futuristic improvements of the kind seen in comic strips and science-fiction magazines; rather, they are just repairs and maintenence on the existing roads and highways. As for designing and building really creative new networks of roads and high-speed rail systems, myopic state officials have called this vision "pie in the sky." It's not that the money isn't there; it's a question of priorities. California spends $6.1 billion per year on prisons and jails. A few years ago it was only millions. But the prison guards' union, the Association of California Correctional Peace Officers, is one of the largest contributors to political campaigns in California.[1] Since 1984 California has built twenty-one large prisons and only one college. Improved, safer roads and expressways would not stop road raging, but it would diminish the number of deaths and crippling injuries resulting from it and enable the police and the highway patrol to stop road-raging racers before they kill others.

A young man was given his mother's car on his seventeenth birthday. He and his father had spent two years restoring the car to almost pristine condition—considerable time, labor, and money. When he experienced the thrill of being behind the wheel for the first time, it was the beginning of a love affair. That love affair was cut short and ripped apart by a bully driving a pickup truck, one of those huge ones with the large wheels. The pickup was behind him, on his rear bumper. The young man was driving at the posted speed limit, 55 MPH, but the pickup driver wanted to go faster, wanted the young man to get out of his way, wanted to frighten him, bully him, punish him, smash him, crush him, wreck his car. He was shaking his fist, sounding his horn, and making the bellicose third finger arabesque. The young man politely signaled and moved over to the next lane in order to let the truck pass him. The pickup truck, seeing that his victim was extremely young, decided to cut him off and give him a "brake job." He jerked his truck in front of the seventeen-year-old and stomped his brakes. The young man was no match for the older driver. He did not know how to parry and evade this assault. He was forced off the road and his beloved car plummeted down an embankment. He was not seriously injured, but the love of his life, his first car, given to him by his loving parents, was totally destroyed, beyond restoration. It might have been a small consolation if someone had witnessed this and taken the bully's license plate number, and if he had been held to answer for his hideous behavior, but it was not to be. When the boy recovered from shock and his injuries were treated and bandaged, he said, "I was never taught or told anything about this new killer, road rage, or how to handle it. It was nowhere on any of the tests, either the state or at the public school. I had to learn the hard way."[2]

He did not understand that one must get as far away as possible from that kind of driver—behind him, not in front of him—and how to recognize one before he can do any damage. He also was unaware of the measure of cruelty that exists in the world. Placing surveillance cameras on cars would help to identify the worst aggressive drivers.

This incident is a classic example of the behavior pattern of the road rage bully and his intent: to destroy the other car. Anything short of that leaves him unsatisfied.

In California, Texas, and most other states you can have a traffic citation expunged by attending traffic school. I have attended these lectures and, during the lunch breaks, spoken with the students. Most of them confessed, with some embarrassment, that they were speeding or racing. These "traffic schools" usually consist of a very dull recitation of the state traffic codes. In recent years the high priests of California have retained professional comedians to teach some of the classes, to liven it up a bit. But they accomplish very little, except to erase the ticket from a driver's record and rob her of a day of her life. Usually the recipients of these lectures go out and do it again: speeding, racing, or driving recklessly. Some of them suffer the loss of life and limb. Driving school, as it now is administered, does not get to the root cause of road rage and does little to diminish acts of aggressive driving. If done differently it could be highly effective.

When I was drafted into the army we were told that there was an epidemic of syphilis and gonorrhea. This inevitably happens where there are large numbers of young, unmarried men copulating with strangers. The army devised a very good solution. All of the enlisted men were herded into theaters where they were ordered to sit and watch a "VD movie." These VD movies were not sanitized for those who are easily shocked. The narrator's voice began with these words: "You don't believe it's going to happen to you. It's always the other guy—right? Wrong." We were shown the horrifying conditions that can result from engaging in unprotected sex: patients lying in hospital beds who had waited too long before seeking treatment. What we saw was so revolting that when it was time for dinner, most of the men could not bring themselves to eat and barely touched their food. But it worked. The men began using condoms and the number of new cases of sexually transmitted diseases declined. Naturally, with the passage of time, the impact of the VD movies attenuated and it was necessary to periodically herd the men into the theater once again for a "booster shot." It worked. They did not show us charts, graphs, or index cards. They showed the plain, ugly truth about the rewards of recklessness.

The only form of traffic school that will reduce aggressive driving must include films that show the gory, horrifying sights the police see after a car crash: the blood; the broken, dismembered bodies; the exposed viscera; the staring, blind eyes of the dead; the screaming, agonized faces of the dying. Those who have been cited for aggressive driving must see the paraplegics confined to hospitals or wheelchairs because of one foolish, reckless act of mindless rage. All drivers should be required to see a film like this as a condition of license renewal.

The first time I saw the wreckage of a head-on collision, shortly after it happened, I was almost too appalled to speak. One of the vehicles was a truck. The other was a Volkswagen. The inside of the Volkswagen was splattered with blood and various internal viscera. A woman stood and told me, stoically, "This woman is dead, and these are her children. My son is dead." Then she began to sob. This experience had a strong and lasting influence on my driving behavior.

People need to see the inside of one of our barbaric prisons, and what prisons do to the human spirit. They must see those who are brain damaged, babbling nonsense syllables, unable to speak, unable to think. They should see what is possibly the greatest sacrilege in the mind of the average American: the destruction of an expensive new car, crumpled and burning on the highway. They should see the charred remains of the occupants of the car. They should be told that witnesses and police often blame the wrong person and that it could happen to you if you do not stay away from car combat and dangerous driving. They should be told that prosecutors and judges are not high beings, descended from heaven, that they are just lawyers, and not always the best kind. They should hear, either on videotape or live, a lecture by a defense attorney who has had to deal with false witnesses in vehicular homicide trials. They need to understand that they cannot crash a car at high speed and come out unscathed. They need to understand that their instinctive aggression is an impulse that overwhelms reason, but it can be controlled if they recognize and understand the warning signs, the sudden transformation of mind and body into a raging, mad killing machine that shuts down all other thought.

That's the crucial moment when one must restrain it before

all rational thought is blotted out, and not allow oneself to go beyond the point of no return. It is better to go home angry than dead. We do not need a board-certified psychiatrist to tell us that aggressive driving is self-destructive behavior, that only a fool gambles everything—including his life—to atone for a trivial affront by a stranger. There will always be those among us who cannot handle freedom responsibly. We must find ways to manage them without abridging the rights of the rest of us.

As I mentioned earlier, there are twelve-step, four-step, and two-step programs. How about a one-step program?

I have a simple formula that has worked well for me and I believe it would be useful in driver education. Just as a recovering alcoholic knows that he must not take that first drink because if he does he will be drawn helplessly down into that vortex once again, a person susceptible to road rage must not take that first step and retaliate when a rude, belligerent driver angers him—because once you take the challenge and retaliate, it is very difficult to stop. You have dealt yourself into the game and you may not be able to get out until you or the other driver—or both—are destroyed or permanently damaged. The duel is on.

If another driver cuts in front of you, it is possible that she did it without malice. Even if she did it with the intent of insulting you, challenging you, and drives off, gloating over your defeat, aren't there more important issues in your life? If you ignore her, she has failed. If you do not allow yourself to accept the challenge and compete in a deadly road rage duel and refuse to be drawn into a maelstrom, you are the winner because you have shown yourself to have more strength and dignity. Let her be a fool and flaunt her boorish stupidity. You don't have to, and if you don't take the challenge that does not make you a wimp. Even if you should succeed in wrecking her car and her body, you may lose more than she, and you may suffer more. The dead do not suffer.

Just as a recovering alcoholic stands before the group and says, "My name is Egmont. I'm an alcoholic," you should tell yourself: I know I'm susceptible to road rage and I know that if I take that first step and retaliate and allow myself to be drawn into an idiotic duel, I could lose everything, including my life. It's a deadly game. It's a trap. I will make a firm, irrevocable vow not to take that first step if someone passes me and cuts across my bow. The road is a means of transportation, not a racetrack or an abattoir. I will use my aggressive energy to enhance my life, not destroy it.

Before you get into your car, make a strong, irrevocable vow that you will not take the first step, that you will not react when angered but, instead, just remain beyond the belligerent driver's reach. If you do not react, if you do not take the challenge, he has failed; he has no power over you. You are outside his sphere of influence. He is alone with his gross stupidity.

We need to understand that road rage and war are only two manifestations of our natural instinct to fight our own species— not our own tribe but the neighboring tribe, the strangers.

Our failure to teach people to understand and control their aggressive instincts is a reflection of the bankruptcy of our educational institutions. We are animals and our natural state is war. For years, anthropologists and readers of their literature have talked about the mystery of the "missing link" between the anthropoid beast and civilized man. It's no mystery. We are the missing link.

Once, when I was at a large conference in a spacious banquet room, I had a conversation with a member of the state legislature. I told him of my proposal to educate people about the frightful danger and prevalence of hostile driving with the use of films and videotape. Many filmmakers, engineers, designers, and writers would welcome such a challenge with great enthusiasm. I spoke of the need for driver education that would show drivers the horrible, revolting images the police see after a shattering high-speed crash, images that would frighten them badly enough to make them think before charging into battle. The state senator listened and said, "I never thought about that."

Most of us turn a blind eye and a deaf ear to the massacre on our streets and highways. We blame the other car when we should be exercising our will and our responsibility to overhaul and rebuild an environment that generates destruction of property and human lives. Millions of deaths and millions of injuries caused by road rage are not acceptable.

In California an infant was shot to death after his father flipped "the bird" to another driver. In 1994 a couple and their seven-year-old child were driving at a moderate speed when another car tailgated them and fired a gun at them, leaving the child brain damaged. When asked why he fired his gun at them he said, "They were driving too slow." He was not thinking. He just drew down on the other car, forfeiting his own life. In 1994 a young couple driving home from a date stopped for food at a convenience store. When they pulled back on the road a thirty-two-year-old man began tailgating them with bright lights, blinding them, then pulled alongside them and fired fourteen rounds from a semiautomatic, killing the young woman. In Illinois a thirty-five-year-old man and his sister were driving to a restaurant where they worked. Another car cut them off. There was a confrontation. The other driver sprayed the man with mace. The maced driver whacked the other car with a club. He thought it was over but several miles down the road, the other car was waiting. The other car rammed them. The driver suffered multiple fractures. His sister, the mother of a seventeen-year-old boy, was killed. It's not the automobile; it is us. All of this is perfectly normal animal behavior.

I have spent a large part of my life behind the wheel of a car and I have seen probably every kind of altercation between drivers—some trivial, some horribly violent and brutal—perpetrated by people whose rage obliterated all self-awareness and any thought of the probable outcome. There are drivers who possess not much more self-awareness than coyotes and wolves. After all those years of driving I consider myself lucky to be alive and intact. I also have seen many acts of kindness and generosity. I have seen drivers put themselves at risk to assist a stranger under attack by a mad road rage bully.

Two events changed the world: First, the invention of the wheel; then, the invention of the car. Before that time, we lived in small communities with very limited mobility. We lived under the scrutiny of the neighbors. We lived in communities where our ancestors had lived for generations. Everybody knew us. Now, we're the other car. When you're the other car, one among thousands on a crowded freeway, and you're drawn into road rage, everything else vanishes except the imperative of winning by any means, at any cost. If you damage the other car and escape with your own car and your body intact, you may never have to see him again. An otherwise civilized person gets behind the wheel and another self takes charge, another self that you don't recognize as a part of yourself, another self that is violent, frightfully crazy, willing to kill and die rather than be passed. It is not another entity. It is you.

In a large number of accidents that ended in injury or death the driver gave one of these explanations for his behavior:

He was driving too slow.
He passed me.

He was following too close.

He was honking his horn.

He cut me off. Nobody cuts in front of me.

He took my parking space.

He was playing his radio too loud.

He wouldn't dim his lights.

He gave me the finger. Nobody gives me the finger and gets
    away with it.

I had the right of way.

I wanted to teach him a lesson.

He looked at me with disrespect.

Are any of these worth forfeiting your life, your family, your freedom, your assets, or your health?

There are many well-documented cases in which a driver drove his car into a crowd of pedestrians, leaving the dead and wounded in his wake. In some, the driver said he did it because he was tired of waiting. In others, the driver was unable to offer any explanation.

In California a middle-aged man, after years of enduring the rudeness of other drivers, became obsessed with rage. He could no longer shrug it off and get on with his life. He began writing down the license plate numbers of the most blatantly rude offenders. He was able to access their names and addresses because he was an employee of the state and adept with computers. He began sending them letters, threatening to butcher and dismember them. He thought he had won or at least evened the score. He did neither. He was found out, arrested, and taken to the county jail. That's when you really find out what it's like to be abused.

Before you let your anger propel you into battle and do something foolish, consider the fact that you are offering yourself as fodder to a barbaric penal system, which is hungry for human sacrifice and the funding that accompanies it, a system that feeds on paupers, outcasts, and people who do foolish things without stopping to think. It will make you know that you are on the bottom of the heap. It will make you know that it can do anything it wants with you, say anything it wants to say to you, and if you try to rise up and reclaim your dignity it will break you and crush you. If and when you are released, you will be so damaged that you will never be quite the same person. Are you sure you want to do that?

Those who refuse to take that first step and accept the challenge are usually those people who have the things that are too precious to risk: a good marriage, an interesting career, fun things to do, things to look forward to—and an awareness of how brief, fragile, and ephemeral life is. These are the real social controls that restrain us from going over the edge and blowing it all over a trivial affront.

Beating and humiliating another car, making the driver taste the bitter bile of defeat, may give you a momentary high, a rush, a buzz. But whatever you get from that, it's not worth it. Those who succumb to road rage tend to be those who have— or believe they have—little or nothing to lose. Those who refuse to take the challenge generally are those who have too much to lose.

But we all have too much to lose! The miracle of life. The beauty of the earth, all the wonderful things you can see and hear and do, enjoy and look forward to: your spouse, your family, your home, your pet. Nothing is worth throwing away your life, or spending the rest of your days in a wheelchair, dead from the waist down.

We can issue billions of dollars in bonds, put more cops on the streets, build more jails and prisons, hire more therapists and teachers. But in the end it all comes down to the solitary task of knowing yourself, knowing the darker self, knowing the warning signs when the madman rises up. The greatest struggle is within yourself.

To a considerable extent road rage is about bullying, overpowering, defeating, imposing one's will upon another person with the use of force or by intimidation, punishing and humiliating him. The animal instinct that drives road rage manifests itself in other ways. We can learn valuable lessons from observing them. In recent years we have seen an epidemic of shootings in high schools across the nation. In virtually every case, the shooter was the victim of a bully or a gang of bullies, targeted because he was undersized, shy, awkward, defenseless, unfashionably dressed, or in some way different and vulnerable. In nearly every case the victim complained to teachers and the principal, but no action was taken against the bully. In one of these high school shootings the shooter complained that the bullies' in-group called him insulting names, spat on him, and beat him. He said he couldn't take it anymore. There are many similar cases, more than one can count.

In high schools, junior high schools, and colleges, the bullies are the ruling group, feared and treated with obsequious deference by the other students. Teachers tend to like the in-group because they have more in common with them than with the others.

The aggression that motivates the high school bully is the same animal instinct that is the source of road rage, wars, and riots. It is also the raw material of fascism. Fascism is a condition that exists when the bully reigns supreme and no limits are placed on his aggression. Fascism is nothing more than primitive medieval monarchy in modern dress, armed with modern technological weaponry. The tyranny of the high school "jocks" is an exact microcosm of what happens in the larger world of adults. Cops, judges, and bosses generally identify with the bully because they have more in common with him than his victim. They tend to dislike the person who is different, and does not look like the television cliché image of the all-American boy or girl.

There are millions of people who devoutly believe in fascism. They don't candidly call it what it is but wrap it in soothing euphemisms like:

> Compassionate Conservatism
> New World Order
> Law and Order
> Respect for Authority
> Obedience to Authority
> Americanism
> Decency
> Zero Tolerance
> God and Country
> Flag and Cross
> Intervention
> A Thousand Points of Light

These people long for a return to a simpler, more elemental way of life. Fascism is the primitive person's hatred of intelligence, achievement, and change.

We don't know enough about the fundamental causes of human behavior. There can be little doubt that the people living one hundred years from now will laugh at the primitive twentieth-century psychology, and shudder. Hopefully, by that time, we will have dismantled the massive wall of institutionalized bribery that stands in the way of human progress and preserves barbarism.

Hopefully we will have removed all legal obstacles that deny access to information and knowledge. Then, we can begin to deal with the real problems of rage and violence, not only on the road but in other settings as well.

Until then, the best advice you can get is the old saw: Count to ten. Take some deep breaths. Think. Know thyself.

And one thing more. When something happens that raises up overpowering rage and it takes possession of you, you can just disconnect it. Then you can think coolly and clearly and see how idiotic it is to accept the challenge and duel with another driver. You will have a better chance of seeing and knowing how to extricate yourself from a life-threatening situation. Just do it. Disconnect it and leave it behind you. You don't need a pill or a patch or a priest to stop smoking. Your own brain is a better instrument. When you are seized with the overpowering hunger for violence, the overwhelming need to crush, smash, kill, burn, and torture, disconnect it! Once you've done it you will be able to do it again, and again. Sometimes you may fail and become discouraged, but you can try again and succeed again, and in time it will become habitual. Then you will know the pride and satisfaction of acting with real strength and dignity, free at last from the prehistoric killer. Free at last.

POSTSCRIPT

Apparently the media and the medical community are becoming more interested in exploring the mysteries of road rage. This is long overdue: drivers cannot manage and subdue their sudden explosive outbursts of anger if they know nothing about the causes and dynamics of this phenomenon.

A recent study by a group of psychologists, funded by the

National Institute of Mental Health, concluded that it is in the functioning of the brain, not just a fleeting attitude problem, and that it is spontaneous. The study also indicated that "intermittent explosive disorder," as they define it, is far more prevalent than we had believed. Intermittent explosive disorder (IED) "involves multiple outbursts that are way out of proportion to the situation. These angry outbursts often include threats or aggressive actions and property damage."[3]

NOTES

1. California Secretary of State Web site: www.SS/CA.gov. See also Jenifer Warren, "Prison Guards' Pact Criticized by State Auditor," *Los Angeles Times*, July 31, 2002, p. B7.

2. http://www.angelfire.com.

3. This study was broadcast June 6, 2006, on CBS News. You can access it by logging on to http://www.cbssnews.com/stories/2006/06/05/tech/main1684053.shtml. If you are doing research you will find some good sources there.

GLOSSARY

brake job: Cutting in front of another car and then hitting the brakes.

burning rubber: Accelerating rapidly. See also "hitting it," "pedal to the metal," "pushing it to the floor," "punching it," and "spinning your wheels."

camber: The degree of tilt of the tire.

full bore: Full throttle. See also "wide open."

gearhead: A person obsessed with cars. See also "motorhead."

hitting it: Accelerating rapidly. See also "burning rubber," "pedal to the metal," "pushing it to the floor," "punching it, and "spinning your wheels."

loose nut behind the wheel: An incompetent or unsafe driver.

main hoop: A roll bar that passes over the driver's head.

motorhead: A person obsessed with cars. See also "gearhead."

open it up: Run at full throttle.

oversteering: When a car's back wheels drift and skid before the front wheels.

pedal to the metal: Accelerating rapidly. See also "burning rubber," "hitting it," "pushing it to the floor," "punching it," and "spinning your wheels."

playing bumper tag: Following too close. See also "tailgating."

playing "what's my lane?": Constantly changing lanes to try to pass other cars.

punching it: Accelerating rapidly. See also "burning rubber," "hitting it," "pushing it to the floor," "pedal to the metal," and "spinning your wheels."

pushing it to the floor: Accelerating rapidly. See also "burning rubber," "hitting it," "pedal to the metal," "punching it," and "spinning your wheels."

roll axis: The axis on which the car capsizes.

roof hoop: A roll bar extending from the main hoop to the windshield.

running on empty: Out of gas, literally or metaphorically. See also "running on fumes."

running on fumes: Out of gas, literally or metaphorically. See also "running on empty."

shut him down: Won a race. See also "smoked him," and "walked him."

smoked him: Won a race. See also "shut him down," and "walked him."

spinning your wheels: Accelerating rapidly. See also "burning rubber," "hitting it," "pushing it to the floor," "punching it," and "pedal to the metal."

tailgating: Following too close. See also "playing bumper tag."

t-boned him: Rammed another car broadside.

tricked out: Modified for high-power racing.

understeering: When the car's front wheels drift and skid before the rear wheels.

walked him: Won a race. See also "shut him down," and "smoked him."

when the rubber hits the road: When a person or car is put to the test.

wide open: Full throttle. See also "full bore."

RESOURCES

American Automobile Association Foundation for Traffic Safety
http://www.aaafoundation.org
The AAA Foundation for Traffic Safety has produced a video titled *Preventing Road Rage: Anger Management for Drivers*, which teaches drivers about anger management and gives advice for avoiding conflicts with other drivers. The Web site also includes the e-document *Controlling Road Rage: A Pilot Study Prepared by the AAA Foundation for Traffic Safety*, as well as interactive quizzes to test your hostility on the road.

Center for the Advanced Study of Public Safety and Injury Prevention: Aggressive Driving
http://www.albany.edu/tree-tops/dogs.sph/archive/agress.html
A comprehensive list of online resources related to aggressive driving.

RESOURCES

Citizens for Roadside Safety
http://www.guardrail.org/Roadrage.html
This Web page features facts and figures on road rage and a quiz to assess your aggressiveness behind the wheel.

Foremost Insurance Group: Ten Suggestions for Avoiding Road Rage
http://www.foremost.com/safety/rv/rage/htm

Mr. Traffic Discusses Road Rage
http://www.mrtraffic.com/rage.htm
Advice and tips for avoiding road rage from Mr. Traffic, "the #1 Driving and Traffic Safety Media Expert in America."

"My Story"
http://www.angelfire.com/al/alyplace/mystory.html
The story of one teen's experience with road rage.

National Highway Traffic Safety Administration
http://www.nhtsa.dot.gov/people/enforce/aggredriver.html
The National Highway Traffic Safety Administration Web site includes several documents dealing with facts, figures, legal penalties, and tips to avoid aggressive drivers.

Prevent Road Rage
http://www.awesomelibrary.org/road-rage.html
Tips to prevent road rage.

Road Rage: Attitude Toward the World Is Driving Each Driver
http://www.lynetteabel.org/Road-Rage.html
A commentary from the *Biloxi (MS) Sun Herald.*

Road Ragers.com
http://www.roadragers.com
This site features information, advice, quizzes, a discussion board, and a forum to report incidents for public information.

Road Rage Survey
http://www.opinioncenter.com/roadrage/

Smart Motorist: Road Rage
http://www.smartmotorist.com/rag/rag/htm
Links to information about road rage and how to avoid it.

BIBLIOGRAPHY

"Another Case of 'Road Rage.' . . ." WCCO-TV, February 13, 1998. http://www.channel4000 .com /news/stories /news-980213-070851.html.

Ardrey, Robert. *The Territorial Imperative*. New York: Atheneum, 1966.

Argento, Mike. "Road Rage Case Goes to Court." *York Daily Record*, September 30, 2000. http://www.ydr.com/awards/1beath.shtml.

Babula, Joelle. "Drivers Rage Is All the Rage." *Las Vegas Review-Journal*, March 26, 2000, p. 1B.

Balfour, Malcolm. "Cardiologist Punches Bypass Patient in Road Rage." *New York Post*, June 15, 2001.

"Beware of the Road Gods." Cyberprofile. http:// www.rtb.home.texas.net/road_gods3.htm.

Bragg, Rick. "The Last Cowboy." *New York Times*, August 8, 2001.

Bushman, Brad J., and Graig A. Anderson. "Methodology in the Study of Aggression: Integrating Experimental and Nonexperimental

BIBLIOGRAPHY

Findings." In *Human Aggression: Theories, Research, and Implications for Social Policy,* edited by Russell Geen and Edward Donnerstein. New York: Academic Press, 1998.

Byrne, Gerry. "Road Rage." *New Scientist,* December 9, 2000, p. 13.

Canedy, Dana. "Jury Acquits O. J. Simpson in a Trial on Road Rage." *New York Times,* October 25, 2001, p. A-19.

"Charges Filed in 'Road Rage' Case." WCCO-TV, October 10, 1997. http://www.channel4000.com/news/stories/news-971010-213641.html.

Clary, Mike. "Simpson Faces Road Rage Charges." *Los Angeles Times,* February 10, 2001, p. A-3.

Connell, Dominic, and Matthew Joint. *Aggressive Driving: Three Studies.* Washington, DC: American Automobile Association Foundation for Traffic Safety, 1997.

Crump, Spencer. *Ride the Big Red Cars: How Trolleys Helped Build Southern California.* San Diego: Lucent Books, 1966.

———. *Ride the Big Red Cars: The Pacific Electric Story.* Glendale, CA: Trans-Anglo Books, 1970.

Dotto, Lydia. "The Seven Second Solution." *Equinox* (February /March 2000): 32.

Eibl-Eibesfeldt, Irenaus, "Fighting Behavior in Animals." *Scientific American,* December 1961.

"Former SWAT Officer Apologizes for Road Rage Incident." WEWS-TV, June 25, 2002. http://www.newsnet5.com/news /1530069/detail.html.

Friedman, J. L. "Effect of Television Violence on Aggressiveness." *Psychological Bulletin* 96 YEAR: 227–46.

Friedman, Meyer, and D. Ulmer. *Treating Type A Behavior and Your Heart.* New York: Knopf, 1985.

Geen, Russell, and Edward Donnerstein, eds. *Human Agression: Theories, Research, and Implications for Social Policy.* New York: Academic Press, 1998.

Goleman, Daniel. *Emotional Intelligence: Why It Can Matter More Than I.Q.* New York: Bantam Books, 1999.

Gorman, Anna. "Police Chase Victim Gets Settlement." *Los Angeles Times*, April 19, 2001, p. B-1.

Ingram, Carl. "$16 Billion in Transit Bonds Urged." *Los Angeles Times*, March 8, 1999, p. A3.

James, Leon, and Diane Nahl. *Road Rage and Aggressive Driving: Steering Clear of Highway Warfare*. Amherst, NY: Prometheus Books, 2000.

Kuttner, Robert. "Big Trucks, Big Trouble." *Los Angeles Times*, October 25, 1999.

Lankard, Tom, and John Lehrer. "Photo Cop: Think Twice before Racing a Red Light." *Westways* (October 1999): 46.

Larrubia, Evelyn, and Nicholas Riccardi. "Court to Pay Inmates Millions." *Los Angeles Times*, August 15, 2001.

Larson, John A. *Steering Clear of Highway Madness: A Driver's Guide to Curbing Stress and Strain*. Wilsonville, OR: Bookpartners, 1996.

Levene, Art. "How Angry Drivers Are Putting You in Danger." *Redbook*, March 1997, p. 90.

Lorenz, Konrad. *On Agression*. New York: MJK Books, 1963.

Mantell, Michael, with Steve Albrecht. *Ticking Bombs*. New York: Irwin Professional Publishing, 1994.

Martin, Hugo. "No Idle Boast: L.A. Traffic Worst." *Los Angeles Times*, June 21, 2002, p. B-1.

Mascaro, Lisa. "Looming Traffic Crisis." *Los Angeles Daily News*, August 4, 2002, p. 1.

Mistry, Brava. "Soap Opera Romance." *Los Angeles Daily News*, December 1, 1999, p. A-1.

Mosby's Medical Dictionary. St Louis: C. V. Mosby, 1983.

Mrozek, Thom. "Arraignment Delayed for Jack Nicholson." *Los Angeles Times*, April 15, 1994, p. B-3.

National Highway Traffic Safety Administration. *National Automotive Sampling System: Crashworthiness Data Systems*. Washington, DC: US Department of Transportation, 1998.

———. *National Survey of Speeding and Other Unsafe Driving Actions*. 3 vols. Washington, DC: US Department of Transportation, 1998.

BIBLIOGRAPHY

Naval Institute Proceedings, October 2003. http://www.usni.org/ Proceedings/Articles99/protrover.htm.

Nazario, Sonia. "Industry Opposes Push for Anti-Alcohol Campaign." *Los Angeles Times*, May 13, 1999, p. A-19.

Nelson, Don. "New Meaning to the Term 'Road Hog.'" *San Francisco Business Times*, April 26, 1999. http://www.bizjournals.com.

New I.D. in America. Port Townsend, WA: Loompanics Unlimited, 1999.

Northrup, Terrall A. "The Dynamic Identity in Personal Conflict." In *Intractable Conflicts and Their Transformation*, edited by L. Kriesbert, T. Northrup, and S. Thorson. Syracuse, NY: Syracuse University Press, 1989.

Olesky, Walter G. *James Dean*. San Diego: Lucent Books, 2001.

Ornish, Dean. *Stress, Diet, and Your Heart*. New York: New American Library, 1984.

———. *Reversing Heart Disease*. New York: Random House, 1990.

Rathbone, Daniel B., and Jorg C. Huckabee. *Controlling Road Rage: A Literature Review and Pilot Study, Prepared for the AAA Foundation for Traffic Safety*. Washington, DC: Intertrans Group, 1999.

"SAPD SWAT Situation and Arrest." San Antonio Police Department news release, June, 21, 2002. http://www.sanantonio.gov.sapd /pdf/Adv_062002.pdf.

Sharkey, Joe. "You're Not Bad, You're Sick: It's in the Book." *New York Times*, September 8, 1997.

Shaver, Katherine. "Tyson Gets One Year for Assault on Motorists." *Los Angeles Times*, February 7, 1997, p. A-12.

Smith, Stacy L., and Edward Donnerstein. "Harmful Effects of Exposure to Media Violence: Learning of Aggression, Emotional Desensitization and Fear." In *Human Agression: Theories, Research, and Implications for Social Policy*, edited by Russell Geen and Edward Donnerstein. New York: Academic Press, 1998.

Sultan, Karyn. "Woman's Role in Road Rage Up, Statistics Show." *Woman Motorist*, April 18, 2001.

Suro, Robert. "Navy Plays High-Powered New Destroyer; Compulsion Progress Compared to Jump from Sail to Steam." *Washington Post*, January 7, 2000, p. A3.

Tamaki, Julie. "Jack Nicholson Accused of Breaking Man's Windshield." *Los Angeles Times*, February 23, 1994, p. B-1.

———. "Motorist Settles Civil Lawsuit against Jack Nicholson." *Los Angeles Times*, March 11, 1994, p. B-5.

Taylor, Stuart P., and Michael R. Hulzinger. "Psychoactive Drugs and Human Aggression." In *Human Aggression: Theories, Research, and Implications for Social Policy*, edited by Russell Geen and Edward Donnerstein. New York: Academic Press, 1998.

Walczak, Lee. "Auto Racing: Speed Sells." *Business Week*, August 11, 1997. http://www.businessweek.com/1997/32/b3539109.htm.

Warren, Jennifer. "Prison Guards' Pact Criticized by State Auditor." *Los Angeles Times*, July 31, 2002, p. B7.

Zimbardo, Philip G. *Psychology and Life*. Glenview, IL: Scott Foresman, 1985.